VOGUE KNITTING

THE ULTIMATE **QUICK** REFERENCE

COMPLETELY REVISED & UPDATED

THE EDITORS OF
VOGUE KNITTING MAGAZINE

sixth&springbooks | NEW YORK

VOGUE® KNITTING
THE ULTIMATE KNITTING BOOK Completely Revised & Updated

EDITORIAL DIRECTOR
Trisha Malcolm

EXECUTIVE EDITORS
Carla Scott
Lori Steinberg

WRITER
Marjorie Anderson

ART DIRECTION & DESIGN
Diane Lamphron

MANAGING EDITOR
Martha K. Moran

PHOTOGRAPHY
Jack Deutsch Photography

KNITTERS
Christina Behnke
Lisa Buccellato
Claudia Conrad
Loretta Dachman
Melissa McGill
Jaclene Sini
Erin Slonaker
Lori Steinberg
Hannah Wallace

ILLUSTRATORS
Sherry Berger
Glee Barre
Kate Francis /Brown Bird
DesignKathie Kelleher
Carol Ruzicka
Linda Schmidt

TECHNICAL DRAWINGS
Loretta Dachman
Linda Schmidt

YARN EDITORS
Matthew Schrank
Jaclene Sini

INDEX
Carol Roberts

CONTRIBUTING WRITERS
Daryl Brower
Jacob Seifert

PROOFREADER
Erin Slonaker

TRANSCRIBER
Catherine Quartulli Franklin

PRODUCTION MANAGERS
David Joinnides
Joan Krellenstein

MARKETING MANAGER
Beth Ritter

PUBLISHER
Caroline Kilmer

PRESIDENT
Art Joinnides

CHAIRMAN
Jay Stein

SPECIAL THANKS TO
The Craft Yarn Council,
Laura Bryant,
Rosemary Drysdale,
Nancy Marchant,
Deborah Newton,
Erin Slonaker and
Karin Strom. Also to
Debbie Bliss/Knitting
Fever, Jim Bryson/Bryson
Distributing, Cascade
Yarns, Classic Elite Yarns,
CocoKnits, DMC, Istex,
Plymouth Yarn, Sirdar,
and Universal Yarn
for providing all yarns
and knitting tools

VOGUE® KNITTING
THE ULTIMATE QUICK REFERENCE

EDITOR IN CHIEF
Carla Scott

EDITOR
Jacob Seifert

ART DIRECTION & DESIGN
Diane Lamphron

PAGE LAYOUT
Jennifer Markson

INDEX
Carol Roberts

VICE PRESIDENT/ EDITORIAL DIRECTOR
Trisha Malcolm

CHIEF EXECUTIVE OFFICER
Caroline Kilmer

PRODUCTION MANAGER
David Joinnides

PRESIDENT
Art Joinnides

CHAIRMAN
Jay Stein

Library of Congress Cataloging-in-Publication Data

Title: Vogue knitting : the ultimate quick reference / by the editors of Vogue knitting magazine.
Other titles: Vogue knitting international.
Description: First edition. | New York : Sixth&Spring Books, [2019] | Includes bibliographical references and index.
Identifiers: LCCN 2019019706 | ISBN 9781640210516 (flexi-cover)
Subjects: LCSH: Knitting--Handbooks, manuals, etc.
Classification: LCC TT820 .V6268 2019 | DDC 746.43/2--dc23
LC record available at https://lccn.loc.gov/2019019706

Cover photography by Jack Deutsch Photography
Yarn: Purl Soho
Needles: Brittany

5 7 9 10 8 6 4
FIRST EDITION
Printed in China

FOLLOW US

Table of Contents

7

EMBELLISHMENTS
169

8

TABLES AND
TOOLS   177

Special Features of This Book

Vogue Knitting: The Ultimate Quick Reference has been designed to provide knitters with the most-used knitting information from the completely revised and updated edition of *Vogue Knitting: The Ultimate Knitting Book* in a compact, portable guide. The perfect size to slip into a knitting bag, this book offers at-a-glance guidance on every step of completing a knitting project—from casting on and determining gauge to following knitting instructions, correcting errors, and adding embellishments. You'll find sections devoted to color knitting, knitting in the round, and finishing techniques as well as comprehensive lists of knitting abbreviations, terms, and internationally recognized symbols.

Vogue Knitting: The Ultimate Quick Reference incorporates the best features of *Vogue Knitting: The Ultimate Knitting Book* into its concise format. You'll find the same detailed instructions, clear illustrations, and helpful tip boxes. In addition, each chapter of this guide has been color-coded for easy reference—each beginning with a colored opener and containing coordinating bars along the outer side edge of each page.

The binding of this edition allows it to lie flat in front of you, leaving your hands free to work as you follow instructions. The inclusion of a needle inventory means you will never have to wonder what needles you might already own. A flap added to the back cover boasts a ruler, a stitch gauge, and a needle gauge.

Techniques featured in *Vogue Knitting: The Ultimate Quick Reference* were selected to accommodate a range of knitting abilities. Wherever possible, variations on basic techniques have been included, resulting in a collection of instructions that serves beginning knitters and those with greater experience equally well. Whether practicing your first knitting stitches, searching for a creative alternative to a common technique, or simply looking for the answer to a question, *Vogue Knitting: The Ultimate Quick Reference* will provide you with thorough information, at a glance, wherever your knitting happens to take you.

Basic Techniques

Holding Yarn and Needles

Everyone has a different way of holding the yarn and knitting needles. This is the most difficult thing to master when learning to knit, and it's important that you find a method that works for you.

The way you hold the yarn and needles will partly depend on which of two basic ways you choose to knit. If you use the **English method**, you hold the yarn in your right hand; with the **Continental method**, you hold it in your left. If you are left-handed, and you cannot master either the English or Continental method, you can use an alternative technique, which will be discussed later in this chapter.

Your own preferences will also affect your holding position. For example, you may find it easier to knit close to the tips of the needles, or you may prefer to work with the stitches farther back on the shafts. You may use only one finger to control the yarn, or you may use several fingers to obtain the same control. Any method is correct as long as the yarn flows evenly and the tension is consistent. Work in the way that is easiest for you. Once you become comfortable holding your needles, you will automatically increase your knitting speed.

Two traditional methods of holding yarn and needles are shown below.

ENGLISH

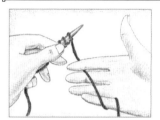

1 Hold the needles with the stitches in your left hand as shown. Wrap the yarn around your little finger and then around the index finger on your right hand.

2a Hold the working needle with your right hand as shown, controlling the tension with your right index finger.

2b Another method is to place the working needle between the thumb and index finger of your right hand as if you were holding a pencil.

CONTINENTAL

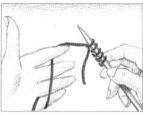

1 Hold the needle with the stitches in your right hand. Wrap the yarn around your little finger and then around the index finger of your left hand. Transfer the needle back to your left hand.

2 Hold the working needle with your right hand as shown, controlling the tension with your left index finger.

Casting On

Before you begin to knit, you must first place loops on a needle to make a foundation row called a **cast on**. You can choose from many different cast-on methods, some worked with one needle and others with two. Several methods presented here are basic, multipurpose cast ons; some are decorative cast ons serving special functions. You may want to try all methods, but if you are like most knitters, you will probably use one or two cast ons for most purposes.

The cast-on row affects all the rows that follow, so it is essential to create the neatest edge possible. If you are a beginner, choose a basic cast on and practice keeping the tension of the loops even before you begin to knit. If your cast-on stitches are too tight, you may have difficulty working

the first row. Try casting on with two needles held together and removing one of them before you begin to knit, or try using a larger needle. If your cast-on stitches are too loose, the edge will stretch out. You can tighten your cast on by using a smaller needle and changing to the correct size on the first row.

Once the loops are on the needle, you must decide which will be the right and wrong side of your work. Many cast-on methods form a loopy edge on one side (much like that of a purl stitch), but the other side is flatter and smoother. Pick the one you like best. Make a mental note of whether the cast-on tail is on the right or left side of your work to help you keep track of right and wrong sides.

SLIP KNOT

The first stitch of most cast-on methods is a **slip knot**. For some cast-on methods, you must leave a predetermined length of yarn free (a long tail) before working the slip knot. A general guide is to allow a length of approximately **three times** the planned width of the cast-on edge. For the other methods, only an 8–10-inch (20–25-cm) length is necessary.

1 Hold the short end of the yarn in your palm with your thumb. Wrap the yarn twice around the index and middle fingers.

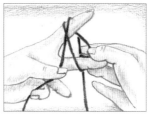

2 Pull the strand attached to the ball through the loop between your two fingers, forming a new loop.

3 Place the new loop on the needle. Tighten the loop on the needle by pulling on both ends of the yarn to form the slip knot. You are now ready to begin one of the following cast-on methods.

TECHNIQUE

LEFT-HANDED CAST ON

1 Make a slip knot on left needle, leaving a long tail. Wind tail end around right thumb from front to back. Wrap yarn from ball over your index finger and secure both ends between palm and fingers.

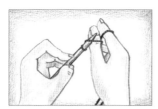

2 Insert needle upwards into loop on your thumb.

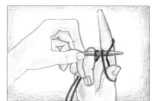

3 Insert the needle downwards into loop on your index finger and draw it through the loop on your thumb. Continue in this way until all stitches are cast on.

DOUBLE CAST ON OR LONG-TAIL CAST ON

The double or long-tail cast on provides a firm yet elastic edge and is frequently recommended for beginners.

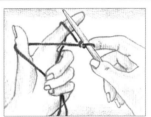

1 Place a slip knot on right needle, leaving a long tail. Wrap tail over your left thumb, wrap yarn from ball over your left index finger, and secure ends in your palm.

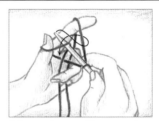

2 Insert the needle upwards in the loop on your thumb. Then with the needle, draw the yarn from the ball through the loop to form a stitch.

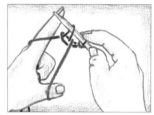

3 Take your thumb out of the loop and tighten the loop on the needle. Continue in this way until all the stitches are cast on.

DOUBLE CAST ON: THE THUMB METHOD

The thumb method has the same finished look as the double cast on shown above.

1 Make a slip knot on the right needle, leaving a long tail. Wind the tail end around your left thumb as shown. Wrap the yarn from the ball over your right index finger and secure both strands in your palms.

2 Insert the needle upwards through the loop on your thumb.

3 Using your right index finger, wrap the yarn from the ball over the needle knitwise. Pull the yarn through the loop on your thumb to form a stitch. Tighten the loop on the needle by pulling on the short end. Continue in this way until all the stitches are cast on.

SINGLE OR BACKWARDS-LOOP CAST ON

This is the simplest but not the neatest method of casting on. It is a good technique to use when casting on in the middle of a row or teaching children.

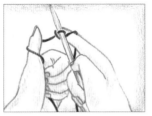

1 Place a slip knot on the right needle, leaving a short tail. Wrap the yarn from the ball around your left thumb as shown and secure it in your palm with your other fingers.

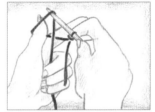

2 Insert the needle upwards through the strand on your thumb.

3 Slip this loop from your thumb onto the needle, pulling the yarn from the ball to tighten it. Continue in this way until all the stitches are cast on.

KNIT-ON CAST ON

With the knit-on method you use two needles and one strand of yarn.

1 Make a slip knot on the left needle. *Insert the right needle knitwise into the stitch on the left needle. Wrap the yarn around the right needle as if to knit.

2 Draw the yarn through the first stitch to make a new stitch, but do not drop the stitch from the left needle.

3 Slip the new stitch to the left needle as shown. Repeat from the * until the required number of stitches is cast on.

CABLE CAST ON

The cable cast on forms a sturdy yet elastic edge. It is useful for ribbed edges.

1 Cast on 2 stitches using the knit-on cast on described above. *Insert the right needle *between* the 2 stitches on the left needle.

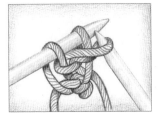

2 Wrap the yarn around the right needle as if to knit and pull the yarn through to make a new stitch.

3 Place the new stitch on the left needle as shown. Repeat from the *, always inserting the right needle in between the last 2 stitches on the left needle.

TUBULAR CAST ON

The tubular cast-on method creates a neat edge for knit 1, purl 1 rib. However, this cast on is not recommended for bulky yarns because the edge may flare. Note that this is only one of the multiple ways to work the tubular cast on.

1 With contrasting yarn, cast on half the required stitches (plus 1 extra, if an odd number of stitches) using the single or backwards-loop cast on. Cut the yarn. With the main color yarn at the back, knit 1, *bring yarn to front, knit 1; repeat from the * to the end of row. Turn.

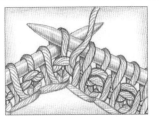

2 Next row *Knit 1, bring yarn to front, slip next stitch purlwise, bring yarn to back between the needles; repeat from the *, end knit 1.
Next row Bring yarn to front, *slip 1, bring yarn to back, knit 1, bring yarn to front; repeat from the * to last stitch, slip last stitch.

3 Work the two rows in step 2 once more. Then work in knit 1, purl 1 rib. After ribbing a few rows, remove the contrasting yarn.

INVISIBLE CAST ON

This cast on creates a rounded edge and is best used when elasticity and strength are needed. You will need two pairs of needles, one pair the size recommended for the yarn weight, and one pair two sizes smaller.

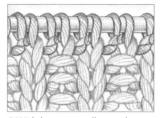

1 With larger needles and contrasting yarn, cast on half the number of stitches required. Work knit 1, purl 1 rib for 3 or more rows. Cut the yarn. With the smaller needle and the main color, knit 1, purl 1 in each stitch, doubling the cast-on stitches.

2 Knit the knit stitches and slip the purl stitches with the yarn in front of the work. Repeat for 4 rows more, then work in ribbing for required length. Remove the contrasting yarn.

OPEN OR PROVISIONAL CAST ON

The open cast on is used when stitches are to be picked up and worked later, such as for hems.

1 Cut a strand of contrasting scrap yarn about four times the required width. With the working yarn, make a slip knot and place it on two needles, or one needle that is three sizes larger than the size you are using.

2 Hold the scrap yarn beside the slip knot and take the working yarn under it and over the needles from front to back. Bring the working yarn in front of the waste yarn.

3 Repeat step 2 until all the stitches are cast on. Take out 1 needle before knitting the first row. Remove the scrap yarn only when the piece is finished and you are ready to pick up stitches along the edge.

CROCHET-CHAIN CAST ON

In this cast-on method, a crochet hook is used to cast the stitches onto the needle. The edge resembles the edge produced by the cable cast on.

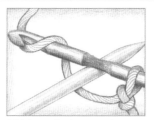

1 Make a slip knot on the crochet hook. Hold the needle and yarn in your left hand with the yarn under the needle. Wrap the yarn around the hook as shown. Pull the yarn through the slip knot.

2 Bring the yarn to the back under the needle, wrap the yarn as before, and pull it through the loop on the hook. Repeat this step until you have cast on the desired number of stitches minus 1.

3 Bring the yarn to the back. Slip the loop from the hook to the needle as shown.

PROVISIONAL CAST ON

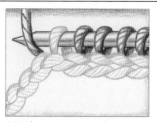

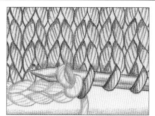

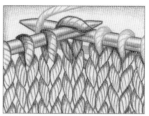

This is the most common provisional cast on used when stitches are to be worked later.

1 With scrap yarn and crochet hook, chain the number of stitches to cast on plus a few extra. Cut a tail and pull the tail through the last chain. With knitting needle and yarn, pick up and knit the stated number of stitches through the "bumps" on the back of the chain.

2 To remove the scrap yarn chain, when instructed, pull out the tail from the last crochet stitch. Gently and slowly pull on the tail to unravel the crochet stitches, carefully placing each released knit stitch on a needle.

3 Join new yarn and work the live stitches as instructed.

I-CORD CAST ON

This cast on creates a finished edge that looks like piping.

1 Make a 3-stitch I-cord with the number of rows equaling the number of stitches to cast on.

2 Drawing the yarn across the back, bind off the I-cord, but do not fasten off—one stitch remains on the needle.

3 Insert the needle tip through a stitch in the next row of the I-cord, wrap yarn knitwise around needle, and draw strand through the I-cord stitch. Continue in this way until the desired number of stitches is on the needle. Work through the same stitch in each I-cord row for a neat cast on.

TIP

IMPROVING YOUR CAST ON

• A cast-on edge should be firm, **but not tight.** If the cast on is too tight, it will eventually snap and unravel.

• If you tend to cast on tightly, use a **larger needle** than suggested, or two needles held together. After casting on, switch back to the correct size.

• **To create a firmer edge,** cast on with a double strand of yarn.

• The cast on should **not be too loose,** or the edge will flare out unattractively.

• Use a firmer cast on with yarns that have **less resilience,** such as cottons and silks. You can also use smaller needles or cast on fewer stitches (increasing to the required number after the last row of ribbing or edging).

• It is best to use **longer needles** when casting on a large number of stitches.

• Use a **stitch marker** after every tenth stitch to help in counting.

• Leave a 12–16-inch (30–40-cm) tail to use for sewing seams. To keep it out of the way, bundle up the tail while working on your piece.

The Basic Knit Stitch

The first stitch you will learn to make is called a **knit stitch**. You can work this stitch in two basic ways (or use an alternative method for left-handers).

The most common technique in English-speaking countries is known as the English or American method. The second method, which has always been associated with European countries, is called the Continental or German method. Each has its merits.

If someone taught you to knit, you probably learned the method used by your teacher. If you are learning now, you can try both methods and decide which is best for you. Usually the first technique you learn will be the easiest for you. (If you learn both methods, however, you will be able to knit colorwork patterns using both hands.)

In the **English method**, your right hand controls the tension of the yarn and wraps it around the needle. The right needle usually rests on your lap or under your arm while you knit. (In some cultures, knitters use long double-pointed needles and a knitting belt around their waists, resting the right needle in a hole in a pouch on the belt.)

With the **Continental method**, you hold the yarn stationary in your left hand and use the right needle to pull the strand through to create a stitch. Although many consider this to be the quickest way to knit, the resulting fabric can sometimes be looser than fabric worked by the English method.

When you're a beginner, learning to knit is awkward no matter which hand you favor, and left-handers might just as well learn one of the above two methods. However, if you find that both of those methods are too difficult, you can use a technique especially for left-handers. Just remember that knitting instructions are written for Continental and English knitting, and left-handers using that method will have to reverse most pattern directions.

To learn the knit stitch, you must prepare by casting on a row of stitches. The directions at the right show you how to knit into each cast-on stitch on your needle, thus completing the first row (this row is always a little tricky to work since the tension has not yet been established). The yarn is always held to the back when knitting. After working the first row, switch the needle with the stitches to your opposite hand, and either work a second row of knit stitches to form garter stitch or go on to the purl stitch.

ENGLISH

1 Hold the needle with the cast-on stitches in your left hand. The first stitch on the left needle should be approximately 1 inch (2.5 cm) from the tip of the needle. Hold the working needle in your right hand, wrapping the yarn around your fingers.

CONTINENTAL

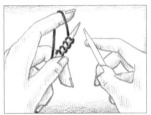

1 Hold the needle with the cast-on stitches in your left hand and the yarn wrapped around your fingers. Hold the working needle in your right hand.

FOR LEFT-HANDERS

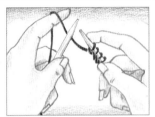

1 Hold the needle with the cast-on stitches in your right hand and the working needle and yarn in your left.

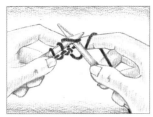

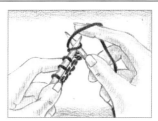

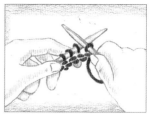

2 Insert the right needle from front to back into the first cast-on stitch on the left needle. Keep the right needle under the left needle and the yarn at the back.

3 Wrap the yarn under and over the right needle in a clockwise motion.

4 With the right needle, catch the yarn and pull it through the cast-on stitch.

5 Slip the cast-on stitch off the left needle, leaving the newly formed stitch on the right needle. Repeat these steps in until all stitches have been worked from the left needle. One knit row is complete.

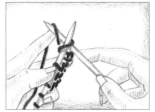

2 Insert the right needle from front to back into the first cast-on stitch on the left needle. Keep the right needle under the left needle, with the yarn in back of both needles.

3 Lay the yarn over the right needle as shown.

4 With the tip of the right needle, pull the strand through the cast-on stitch, holding the new stitch with the right index finger if necessary.

5 Slip the cast-on stitch off the left needle, leaving the newly formed stitch on the right needle. Repeat these steps until all of the stitches have been worked from the left needle. One knit row is complete.

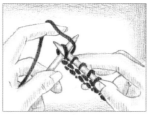

2 Insert the left needle from front to back into the first cast-on stitch on the right needle. Keep the left needle under the right needle and the yarn at the back.

3 Wrap the yarn under and over the left needle in a counterclockwise motion.

4 With the left needle, catch the yarn and pull it through the stitch on the right needle.

5 Slip the cast-on stitch off the right needle. The left needle holds a new stitch. Repeat these steps until all of the stitches have been worked from the right needle. One knit row is complete.

The Basic Purl Stitch

You are ready to learn the second essential stitch—the **purl stitch**. The purl stitch is the reverse of the knit stitch. If you purl every row, your fabric will look the same as if you had knit every row. This is called **garter stitch**. If you alternate one row of purl stitches and one row of knit stitches, you create stockinette stitch, the most commonly used stitch. When you work **stockinette stitch**, the knit rows are the right side of the work and purl rows are the wrong side. (When the purl side is considered the right side, it's called **reverse stockinette stitch**.) When you work the knit stitch and the purl stitch in the same row, you can create stitch patterns with dimension and texture.

When purling, the yarn and the needles are held in the same way as when knitting. The yarn, however, is kept to the front of the work rather than to the back and the right needle is inserted into the stitch from back to front.

ENGLISH

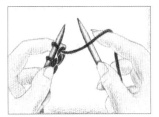

1 As with the knit stitch, hold the working needle in your right hand and the needle with the stitches in your left. The yarn is held and manipulated with your right hand and is kept to the front of the work.

CONTINENTAL

1 As with the knit stitch, hold the working needle in your right hand and the needle with the stitches in your left. The yarn is held and manipulated with your left hand and is kept to the front of the work.

FOR LEFT-HANDERS

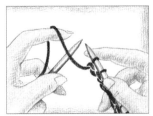

1 As with the knit stitch, hold the needle with the stitches in your right hand and working needle in your left. The yarn is held and manipulated with your left hand and is kept to the front of the work.

1 BASIC TECHNIQUES

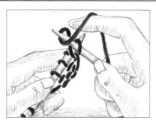
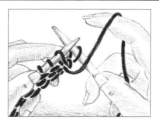
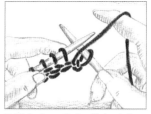

2 Insert the right needle from back to front into the first stitch on the left needle. The right needle is now in front of the left needle and the yarn is at the front of the work.

3 With your right index finger, wrap the yarn counterclockwise around the right needle.

4 Draw the right needle and the yarn backwards through the stitch on the left needle, forming a loop on the right needle.

5 Slide the stitch off the left needle. You have made one purl stitch. Repeat these steps until all stitches have been worked from the left needle. One purl row is complete.

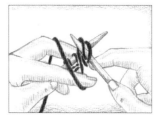

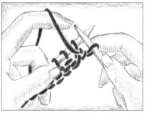

2 Insert the right needle from back to front into the first stitch on the left needle, keeping the yarn in front of the work.

3 Lay the yarn over the right needle as shown. Pull down on the yarn with your left index finger to keep the yarn taut.

4 Bring the right needle and the yarn backwards through the stitch on the left needle, forming a loop on the right needle.

5 Slide the stitch off the left needle. Use your left index finger to tighten the new purl stitch on the right needle. You have made one purl stitch. Repeat these steps until you have worked all of the stitches from the left needle to the right needle. One purl row is complete.

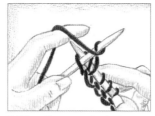

2 Insert the left needle from back to front into the back loop of the first stitch on the right needle.

3 Wrap the yarn clockwise over and under the left needle, holding the yarn taut with your left index finger.

4 Draw the left needle through the stitch, bringing the yarn with it, making a new stitch on the left needle.

5 Slide the stitch off the right needle. You have made one purl stitch. Repeat these steps until all stitches from the right needle have been worked. One purl row is complete.

Joining Yarns

Whenever possible, join new balls of yarn at the **beginning or end of a row**. When the garment is finished, you can easily untie the strands and weave them into the seams.

Sometimes, however, joining the yarn in the **middle of the row** is unavoidable, such as on garments that are knit in the round or with some colorwork patterns. Mid-row joinings should be handled carefully. Join the yarn, whenever possible, in an inconspicuous place, such as at the edge of a cable or in a textured stitch area.

Wherever you join the yarn, it is essential to **weave the ends** in neatly during finishing. Always weave the strands into the wrong side of the fabric by untying any knots and working the strands in opposite directions. If you are using a thick yarn, untwist the plies and weave them in separately.

There are ways to avoid running out of yarn in mid-row. If you're almost to the end of the ball of yarn and you're not sure you can complete the next row, lay your piece flat and fold the remaining yarn back and forth over the knitting. If you have at least **four times** the width of your piece, you will have sufficient yarn to work a row of simple stitch patterns (a row of stitches such as bobbles or cables may require more yarn). Another method is to fold the remaining yarn in half and make a slip knot about 6 inches (15 cm) from the folded end. If you do not reach the knot when working the next row, you know that you will have enough yarn to work one more row.

JOINING WHILE KNITTING

To join a new yarn at the side edge, tie it loosely around the old yarn, leaving at least a 6-inch (15-cm) tail. Untie the knot later and weave the ends into the seam.

1 To join a yarn in the middle of the row, insert the right needle into the next stitch to be worked, wrap the new yarn around the right needle, and start knitting with the new yarn.

2 Work to the end of the row. Tie the old and new strands together loosely before continuing so they will not unravel. Untie and weave the ends in later.

SPLICE

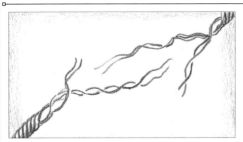

1 To join the same color in the middle of a row, splice the two ends together by untwisting the ends of both the old and the new yarn. Cut away approximately 4 inches (10 cm) from half of each set of strands as shown.

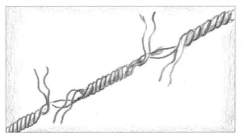

2 Overlap the remaining uncut strands and twist them together in the same direction as the yarn. Continue working with the twisted yarn, weaving in the loose ends later in the finishing.

FELTED JOIN (SPIT SPLICE—UNTREATED WOOL FIBER ONLY)

1 Unravel approximately 2 inches (5 cm) of the plies on the end of each of the two strands to be joined. (Two colors are shown for clarity.) Cut away half the plies on each strand.

2 Place the strands in the palm of the hand next to each other as shown and spit on or wet them.

3 Rub the two wet strands briskly between your hands until the friction and moisture has felted them together. Two colors are used here for clarity.

RUSSIAN JOIN

Thread a yarn needle with the old strand. Thread the needle through the plies of the yarn for about 1 inch (2.5 cm), pulling the tail through to form a loop at the end of the strand.

With a yarn needle, thread the new yarn (shown in blue for clarity) through the loop in the old yarn, then thread the needle through the plies of the new yarn and pull the tail all the way through. Pull both tails to close the loops.

Pull the ends of the strands tight, closing both loops. Trim the tails. Two colors are used here for clarity.

MAGIC KNOT

Tie the old strand around the new strand (shown in blue for clarity) with a simple knot.

Tie the new strand around the old strand as shown.

Pull the strands so the knots slide together. Pull the knots tightly together to form one knot. Trim the tails.

Increases

Increases are used to shape a piece of knitting by adding stitches to make it larger. Some increases are inconspicuous and do not interrupt the pattern, whereas others are meant to be visible and add a decorative touch. (**Decorative increases** are generally worked two or three stitches from the edge of the work.)

Most increases are worked on the **right side** of the work for two reasons. First, it is easier to see the finished look and placement of the increases. Also, it is easier to keep track of your increase rows when you work them at regular intervals, such as on every fourth row.

Often a knitting pattern may not specify the type of increase to be used. Increases that have a definite **right or left slant** can be placed to follow the slant of the fabric. To choose an appropriate one, you should learn a variety of increases and note their characteristics. The chart **symbol** appears for each type of increase shown in this chapter. Use these as a reference when working with charts for patterns that are given in symbols.

If you want to add one or two stitches, use increases, but if you need to add several stitches at one time at the side edge, it is better to cast on the additional stitches.

BAR INCREASE OR KFB: RIGHT LEANING

This is a visible increase. A horizontal bar will follow the increased stitch on the knit side of the work, whether you work the increase on the knit or the purl side.

1 To increase on the knit side, insert the right needle knitwise into the stitch to be increased. Wrap the yarn around the right needle and pull it through as if knitting, but leave the stitch on the left needle.

2 Insert the right needle into the back of the same stitch. Wrap the yarn around the needle and pull it through. Slip the stitch from the left needle. You now have 2 stitches on the right needle.

TECHNIQUE

WORKING IN FRONT AND BACK LOOPS

The front of the stitch is the loop closest to you. Always work into the front loop unless otherwise stated.
To knit into the front loop, insert right needle, left to right, into the stitch on the left needle. To knit into the back loop (loop farthest from you), insert needle, right to left, under left needle and into the stitch. To purl into the front loop, insert needle, right to left, into stitch. To purl into back loop, insert needle from behind into stitch.

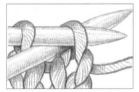

Knitting into the front loop

Purling into the front loop

Knitting into the back loop

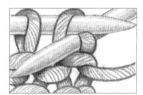

Purling into the back loop

LIFTED INCREASE: RIGHT LEANING ⅄

This increase can be used almost anywhere. However, because you are increasing by pulling up a loop from the previous row, the work may pucker if there are fewer than three rows between each increase.

The lifted increase, worked on the knit side.

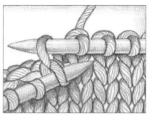

1 To work the increase on the knit side, turn the work on the left needle towards you so that the purl side of the work is visible. Insert the tip of the right needle from the top down into the stitch one row below as shown.

2 Knit this stitch, then knit the stitch on the left needle.

MAKE ONE RIGHT: M1R M

The make one right increase is made between two stitches and is practically invisible. This one slants to the right on the knit side.

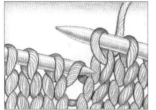

1 Insert the left needle from back to front under the horizontal strand between the last stitch worked and the next stitch on the left needle.

2 Knit this strand through the front loop to twist the stitch.

To make the increase on the purl side, insert the left needle from back to front into the horizontal strand and purl it through the front loop.

MAKE ONE OR MAKE ONE LEFT: M1 OR M1L M

This make-one method is similar to make one right above, but it slants to the left on the knit side.

1 Insert the left needle from front to back under the horizontal strand between the last stitch worked and the first stitch on the left needle.

2 Knit this strand through the back loop to twist it.

To make the increase on the purl side, insert the left needle from front to back under the horizontal strand and purl it through the back loop.

Decreases

Decreasing is a method of reducing the number of stitches (usually one or two at a time) to narrow a piece of knitting.

As with increases, a variety of methods can be used, depending on the purpose they will serve. For example, decreases can **slant** to the left or right, or be **vertical**. When shaping an armhole, you might want to work a left-slanting decrease on the right-hand side of the garment and a right-slanting decrease on the left-hand side of the garment, thus emphasizing the slope of the shaping. If placed one or two stitches in from the edge, the decreases become a decorative detail. This type of visible shaping is called **full-fashioned** shaping. Placing the decreases away from the edge also makes it easier to seam the pieces together.

Of course, the decreases do not have to be visible. A simple decrease (such as knitting two stitches together) can be placed at the edge of the knitting so that it will be invisible once the pieces are sewn together.

Most decreases are worked on the right side of the knitting, but sometimes it is necessary to decrease stitches on the wrong side, as when the decreases are worked on every row. For this reason, we have also shown decreases that can be worked on the purl side of the work.

BASIC SINGLE LEFT-SLANTING DECREASE: K2TOG TBL OR P2TOG TBL

Knitting (or purling) 2 stitches together through the back loops is a decrease that slants the stitches to the left on the knit side of the work. It is abbreviated as k2tog tbl (or p2tog tbl).

On the knit side, with the right needle behind the left needle, insert the right needle through the back loops of the next 2 stitches on the left needle. Knit these 2 stitches together.

On the purl side, with the right needle behind the left needle, insert the right needle into the back loop of the second stitch, and then into the back loop of the first stitch on the left needle, which twists the 2 stitches. Purl these 2 stitches together.

BASIC SINGLE RIGHT-SLANTING DECREASE: K2TOG OR P2TOG

Knitting (or purling) 2 stitches together is the easiest technique and one that every beginner must learn. This basic decrease slants to the right on the knit side of the work. It is abbreviated as k2tog (or p2tog).

On the knit side, insert the right needle from front to back (knitwise) into the next 2 stitches on the left needle. Wrap the yarn around the right needle (as when knitting) and pull it through.

On the purl side, insert the right needle into the front loops (purlwise) of the next 2 stitches on the left needle. Wrap the yarn around the right needle (as when purling) and pull it through.

SINGLE LEFT-SLANTING DECREASE: SKP

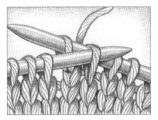

This decrease slants the stitches to the left on the knit side of the work. It is abbreviated as SKP or sl 1, k1, psso (slip 1 stitch, knit 1 stitch, pass slip stitch over knit stitch).

1 Slip 1 stitch knitwise, then knit the next stitch. Insert the left needle into the slipped stitch as shown.

2 Pass the slipped stitch over the knit stitch and off the right needle.

SINGLE LEFT-SLANTING DECREASE: SSK

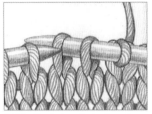

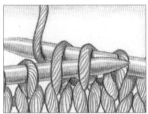

This decrease slants the stitches to the left on the knit side of the work. It is abbreviated as SSK (slip 1, slip 1, knit 2 together).

1 Slip 2 stitches knitwise, 1 at a time, from the left needle to the right needle.

2 Insert the left needle into the fronts of these 2 slipped stitches as shown and knit them together.

SINGLE LEFT-SLANTING DECREASE: SSP

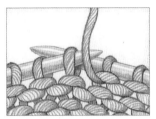

This decrease, worked on the purl side, slants the stitches to the left on the knit side.

1 Slip 2 stitches knitwise, one at a time, from the left needle to the right needle. Return these 2 slipped stitches to the left needle as shown, keeping them twisted.

2 Purl these 2 stitches together through the back loops.

SINGLE RIGHT-SLANTING DECREASE: KNIT SIDE ⟨image⟩

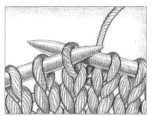

This decrease slants stitches to the right on the knit side.

1 Knit 1 stitch, slip 1 stitch knitwise; return the slipped stitch (keeping it twisted) and the knit stitch (as shown) to the left needle.

2 Pass the slipped stitch over the knit stitch and off the left needle as shown. Slip the knit stitch purlwise to the right needle.

SINGLE RIGHT-SLANTING DECREASE: PURL SIDE ⟨image⟩

This decrease, worked on the purl side, slants stitches to the right on the knit side.

1 Slip the next stitch on the left needle purlwise, then purl 1 stitch as shown.

2 With the left needle, pass the slipped stitch over the purl stitch and off the right needle.

DOUBLE LEFT-SLANTING DECREASE: SK2P ⟨image⟩

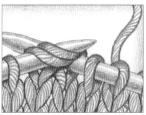

This method decreases 2 stitches and slants to the left on the knit side.

1 Slip the next stitch knitwise, then knit the next 2 stitches together as shown to decrease 1 stitch.

2 Pass the slipped stitch over the decreased stitch to decrease the second stitch.

DOUBLE LEFT-SLANTING DECREASE

This method, worked on the purl side, decreases 2 stitches and slants to the left on the knit side.

1 Purl 2 stitches together and return this decreased stitch to the left needle as shown.

2 Pass the second stitch on the left needle over the decreased stitch and off the needle. Then return the decreased stitch to the right needle.

DOUBLE DECREASE: KNIT SIDE

This method, decreases 2 stitches and slants to the right on the knit side.

1 Slip 1 stitch knitwise, knit the next stitch, pass the slipped stitch over the knit stitch (SKP). Return this decreased stitch to the left needle.

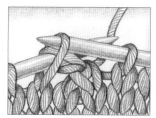

2 Pass the second stitch on the left needle over the decreased stitch and off the needle. Return the decreased stitch to the right needle.

DOUBLE VERTICAL DECREASE: S2KP

This method decreases 2 stitches and creates a vertical stitch.

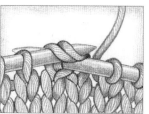

1 Insert the right needle into the next 2 stitches on the left needle as if you were knitting them together and slip them to the right needle.

2 Knit the next stitch on the left needle. With the left needle, pull both slipped stitches over the knit stitch as shown.

Binding Off

Binding off links stitches that are no longer to be worked and keeps them from unraveling. The resulting edge can be connected to other pieces of knitting or it can stand on its own. The bound-off edge should be **elastic**, but firm—not too loose or too tight. Knitters often tend to bind off too tightly. A way to reduce this tendency is to use a larger needle to bind off. Unless otherwise stated, you should bind off in the **stitch pattern** used for the piece.

Binding off is also used for shaping armholes, necks, and shoulders. It can be the first row of a buttonhole, or it can be used to create three-dimensional stitch patterns.

Although several basic bind offs are multipurpose, others serve special functions or are used to form decorative edges.

Some bind offs are worked with two or more knitting needles, whereas others require the use of one knitting needle along with a crochet hook or sewing needle.

When you bind off all the stitches in the row, pull the yarn through the last stitch to **fasten off** the piece.

BASIC KNIT BIND OFF

This is the most common bind-off method and the easiest to learn. It creates a firm, neat edge.

1 Knit 2 stitches. *Insert the left needle into the first stitch on the right needle.

2 Pull this stitch over the second stitch and off the right needle.

3 One stitch remains on the right needle as shown. Knit the next stitch. Repeat from the * until you have bound off the required number of stitches.

BASIC PURL BIND OFF

The purl bind off creates a firm edge and is used on purl stitches.

1 Purl 2 stitches. *Insert the left needle from behind the right needle into the back loop of the first stitch on the right needle as shown.

2 Pull this stitch over the second stitch and off the right needle.

3 One stitch remains on the right needle as shown. Purl the next stitch. Repeat from the * until you have bound off the required number of stitches.

SUSPENDED BIND OFF

The suspended bind off is similar to the basic knit bind off but is more flexible. You can use this method if you have a tendency to bind off too tightly.

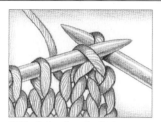

1 Work the first 2 stitches. *Pull the first stitch over the second stitch, but do not drop it from the left needle.

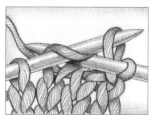

2 Knit the next stitch on the left needle.

3 Slip both stitches off the left needle. Two stitches remain on the right needle, and 1 stitch has been bound off. Repeat from the * until you have bound off all the stitches.

DECREASE BIND OFF

The decrease bind off is a decorative one that is ideal for conspicuous edges such as pockets or trims.

1 *Knit 2 stitches together through the back loops, as shown. One stitch remains on the right needle.

2 Slip the stitch from the right needle to the left needle, making sure it is not twisted. Repeat from the * until the required number of stitches are bound off.

ONE-OVER-TWO BIND OFF

This bind off pulls the stitches together for a gathered edge. It is used with pattern stitches that have a great deal of lateral spread, such as allover traveling cables or openwork stitches.

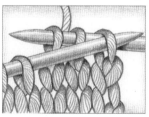

1 Work 3 stitches. *Insert the left needle into the first stitch.

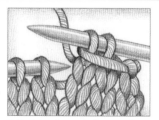

2 Pull the first stitch over the next 2 stitches and off the right needle.

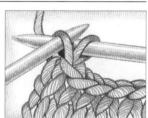

3 Work 1 more stitch onto the right needle, then repeat from the * until you have bound off the required number of stitches. If binding off every stitch, work the last 2 stitches using the basic knit bind off, as shown.

SINGLE CROCHET BIND OFF

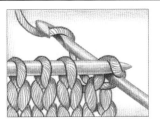

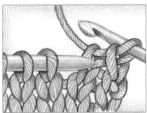

The crochet bind off is good for yarns that are not resilient, such as cottons and silks, as it creates an elastic edge.

1 Use a crochet hook of comparable size to your knitting needle. With the yarn in your left hand, insert the hook knitwise into the first stitch on the needle. Pull the yarn through to make a loop on the hook and let the old stitch fall from the needle.

2 *Work the same way into the next stitch, but pull the loop through both the stitch on the needle and the loop on the hook. One loop remains on the hook. Repeat from the * until the desired number of stitches are bound off.

DOUBLE CROCHET BIND OFF

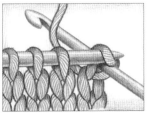

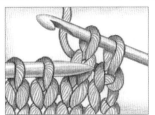

The double crochet bind off is decorative and should be used for open edges.

1 With the yarn in your right hand, insert the hook knitwise into the first stitch and wrap the yarn around the hook as if to knit. Draw a loop through and let the old stitch fall from the needle.

2 *Work the next stitch in the same way. You now have 2 loops on the hook.

3 Wrap the yarn around the hook as before and pull it through both loops on the hook. Repeat from the * until you have bound off the required number of stitches.

SLOPED BIND OFF

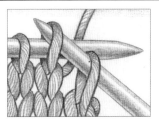

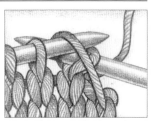

The sloped bind off is ideal for shoulder and neck shaping. It avoids the stair-step edge that is formed by a series of bind offs by making a smooth transition from one bind-off row to the next.

1 *One row before the next bind-off row, work to the last stitch of the row. Do not work this stitch. Turn the work.

2 With the yarn in back, slip the first stitch from the left needle purlwise as shown.

3 Pass the unworked stitch of the previous row over the slipped stitch. The first stitch is bound off. Bind off the desired number of stitches for that row. Work to the end of the row. Repeat from the *.

YARN OVER BIND OFF

The yarn over bind off creates an elastic edge and works well for necklines and lace patterns.

1 Knit 2 stitches and pass the first stitch over the second. *Yarn over on the right-hand needle.

2 Pass the stitch over the yarn over.

3 Knit the next stitch and bind it off by passing the last stitch over it. Repeat from the * in step 1 until all stitches are bound off.

KNIT ONE, PURL ONE, BIND OFF: SEWN BIND OFF

This method produces a subtle finish that is perfect for edges worked in single ribbing such as neckbands. A yarn needle is used in place of the right needle.

1 Cut the yarn leaving a tail three times the width of the ribbings. Thread a yarn needle with the tail and draw the yarn through the first (knit) stitch purlwise. With the yarn needle behind the knit stitch, draw the yarn through the purl stitch knitwise.

2 *With the yarn needle, slip the first knit stitch knitwise and then insert the yarn needle into the next knit stitch purlwise as shown. Pull the yarn through.

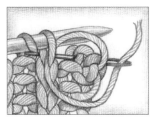

3 With the yarn needle, slip the first stitch purlwise. Go behind the knit stitch and insert the yarn needle knitwise into the next purl stitch as shown. Pull the yarn through. Repeat from the * in step 2 until all the stitches are bound off.

BINDING OFF TWO PIECES TOGETHER: THREE-NEEDLE BIND OFF

This bind off is used to join two edges that have the same number of stitches, such as shoulder edges that have been placed on holders.

1 With the right side of the two pieces facing each other, and the needles parallel, insert a third needle knitwise into the first stitch of each needle and wrap the yarn around the needle as if to knit.

2 Knit these 2 stitches together and slip them off the needles. *Knit the next 2 stitches together in the same way as shown.

3 Slip the first stitch on the third needle over the second stitch and off the needle. Repeat from the * in step 2 across the row until all the stitches are bound off.

This method is used for finishing a knit 2, purl 2 rib. A yarn needle is used in place of the right needle.

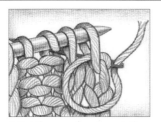

1 Cut the yarn leaving a tail three times the width of the ribbing. Thread a yarn needle with the tail and draw it through the first (knit) stitch purlwise. With the yarn needle behind the two knit stitches, draw the yarn through the first purl stitch knitwise.

2 *With the yarn needle. Slip the first knit stitch knitwise. Insert the yarn needle purlwise into the second knit stitch as shown. Pull the yarn through.

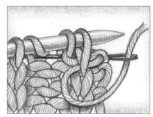

3 Take the yarn needle behind the knit stitch; insert it purlwise into the first purl stitch and knitwise into the second purl stitch as shown. Pull the yarn through.

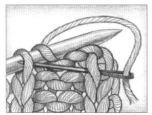

4 With the yarn needle, slip the first knit stitch knitwise. Insert the yarn needle purlwise into the next knit stitch as shown. Drop the first purl stitch from the left needle. Pull the yarn through.

5 Insert the yarn needle purlwise into the first purl stitch as shown. Pull the yarn through. Drop the stitch from the needle.

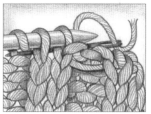

6 Take the yarn needle behind the next column of knit stitches. Insert it knitwise into the next purl stitch as shown. Pull the yarn through. Repeat from the * in step 2 until all the stitches are bound off.

TECHNIQUE

NEATENING THE LAST LOOP

When you have bound off all the stitches and only **one stitch remains** on the right needle, you must secure this stitch so that the row will not unravel. You can **pull the yarn through the last stitch,** but this often leaves a loose loop. To tighten up this loose loop and complete the bind off at the same time, bind off until one stitch remains on the left needle. Slip this last stitch to the right needle. There are now two stitches on the right needle. With the left needle, pick up the left loop of the stitch **one row below** the slipped stitch. Return the slipped stitch to the left needle and knit the picked-up loop and the slipped stitch together. Bind off the last stitch on the right needle and pull the yarn through the last stitch.

Cables

Cables are a textured, traveling stitch pattern that is formed by **crossing** stitches from one position to another and knitting them out of order.

BASIC CABLE STITCHES AND SYMBOLS*

2-st RT 2-st right twist: On RS rows, k2tog leaving sts on LH needle, k first st again, sl both sts from needle. On WS rows, wyif skip next st and purl the 2nd st, then purl skipped st, sl both sts from needle tog.

2-st LT 2-st left twist: With RH needle behind LH needle, skip the first st and k the 2nd st tbl, insert RH needle into backs of both sts, k2tog tbl.

2-st RPT 2-st right purl twist: Sl 1 st to cn and hold to *back* of work, k1, p1 from cn.

2-st LPT 2-st left purl twist: Sl 1 st to cn and hold to *front* of work, p1, k1 from cn.

3-st RT 3-st right twist: Sl 2 sts to cn and hold to *back* of work, k1, then k2 from cn.

3-st LT 3-st left twist: Sl 1 st to cn and hold to *front* of work, k2, k1 from cn.

3-st RC 3-st right cable: Sl 1 st to cn and hold to *back* of work, k2, k1 from cn.

3-st LC 3-st left cable: Sl 2 sts to cn and hold to *front* of work, k1, k2 from cn.

3-st RPC 3-st right purl cable: Sl 1 st to cn and hold to *back* of work, k2, p1 from cn.

3-st LPC 3-st left purl cable: Sl 2 sts to cn and hold to *front* of work, p1, k2 from cn.

4-st RC 4-st right cable: Sl 2 sts to cn and hold to *back* of work k2, k2 from cn.

4-st LC 4-st left cable: Sl 2 sts to cn and hold to *front* of work, k2, k2 from cn.

4-st RPC 4-st right purl cable: Sl 3 st to cn and hold to *back* of work, k1, p3 from cn.

4-st LPC 4-st left purl cable: Sl 1 st to cn and hold to *front* of work, p3, k1 from cn.

4-st RPC 4-st right purl cable: Sl 2 sts to cn and hold to *back* of work, k2, p2 from cn.

4-st LPC 4-st left purl cable: Sl 2 sts to cn and hold to *front* of work, p2, k2 from cn.

5-st RC 5-st right cable: Sl 2 sts to cn and hold to *back* of work, k3, then k2 from cn.

5-st RPC 5-st right purl cable: Sl 2 sts to cn and hold to *back* of work, k3, p2 from cn.

5-st LPC 5-st left purl cable: Sl 3 sts to cn and hold to *front* of work, p2, k3 from cn.

5-st LPC 5-st left purl cable: Sl 3 sts to cn and hold to *front* of work, p2, k3 from cn.

tie st: Sl 5 sts to cn and hold to *back* of work, wrap yarn around these 5 sts 3 times, return sts to LH needle, then work them as foll: K1, p3, k1.

6-st RC 6-st right cable: Sl 3 sts to cn and hold to *back* of work, k3, k3 from cn.

6-st LC 6-st left cable: Sl 3 sts to cn and hold to *front* of work, k3, k3 from cn.

* See additional symbols on page 93.

TECHNIQUE

HOW A CABLE SYMBOL IS MADE

Each box = 1 stitch and 1 row

The center slanting line shows the direction of the cable: this line slants to the left, so the stitches must be held to the front.

The two straight lines on the lower left-hand side show how many stitches are slipped to the cable needle and how to work them, in this case 2 stitches are slipped to the cable needle and held to the front of the work.

The two straight lines on the upper right-hand side show how many stitches are to be worked after the stitches are slipped to the cable needle and how to work them. In this case the next 2 stitches are knit from the left-hand needle.

Then you are ready to work the stitches from the cable needle, in this case the 2 stitches are knit from the cable needle. The 4-St Left Cable is complete.

Here the center slants to the right, so the stitches must be held to the back. The two straight lines on the upper left-hand side show how many stitches are slipped to the cable needle. In this case, two stitches are held to the back. Then knit the next two stitches on the left needle (the two straight lines on the lower right). Finally, knit 2 stitches from the cable needle. The 4-St Right Cable is complete.

BACK (RIGHT) CABLE

6-st RC

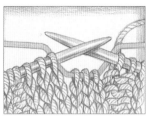

1 Slip 3 stitches to the cable needle and hold to the *back*.

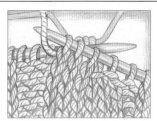

2 With the cable needle at the back, knit the next 3 stitches from the left-hand needle.

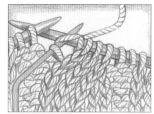

3 Knit the next 3 stitches from the cable needle.

FRONT (LEFT) CABLE

6-st LC

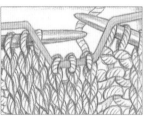

1 Slip 3 stitches to the cable needle and hold to the *front*.

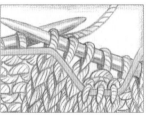

2 With the cable needle at the front, knit the next 3 stitches from the left-hand needle.

3 Knit the 3 stitches from the cable needle.

PLAIT CABLE

This plait cable is worked over 8 sts, alternating right-side rows of two 4-st RCs with one 4-st LC worked in the center of the cable panel.

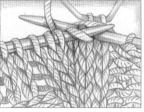

1 Work to the cable panel. Slip 2 stitches to the cable needle and hold to the *back*, then knit the next 2 stitches from the left-hand needle as shown.

2 Knit 2 from the cable needle to complete the first 4-st RC, then knit the next 2 stitches from the left-hand needle.

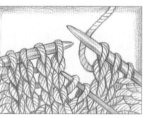

3 In the next RS row, work to the cable panel. Knit 2 stitches, slip the next 2 stitches to the cable needle and hold to the *front*, as shown, then knit 2 from the right-hand needle, knit 2 from cable needle, knit 2.

DIMINISHING CABLE

6-st LC becomes a 4-st LC

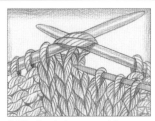

1 Slip 3 stitches to cable needle and hold to *front*, k2tog as shown, then knit 1.

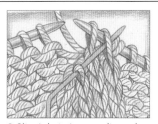

2 Slip 1, knit 1, pass slipped stitch over the first 2 stitches on the cable needle.

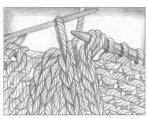

3 Knit next stitch from cable needle.

4-ST RIGHT CABLE (WITHOUT A CABLE NEEDLE)

This 4-st RC was worked without a cable needle.

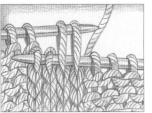

1 Work to cable panel. With yarn in back, place the 4 cable sts on the right-hand needle, then working behind the second 2 cable stitches, insert the left-hand needle through the first 2 cable stitches.

2 Carefully pull the right-hand needle out of the second 2 cable sts and place them on the left-hand needle to the right of the 2 cable stitches already on the left-hand needle.

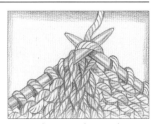

3 Knit the 4 stitches in the new orientation.

4-ST LEFT CABLE (WITHOUT A CABLE NEEDLE)

This 4-st LC was worked without a cable needle.

1 Work to cable panel. With yarn in back, place 4 cable sts on the right-hand needle, then with the left-hand needle in front of the second 2 cable stitches, insert it through the first 2 cable stitches.

2 Carefully pull the right-hand needle out of the second 2 cable stitches and place them on left-hand needle to the right of the 2 cable stitches already on the left-hand needle.

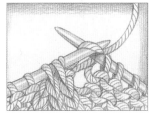

3 Knit the 4 stitches in the new orientation.

Stranded Knitting

In stranded knitting, more than one color is worked in a single row. The unused colors are carried along the back of the work, forming **floats**.

STRANDING: ONE HANDED

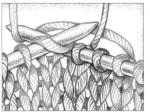

1 Knit Side: Drop working yarn. Bring new color (now the working yarn) over top of dropped yarn and work to the next color change.

2 Drop the working yarn. Bring the new color under the dropped yarn and work to the next color change. Repeat steps 1 and 2.

1 Purl Side: Drop working yarn. Bring new color (now the working yarn) over top of dropped yarn and work to the next color change.

2 Drop the working yarn. Bring the new color under the dropped yarn and work to the next color change. Repeat steps 1 and 2.

STRANDING: TWO HANDED

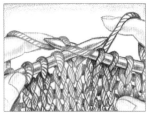

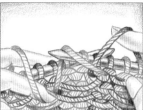

1 Knit Side: Hold the working yarn in your right hand and nonworking yarn in your left. Bring the working yarn over the top of the yarn in your left hand and knit with the right hand to the next color change.

2 Yarn in your right hand is now the nonworking yarn; yarn in your left hand is the working yarn. Bring working yarn under non-working yarn and knit with the left hand to next color change. Repeat steps 1 and 2.

1 Purl Side: Hold the working yarn in your right hand and nonworking yarn in your left. Bring the working yarn over the top of the yarn in your left hand and purl with the right hand to the next color change.

2 Yarn in your right hand is now the nonworking yarn; yarn in your left hand is the working yarn. Bring working yarn under nonworking yarn and purl with the left hand to the next color change. Repeat steps 1 and 2.

STRANDING: BOTH STRANDS IN RIGHT HAND

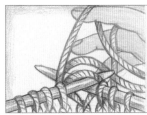

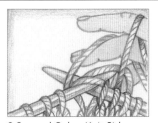

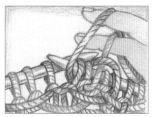

1 Main Color, Knit Side: Hold working yarn over index finger and second color over middle finger. Insert right-hand needle as if to knit and, bringing yarn over second color, wrap main color around needle tip and knit the stitch.

2 Second Color, Knit Side: Hold strand on index finger out of the way, insert the right-hand needle as if to knit and, bringing the strand on middle finger under the main color strand, knit the stitches.

1 Main Color, Purl Side: Hold working yarn over index finger, second color over middle finger. Insert tip of RH needle in stitch as if to purl; with index finger, wrap main color around needle as if to purl, bringing yarn over second color, purl.

2 Second Color, Purl Side: Hold strand on the index finger out of the way, bring strand on the middle finger under the main color strand and purl the stitches.

STRANDING: BOTH STRANDS IN LEFT HAND

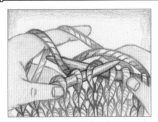

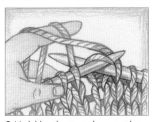

1 Knit Side: Hold both strands over the index finger with the main color to the left of the second color. Insert the right-hand needle into the next stitch as if to knit and, bringing the main color strand over the second color, draw it knitwise through the stitch.

2 Hold both strands over the index finger with the main color to the left of the second color. Insert the right-hand needle into the next stitch as if to knit and, bringing the second color strand under the main color, draw it through the stitch.

1 Purl Side: Hold both strands over index finger with main color to left of second color. Insert right-hand needle into next stitch as if to purl and, bringing main color strand over the second color, draw it purlwise through the stitch.

2 Hold both strands over the index finger with the main color to the left of the second color. Insert the right-hand needle into the next stitch as if to purl, and bringing the second color strand under the main color, draw it through the stitch.

WEAVING

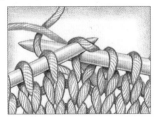

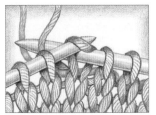

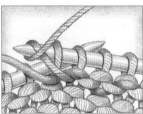

1 Hold working yarn in one hand and yarn to be caught in the other. To catch yarn above a knit stitch, bring it over right needle. Knit the stitch with the working yarn, bringing it under the caught yarn.

2 The caught yarn will go under the next knit stitch. With the working yarn, knit the stitch, bringing the yarn over the caught yarn. Repeat steps 1 and 2 to the next color change.

1 To catch the yarn above a purl stitch, bring it over the right needle. Purl the stitch with the working yarn, bringing it under the caught yarn.

2 To catch the yarn below a purl stitch, purl the stitch with the working yarn, bringing it over the caught yarn. Repeat steps 1 and 2 to the next color change.

CATCHING FLOATS (TWISTING)

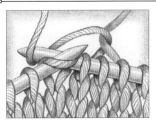

On the knit side, twist the working yarn and the carried yarn around each other once. Then continue knitting with the same color as before.

On the purl side, twist the yarns around each other as shown, then continue purling with the same color as before.

Intarsia

Intarsia is a colorwork technique in which blocks of color are worked with **separate** balls of yarn or bobbins. The yarns are not carried across the back of the work between color changes and must be **twisted** around each other at each change to prevent holes in the work.

When changing colors in a **vertical line,** the yarn must be twisted at the color change on every row to avoid a hole in the work. When changing colors in a **diagonal line,** the yarns must only be twisted on every other row. If the diagonal slants to the right, twist the yarn only on the knit rows. If the diagonal slants to the left, twist the yarn only on purl rows.

CHANGING COLORS IN A DIAGONAL LINE

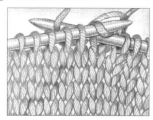 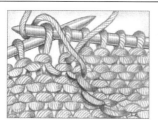 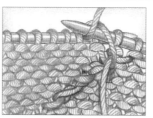 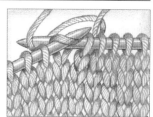

1 When working a right diagonal on the knit side, bring the new color over the top of the old color and knit to the next color change.

2 On the purl side, pick up the new color from under the old color and purl to the next color change.

1 When working a left diagonal on the purl side, bring the new color over the top of the old color and purl to the next color change.

2 On the knit side, pick up the new color from under the old color and knit to the next color change.

CHANGING COLORS IN A VERTICAL LINE

 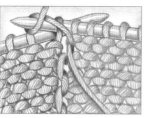

1 On the knit side, drop the old color. Pick up the new color from under the old color and knit to the next color change.

2 On the purl side, drop the old color. Pick up the new color from under the old color and purl to the next color change. Repeat steps 1 and 2.

TECHNIQUE

HAND-WOUND BOBBIN OR BUTTERFLY

1 Hold the end of the yarn with your thumb. Bring the yarn around your forefinger and middle finger. Wrap it in the opposite direction around your ring finger and little finger. Continue wrapping the yarn in a figure eight until you have enough.

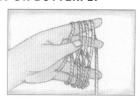

2 Cut the yarn, leaving about an 8-inch (20-cm) tail. Remove the yarn from your fingers, wrap the tail several times around the center, and tie a knot as shown.

3 Pull the unknotted end of the strand to release the yarn as needed.

JOINING A NEW COLOR: VERSION A

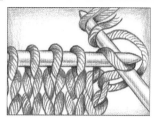

1 Wrap first the old and then the new yarn knitwise and work the first stitch with both yarns.

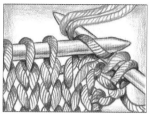

2 Drop the old yarn. Work the next 2 stitches with both ends of the new yarn.

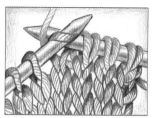

3 Drop the short end of the new color and continue working with the single strand. On the following row, work the 3 double stitches as single stitches.

JOINING A NEW COLOR: VERSION B

1 Cut the old yarn, leaving about 4 inches (10 cm). Purl the first 2 stitches with the new yarn. *Insert the needle purl-wise into the next stitch, lay the short ends of both the old and new colors over the top of the needle and purl the next stitch under the short ends.

2 Leave the short ends hanging and purl the next stitch over them.

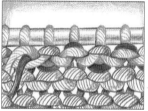

3 Repeat from the * until you have woven the short ends into the wrong side of the piece.

JOINING A NEW COLOR: VERSION C

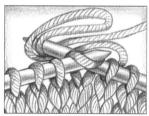

1 Work to 3 stitches before the place where you want to join the new yarn. Work these stitches with the yarn folded double, making sure you have just enough to work 3 stitches.

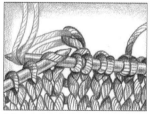

2 Loop the new yarn into the loop of the old yarn, leaving the new yarn doubled for approximately 8 inches (20 cm). Knit the next 3 stitches with the doubled yarn. Let the short end of the new yarn hang and continue knitting with 1 strand.

3 On the next row, carry the first yarn across the back of the work from the place where it was dropped on the previous row and twist it together with the second yarn. Work the doubled stitches as single stitches.

Stripes

Horizontal stripes are one of the easiest types of color knitting because you do not have to **carry** yarns across the row as you work. You can cut the yarn as you finish each stripe, but this means weaving in many ends after the pieces are complete. To avoid this, carry the yarns you are not using along the side of the work.

When working vertical stripes, you must either **carry the colors** across the back of the work or use separate balls or **bobbins** for each stripe. If each stripe is an inch (2.5 cm) or less, you can carry the yarns across the back. With wide stripes you should use bobbins for each color and **twist** the colors around each other on every row.

CASTING ON FOR VERTICAL STRIPES

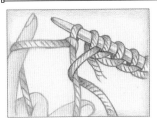

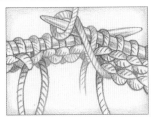

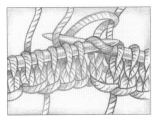

1 Using double or long-tail cast on and with end of yarn coming from the skein over thumb, cast on first color. Make a slip knot on needle with second color. To cast on second stitch, twist the old and new colors as shown.

2 If working in stockinette stitch, purl the first row, twisting the yarns at each color change, as shown. Pull the yarn tightly to prevent gaps.

3 On the second (knit) row, twist the yarns by bringing the working yarn over the old yarn.

CORRUGATED RIBBING

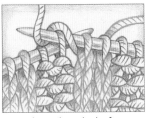

1 On the right side, before a purl stitch, drop the old color. Bring the working color under the old color and to the front of the work between the needles. Purl the next 2 stitches.

2 Before a knit stitch, bring the old color to the back of the work and leave it. Bring the working color under the old color and knit the next 2 stitches.

1 On the wrong side, before a knit stitch, drop the old color. Bring the working color over the top of the old color and to the back of the work as shown. Knit the next 2 stitches.

2 Before a purl stitch, drop the old color, bring the working color over the top of the old color, and purl the next 2 stitches.

TECHNIQUE

CARRYING COLORS ALONG THE SIDE

1 When changing colors with narrow, even-numbered stripes, drop the old color. Bring the new color under the old color, being sure not to pull the yarn too tightly, and knit the next stripe.

2 When working thicker stripes (more than 4 rows), carry the old yarn up the side until it is needed again by twisting the working yarn around the old yarn every couple of rows, as shown.

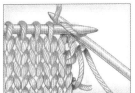

Mosaic Knitting

This form of colorwork requires no bobbins, no stranding, and no changing of colors in the middle of a row. Color changes are made at the **side edge every other row.** You can work a mosaic motif in stockinette, reverse stockinette, garter stitch, or a combination of these stitches.

Only **two colors** are used in a motif. Each color is used alone for two entire rows. The first stitch of the chart is a guide to which color will be worked on that row. Reading the chart (below), all the stitches in the dark color are worked (either knit or purl) over two rows while the light color is slipped purlwise over the same two rows. In the next two rows, the light color is worked and the dark color is slipped. The first and last stitch of every row is always worked, never slipped.

Usually only the right-side rows are charted. When working wrong-side rows, you do not need to look at the chart. The colors are either slipped or worked exactly as they were in the preceding row.

When you slip stitches, always hold the working **yarn to the wrong side** of the work; that is, to the back on right-side rows and to the front on wrong-side rows.

Begin a mosaic pattern by knitting a foundation of one or two rows with the color that will be slipped in the first row. This is necessary because you should not slip stitches immediately after the cast-on row.

To change colors at the end of a row, drop the yarn in use and pick up the other yarn behind it.

Mosaic knitting patterns can be worked in the round. Follow the chart by reading every round from right to left. The second (even-numbered) rounds are the same as the odd-numbered rounds for each color. If you are working in stockinette, for example, the second round will be knit and not purled.

WORKING MOSAIC KNITTING IN STOCKINETTE STITCH

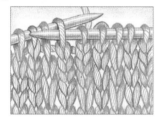

1 On the right-side row (here chart row 13), knit all the stitches in the light color and slip all the stitches in the dark color purlwise with the yarn at the back.

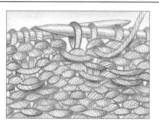

2 On the wrong-side row (here chart row 14), purl all the stitches in the light color and slip all the stitches in the dark color purlwise with the yarn at the front.

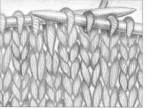

1 On the right-side row (here chart row 15), knit all the stitches in the dark color and slip all the stitches in the light color purlwise with the yarn at the back.

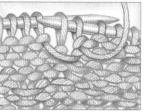

2 On the wrong-side row (here chart row 16), purl all the stitches in the dark color and slip all the stitches in the light color purlwise with the yarn at the front.

MOSAIC CHART

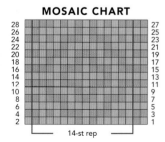

28 26 24 22 20 18 16 14 12 10 8 6 4 2
27 25 23 21 19 17 15 13 11 9 7 5 3 1

14-st rep

This swatch was made following the chart in stockinette stitch; that is, knitting the right-side rows and purling the wrong-side rows.

This swatch was made following the chart in garter stitch; that is, knitting every row.

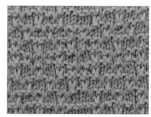

Working the light-color rows in garter stitch and the dark-color rows in stockinette stitch creates a dimensional effect.

Yarn Overs in Lace ⬚

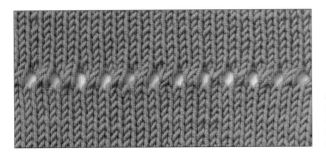

A row of yarn overs followed by compensating decreased stitches.

BETWEEN TWO KNIT STITCHES

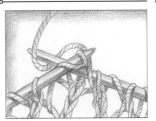

Bring the yarn from the back of the work to the front between the two needles. Knit the next stitch, bringing the yarn to the back over the right-hand needle as shown.

BETWEEN A KNIT AND A PURL STITCH

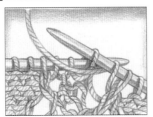

Bring the yarn from the back to the front between the two needles, then to the back over the right-hand needle and to the front again as shown. Purl the next stitch.

AT THE BEGINNING OF A PURL ROW

To work a yarn over at the beginning of a purl row, keep the yarn at the back of the work. Insert the right-hand needle purlwise into the first stitch on the left-hand needle. Purl the stitch.

BETWEEN A PURL AND A SLIP ONE, KNIT ONE, PASS SLIPPED STITCH OVER

Leaving the yarn at the front of the work, slip the next stitch knitwise. Bring the yarn to the back over the right-hand needle and knit the next stitch. Pass the slipped stitch over to complete the decrease.

BETWEEN TWO PURL STITCHES

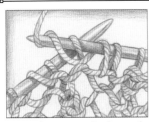

Leave the yarn at the front of the work. Bring the yarn to the back over the right-hand needle and to the front as shown. Purl the next stitch.

AT THE BEGINNING OF A KNIT ROW

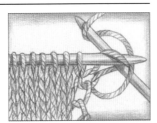

Keep the yarn at the front of the work. Insert the right-hand needle knitwise in the first stitch. Bring the yarn to the back over the right-hand needle and knit the next stitch.

MULTIPLE YARN OVER

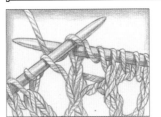

1 Wrap the yarn around the needle as for a single yarn over, then wrap the yarn around the needle again as many times as needed to create the indicated number of yarn overs.

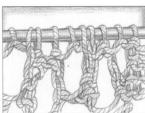

2 On the following row, alternate knitting and purling into the multiple yarn over.

Decreases in Lace

K2TOG BEFORE A YARN OVER

1 With yarn at back, insert needle in next 2 stitches as if to knit.

2 Wrap needle to knit and draw through both stitches.

SSK AFTER A YARN OVER

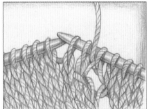

1 With the yarn in front, slip the next 2 stitches knitwise one at a time.

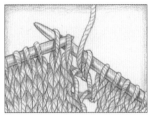

2 Insert the left-hand needle through the front of the two slipped stitches. Bring the yarn to the back over the needle and knit the 2 stitches together.

SKP AFTER A YARN OVER

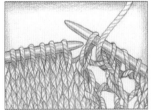

1 Bring yarn to front between the needles and slip the next stitch knitwise.

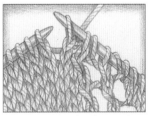

2 Bring yarn to back over the right-hand needle and knit the first stitch on the left-hand needle.

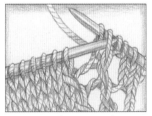

3 Keeping the yarn at the back of the work, insert the left-hand needle in the slipped stitch and pass the slipped stitch over the knit stitch.

K3TOG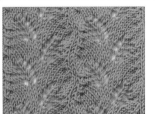

1 With the yarn at the back of the work, insert the right-hand needle knitwise through the next three stitches on the left-hand needle.

2 Wrap the yarn knitwise and draw it through all 3 stitches.

SK2P AFTER A YARN OVER

1 Bring the yarn to front between the needles and slip the next stitch knitwise. Insert the right-hand needle knitwise through the next 2 stitches on the left-hand needle. Bring the yarn from front to back over the right-hand needle and knit them together.

2 With the yarn at the back, pass the slipped stitch over the k2tog.

S2KP

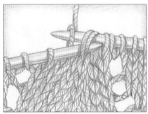

1 Keeping the yarn at the back, insert right-hand needle in next 2 stitches as if to knit them together, and slip them off the left-hand needle.

2 Knit the next stitch on the left-hand needle. Insert the left-hand needle through the 2 slipped stitches and pass them over the knit stitch.

Lace Borders and Edgings

The simplest way to finish a lace piece is to use a stretchy bind-off or decorative crocheted chain. It is more pleasing, however, to add a border or edging to the bottom of a shawl or scarf to give interest to the edges. Lace borders and edgings are not restricted to shawls or scarves, or to items knit in lace-weight yarn. They can be used to decorate garments or accessories according to personal preference.

CROCHET-EDGE BIND OFF

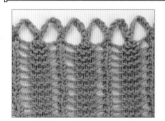
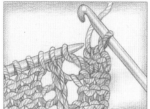
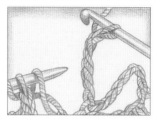

1 Work a single crochet through the first three stitches.

2 Chain 8.

3 Insert crochet hook through the next 3 stitches to begin the next single crochet.

BORDER WORKED DOWN FROM A PROVISIONAL CAST ON

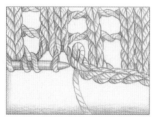
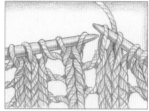

The finished join after the border has been worked.

1 Carefully remove scrap yarn, placing the released stitches on a knitting needle.

2 Rejoin yarn to knit cast-on stitches, taking care to make sure the stitches are not twisted on the needle. The next stitch shown on the left needle should be knit through the back loop to untwist it.

PERPENDICULAR EDGING JOINED WHILE WORKING

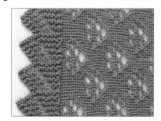
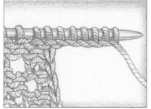

Notice the straight edge attached to the lace motif and the pointed edge on the opposite side of the edging.

1 Cast on the indicated number of stitches at the end of the last row and turn.

2 Work last edging stitch together with next stitch from shawl to join edging to shawl. The remaining live stitches are on the needle. Turn.

3 After turning the work, slip the joining stitch and continue the next edging row.

Shaping in Lace

Lace stitch patterns are constructed from matching pairs of yarn overs and decreases. If you are knitting a garment that requires shaping, such as decreases for armholes on a sweater bodice or increases in a sleeve knit from cuff to armhole, you have to consider the effect of both as you remove or add stitches.

If you **eliminate the lace decrease** when you decrease to shape your piece, you must **eliminate the corresponding yarn over**.

If you can make both the decrease and its yarn over independent of the shaping decrease, then make both of them. If you cannot, then make only the shaping decrease.

The simplest way to shape lace, which works well if the stitch pattern has a small repeat, is to **replace** the lace repeat with stockinette stitches. For example, if the stitch pattern has an eight-stitch repeat, knit eight stitches in stockinette at the beginning and end of the row or round. Decrease within that stockinette panel.

It is best to decrease or increase one or two stitches **in from the edge** so that there is a smooth edge for seaming.

The same rules apply when you increase in a lace stitch pattern. If the number of stitches added does not accommodate both the lace decrease and the yarn over, then just add plain stockinette (or "ground") stitches.

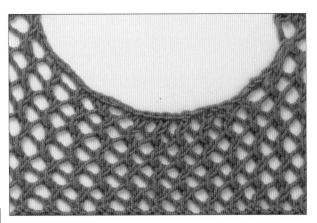

When shaping in lace, increases may be eliminated to ensure the proper stitch count. The stitches on the chart shaded in pink show where to knit 1 instead of working in the pattern. Note that on the left side of the chart, the pink stitches are actually the loops left after binding off, which are considered one knit stitch.

DECREASING IN LACE

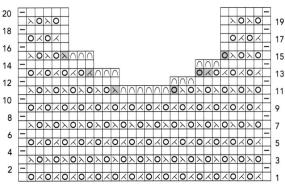

STITCH KEY

☐	k on RS, p on WS
▨	k instead of stitch in pattern
⊟	p on RS, k on WS
⊿	k2tog
⊠	SKP
⊙	yo
⌒	bind off 1 st

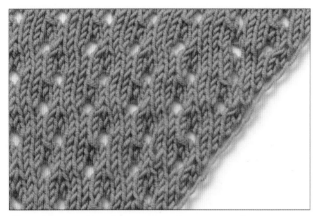

Chart shows working increases into lace pattern. Repeats are added when there are enough stitches for a yarn over with compensating decrease.

INCREASING IN LACE

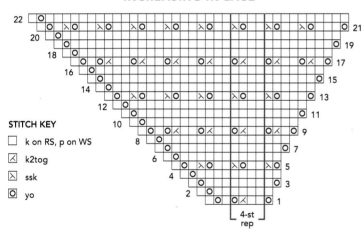

STITCH KEY

- ☐ k on RS, p on WS
- ⟋ k2tog
- ⟍ ssk
- ⊡ yo

CASTING ON AND BINDING OFF IN LACE

Many of the cast-on methods used for lace knitting are the same as those used for any type of knitting: long-tail cast on, cable cast on, backwards-loop cast on, etc. In casting on for lace, however, it is essential that you **cast on loosely.** More specifically, the space between the cast-on stitches should be at least 1/8 inch (1/3 cm) so that the edge of the work won't be too tight. Try casting on with needles that are **one or two sizes larger** than those used in your project or casting on over two needles. Some lace patterns will start with a provisional cast on so that the edge may be picked up to add edging or grafted to another piece of lace. Top-down shawls may start with the garter tab cast on.

The bind off on a lace piece also should be **flexible** so that it doesn't pull your work. You may find it easier in lace knitting (with the pattern only on the right side of the work) to bind off on the purl or wrong-side row rather than on the right-side row. In that way, you will not have to bind off yarn overs. Many of the bind off methods used for other types of knitting work well on lace, such as the yarn over bind off or the suspended bind off. Some shawls may also have a crocheted chain as a decorative bind off and edge. As in casting on for lace, you may find you achieve a sufficiently loose bind off by working with a needle that is **one or two sizes larger** than your working needle.

Correcting Mistakes in Lace Knitting

Making a mistake in lace knitting can cause more frustration than making an error in other kinds of pattern stitches. If you discover your mistake after knitting several rows, you may have to rip out stitch by stitch to avoid dropping yarn overs or changing your stitch count. Ripping back a row with multiple decreases may cause more problems than the one you sought to correct, because if you do not undo the decrease carefully you may find you no longer have the correct number of stitches.

A bit of advice that is the knitting equivalent of "measure twice, cut once" is to not make the mistake in the first place. There is a relatively painless way, however, to correct mistakes in lace knitting—use a **lifeline**. Lifelines are useful in all types of knitting, but they are especially helpful when knitting lace, particularly complex lace patterns in shawls, wraps, or scarves. If you find that you've made a mistake after knitting several more rows or rounds, you can simply remove your stitches from the needle and rip back to the lifeline. The lifeline will hold your stitches, whether they are knits and purls, decreases, or yarn overs, and you can return the stitches to the needle and reknit from that point on.

The decision on how often to place lifelines when knitting lace is up to you. Many knitters like to insert them at regular intervals, such as the beginning of every pattern repeat. Others find that they are most helpful if placed in a particularly complex row—one that you would not really want to knit again. The rows of shawls knit from the top down or the rounds in circular shawls become longer as you progress with your garment, and using frequent lifelines to avoid correcting mistakes in rows or rounds like these can save hours of work.

In choosing a type of lifeline, consider the yarn you are using for your piece. The lifeline should be **thinner than the knitting yarn**, and it should be **smooth and easy to pull out**. Cotton embroidery thread, thin silk yarn, or dental floss are all good choices, and the lifeline should be in a **contrasting color** to your working yarn so that it is easy to see.

The steps for inserting a lifeline are on page 99. If you are using stitch markers in your work, be sure not to thread the lifeline through them. Some brands of interchangeable circular needles have hole at the base of the needle point, and the contrast yarn or floss can be threaded through the hole. In that way, you can add the lifeline automatically as you knit. Using a needle having a different color from the yarn you are using makes it easier to see the stitches and can also cut down on mistakes.

Many common mistakes, such as those shown below, can be corrected without ripping out your work. If you have missed a yarn over, decreased in the wrong direction, or forgotten to decrease, it is possible to correct the error on the next right-side row or round. Using **stitch markers** and checking to see that you have the **correct number of stitches** for each pattern repeat will prevent one of these simple errors from becoming a problem that could require rows or rounds of ripping.

CORRECTING ERRORS

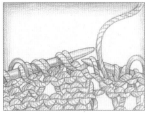

A yarn over was missed in the previous row. To correct it, in the place where the yarn over should be, insert the right-hand needle under the strand from back to front and place it on the left-hand needle.

In the previous row, the knitter forgot to pass the stitch over. Work to the missed SK2P, turn the work to pass the slipped stitch over the k2tog, then turn back to continue the row.

1 The decrease two rows below has been worked in the wrong direction. Work to the error. Run a smaller needle through the 2 stitches for the decrease and the stitches on each side of it drop the decreased stitches down to the needle.

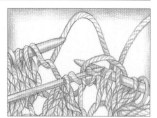

2 Work the correct decrease using the strand of yarn from the row of the error. Work the next row with the strand from that row. Continue to work the next row.

1 BASIC TECHNIQUES

Knitting In The Round

Unlike flat knitting, in which you knit back and forth on straight needles to form rectangular pieces, circular knitting forms **seamless tubes of knitting** that can be shaped using increases and decreases or short rows. In this way, you can knit tubular sweater bodies and sleeves, socks, hats, and mittens, as well as non-wearable items such as knitted toys and bags. To knit circularly, you need a set of double-pointed needles (dpns) or circular needles. After **joining your cast-on row** to make a round, you create spirals of knitting to form the tube.

In the past, only **double-pointed needles** were available for circular knitting. The modern **circular needle**, which consists of two short needles attached to a flexible cord, did not enter the market until the twentieth century and became popular in recent decades thanks to improvements in the flexibility of the cable and materials used to make the needle tips. Sets of **interchangeable circular needles** are available in which needle tips of different sizes can be screwed into or attached to the cords.

CASTING ON AND KNITTING WITH DPN

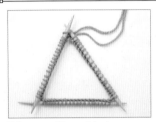

When working with dpn, divide the stitches evenly over 3 or 4 needles. Here, the work is divided over 3 needles that form a triangle. When divided over 4 needles, the needles will form a square.

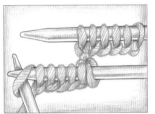

1 Cast on the required number of stitches on the first needle, plus 1 extra. Slip extra stitch to next needle. Continue in this way, casting on the required number of stitches on the last needle.

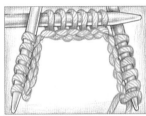

2 Arrange the needles as shown, with the cast-on edge facing the center of the triangle (or square).

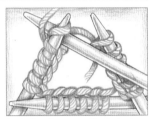

3 With a free needle, knit the first cast-on stitch and pull yarn tightly. Place a marker after or in first stitch to mark the beginning of the round. Work in rounds, slipping the marker each round.

TIP

AVOIDING LADDERS

One problem that may occur when working with double-pointed needles is laddering. A ladder is a **column of stretched stitches** that can form where one needle meets another—and so this problem can occur using circular needles as well, but only in one or two columns rather than three or four. Ladders usually form if your tension is looser at the point where you switch from one needle to the next than for stitches in the rest of the round.

Although most knitters get ladders from too-loose stitches, it is possible to tighten too much and distort your knitting so that a column of tight stitches forms at the junction between the two needles.

You can avoid ladders by tightening the first and second stitch when you switch needles. Just give the yarn a slight tug and then continue to knit.

You can also try to avoid ladders by using five double-pointed needles instead of four so that your tension is divided more evenly.

Moving the stitches from one needle to another changes the placement of the first and last stitches on each needle. In this way, you are not stretching the same stitch on each round.

Often just gaining experience by practicing knitting in rounds will eliminate the ladders.

CASTING ON AND KNITTING WITH CIRCULAR NEEDLES

  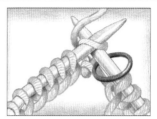 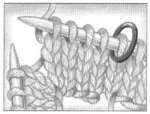

Cast on as you would for straight knitting. Distribute the stitches evenly around the needle, **being sure not to twist them**. The last cast-on stitch is the last stitch of the round. Place a marker here to indicate the end of the round.

If the cast-on stitches are twisted, as shown, you will find that after you knit a few inches the fabric will be twisted. You will have to rip out your work to the cast-on row and straighten the stitches.

To join the cast-on row for the first round, hold the needle tip with the last cast-on stitch in your right hand and the tip with the first cast-on stitch in your left hand. Knit the first cast-on stitch, pulling the yarn tightly to avoid a gap.

Work until you reach the marker. This completes the first round. Slip the marker to the right needle and work the next round.

USING TWO CIRCULAR NEEDLES

 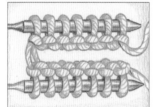 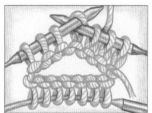 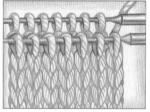

When working with two circular needles, it helps to use two needles that look different from each other. The needles in these drawings have cables of different colors for the sake of clarity.

1 Cast on the required number of stitches, slip half to second needle. Slide stitches so the ends that are not joined are at the tips of each needle. Join the ends to begin working in the round.

2 Slide the stitches on the back needle to the cable. Using the other end of the front needle (with purple cable) knit the stitches on that needle.

3 Turn, slide stitches on needle with purple cable (now the back needle) to the cable.
   Slide the stitches on front needle (yellow cable) to tip and, using the working yarn and other end of front needle, knit across the needle. Continue to work rounds in this manner.

TECHNIQUE

JOINING METHODS FOR CIRCULAR KNITTING

When joining after casting on, make sure your stitches are not twisted around the needle. To help keep the stitches untwisted, keep the cast-on edge facing you, or work one or two rows before joining, then sew the gap.

On the first round, work the first few stitches with both the working yarn and the cast-on tail to create a neater join.

Another way to make a neat join is to cast one extra stitch onto the last needle. Slip this stitch to the first needle and knit it together with the first cast-on stitch. These joins, in addition to the crossover join shown here, can be used with circular needles as well as double-pointed needles.

In the **crossover joining method**, the first and last cast-on stitches swap positions. Stitches are divided on two needles. Slip the first cast-on stitch from left-hand to right-hand needle. The left needle tip is inserted in the last cast-on stitch, where it is available to pass the stitch over the slipped first stitch and onto the left needle.

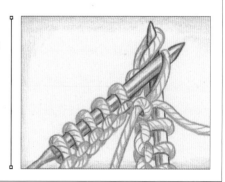

Magic Loop

Magic loop knitting is usually done with a circular needle having a cable that is longer than 29 inches (74 cm), although some knitters use longer cables and some use cables as short as 24 inches (60 cm). The length of your needle should be three or **four times the circumference** of your project. The ideal needle will have a thin, flexible cable.

This method is excellent for knitting small-circumference tubes, such as those found in socks or mittens. It is also easy to knit two socks or sleeves at a time.

A drawback of the magic loop method is that it can become tedious to pull all the loops through the work. In addition, you must work with care to avoid stretching out your work near the loops. It might be necessary to buy new needles if those you have on hand have cables that are too short for magic loop. This method also causes wear and tear on the cables of your circular needles, making it necessary to replace them.

MAGIC-LOOP METHOD

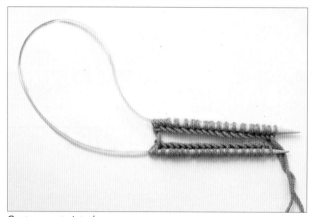

Cast on, untwisted

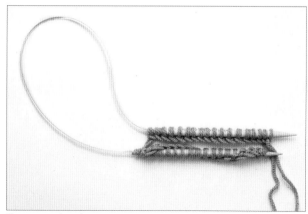

Cast on, twisted

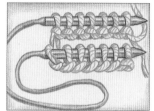

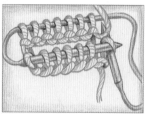

1 Cast on the required number of stitches on one circular needle. Slide the stitches to the cable of the needle. Slide the points of the needles so each point holds **half** of the cast-on stitches. Be sure that the working yarn is on the back needle.

2 Join ends to begin working in the round.

The back stitches are on the cable and the front stitches on the left needle point, with the right needle point ready to knit the front stitches. The working yarn is at back and wrapped to knit.

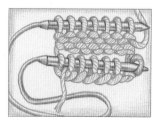

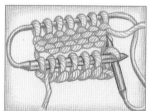

3 Knit across the front stitches, slide the back stitches to the needle point, and turn the work.

The first half of the stitches have been knit, the second half of the stitches are pushed to the point and the work is turned.

4 Slide the stitches just knit to the cable and begin to knit the second half of the stitches (now on the front needle).

Steeking

A **steek** is a vertical column of extra knitted stitches that are intended to be cut open when a garment is being finished. Steeks are often used in stranded knitting to create armholes, necklines, and cardigan fronts, and they are most common in traditional types of knitting such as Fair Isle or Scandinavian knitting. There are no limits to the use of steeks, however, and you can use them in any type of modern item knit in the round, stranded or not. After the steek is cut on a sweater, stitches are picked up around the cut edge; sleeves then can be knit from the armhole to cuff and buttonbands and neck edges can be added.

The simplest type of steek is an **unreinforced steek**, in which the steek is cut without any added sewing or crocheting. Steeks of this sort tend to full and stick together. Shetland yarns or the all-wool yarns used for traditional Scandinavian sweaters are examples. Even with yarns like these, many knitters will trim the steek and finish it with an **overcast stitch**, such as that shown below.

Other methods of finishing steeks use **crocheting and sewing**. In a crocheted steek, the edge to be cut is finished with two rows of single crochet, and then the steek is cut open between those two rows. Alternatively, straight or zigzag sewing machine stitches may be used to reinforce the steek. The steek is then cut open between the machine stitches. Reinforced steeks may be used with untreated 100% wool yarns, however, they are necessary to prevent unraveling in steeking items that are knit from superwash wools or any nonwool yarn.

Traditional sweaters may have ribbons or facings covering the steeked edge on the inside of the work.

To create a steek on a stranded sweater, cast on 8 to 10 stitches at the beginning of the armhole or cardigan opening. The first and last of these stitches are edge stitches that will be picked up later. When the knitting is complete, the steek will be cut up the center.

UNREINFORCED STEEKS

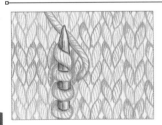

To create a steek on a stranded sweater, cast on 8–10 stitches at the beginning of the armhole or cardigan opening. The first and last of these are edge stitches that will be picked up. For an unreinforced steek, such as that shown here, pick up and knit 1 stitch for each row along the edge of the steek panel.

The center of the steek panel, after it has been cut.

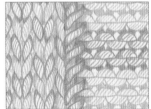

Fold the cut steek to the wrong side of the work and sew down using an overcast stitch, as shown, or cross stitch.

MACHINE-STITCHED REINFORCED STEEKS

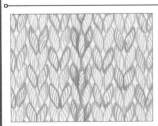

Mark the center stitch of the steek with a running stitch in a contrasting scrap yarn.

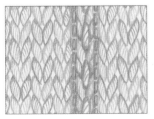

Using a small straight or zigzag stitch, begin at the lower edge and machine stitch through the stitches on one side of the center, across the center, and down through the knit stitches on the other side of center. Remove the contrast yarn and cut through the center stitch. Fold the steek panels to the wrong side and hand sew them to secure.

CROCHET-REINFORCED STEEKS

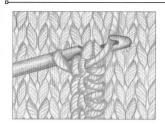

Pull up a loop of working yarn through the lower edge of the steek panel. Insert crochet hook in one leg of the center stitch and one leg of the adjacent stitch. Draw a loop through, yarn over and draw through both loops. Continue to work in this manner through the legs of the stitches in the row above, until one side of the steek has been worked.

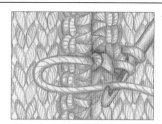

Work from top to the lower edge along the open leg of the center stitch and one leg of the adjacent stitch.

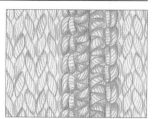

The two rows of single crochet form an edge. Cut the center to complete the process.

The crochet steek being cut.

Jogless Join

Although it may seem as if you are knitting in circles when you knit in the round, you are actually making a series of spirals. As a result, there will be a step or "jog" at the start of each new round. The jog is particularly noticeable if you are knitting stripes or a two-color motif. In some instances, you can hide the jog by placing it at the underarm, as in a sleeve that is knit in the round. If you are knitting a stranded cardigan in the round, start your new round within the steek. When the steek is cut, the jog will be lost in the finishing.

If it is possible to start and end a round at a point where you are always knitting in the same color, as in a traditional mitten that may have a vertical stripe between the front and back, the jog also will be disguised. In other cases, you can **manipulate the stitches at the end of the round** to minimize the transition. There are several methods to accomplish this. A common technique is to knit into a stitch in the round below the one you are working on when you start a new round. Another relies on slipping the first stitch of the new round.

TWO METHODS TO AVOID A JOG

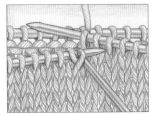

1 Knit the first round in the new color. Insert the working needle in the right-hand leg of the first stitch in the row below and lift it on to the left-hand needle.

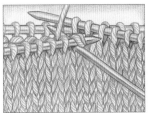

2 Insert the working needle in the first stitch of the last round and the stitch below and **knit the 2 stitches together.**

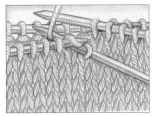

1 Knit the first round in the new color. **Slip the first stitch** of the round purlwise and knit the second stitch.

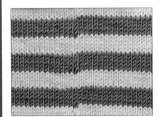

Striped swatch worked in the round in stockinette stitch. The jog at the beginning of the round when changing colors is visible.

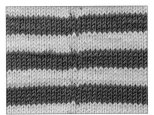

Striped swatch worked in the round in stockinette stitch using a jogless join.

Advanced Techniques

Entrelac

The name "entrelac" comes from the French word *entrelacer*, which means to interlace. This technique creates a **basketweave pattern** made up of **triangles** and **rectangles**. The shapes are positioned at right angles, giving the rectangles the appearance of diamonds.

Entrelac is often knit in stockinette stitch, but it is possible to construct the rectangles and triangles from garter stitch, seed stitch, or any textured stitch, including cables, and incorporate lace motifs into entrelac rectangles. Beads or embroidery can embellish entrelac pieces. Entrelac rectangles and triangles can be knit from yarns of different colors, variegated yarns, or self-striping yarns. Entrelac pieces also look good when felted, and they are often used to make bags and other accessories.

Entrelac knitting is less complex than it looks. It requires only casting on, knitting and purling, picking up stitches, increasing and decreasing, and binding off. The resulting work can be used in garments or accessories, either on its own or combined with other stitches. For example, a sweater made from entrelac pieces can have ribbing or a border in another stitch. Entrelac knitting is an excellent way to use up leftover yarn from other projects.

To knit a rectangular piece in entrelac, you begin with a line of **base triangles**. Once these triangles are complete, you work a **right-hand corner triangle**, then the first row of rectangles. The picked-up stitches form the width of the rectangle and the rows of knitting determine the length. Another row of triangles will form the top edge of the piece. **Triangles** are also used on the right and left of the piece to form the vertical edge. It is also possible to knit entrelac pieces in the round.

In the examples shown, the triangles and rectangles are multiples of eight, but you can change the size to make your work larger or smaller. The number of stitches you cast on should be a **multiple of the width** of your rectangle. For example, if you have rectangles that are 10 stitches wide and you want your piece to have 12 rectangles, cast on 120 stitches. The number of rows in each rectangle will always be **twice** the number of stitches.

Many knitters prefer to work stockinette entrelac pieces only on the right side of their piece, rather than turn it for the wrong-side rows. They do so by knitting backwards rather than purling (page 57).

BASE TRIANGLES

 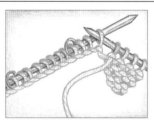  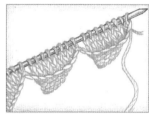

Cast on the number of stitches needed to create the desired number of base triangles. Three are used in the illustrated example. Place markers to separate the base triangles. Here 8 stitches are used for each triangle.

To work the first base triangle, purl 2 stitches on the wrong side. Turn and knit 2 stitches. Turn and purl 3 stitches. Continue in this manner, working one more stitch in every wrong-side row, until all the stitches in this triangle have been purled. Do not turn, but begin to work the next triangle.

Work the remaining base triangles same as the first.

The base triangles will not lie flat when they are on the needle.

RIGHT-HAND CORNER TRIANGLES

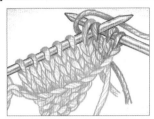

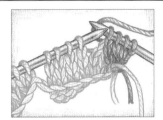

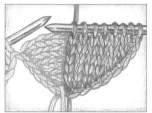

With the RS facing, knit 2 stitches and turn. Then, purl 2 stitches and turn. On right-side rows, increase 1 stitch in the first stitch by knitting into the front and back of the stitch (kfb). Then slip the next stitch knitwise, slip the first stitch of the base triangle knitwise, insert the left-hand needle through the front loops of both stitches, and knit them together through the back loops as shown (ssk). Turn and purl the WS row. Turn.

Kfb in the first stitch, knit to the last stitch, ssk the last stitch on the right-hand needle with the next stitch of the base triangle, as before. Turn and purl to the end.

Repeat these two rows, working one stitch more before the ssk until all the stitches of the base triangle have been worked. Do not turn. One right-hand corner triangle is complete.

RIGHT-SIDE RECTANGLES

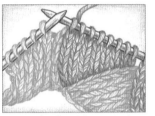

Pick up and knit 8 stitches along the left side of the first base triangle. Turn and purl to the end of the row.

To join the first RS rectangle to the second base triangle, knit to the last stitch on the right-hand needle, work ssk with this stitch and the first stitch of the base triangle. Then, turn and purl 8 stiches on the WS row.

Repeat the last two rows until the 8 stitches of the base triangle have been worked. Work the remaining RS rectangles across the row in the same manner.

Right-side rectangles on needle ready to begin a left-hand corner triangle.

LEFT-HAND CORNER TRIANGLE

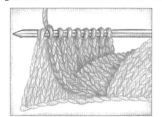 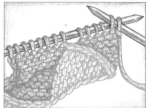 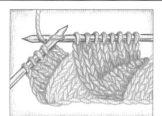 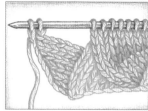

Pick up and knit 8 stitches along the left-side edge of the last base triangle. Then turn the work.

Decrease stitches on the left-hand corner triangle by working a p2tog and purling to the end of the WS row.

Turn to the right side and knit the remaining stitches.

Repeat the last two rows until 2 stitches remain on the right side. Turn and purl these 2 stitches together using the color for the next tier of rectangles.

WRONG-SIDE RECTANGLES

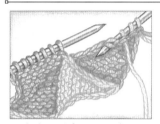 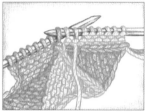 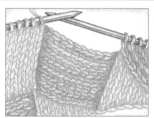

With the WS facing, pick up and purl 7 stitches along the left-hand side of the left-hand corner triangle—8 stitches on needle. Turn and knit.

Turn and purl to the last stitch on the right-hand needle, purl this stitch together with the next stitch of the right-side rectangle. Turn and knit 8 stitches.

Repeat these two rows until all the picked-up stitches have been worked. Do not turn. One wrong-side rectangle is complete. Repeat across the row of right-side rectangles.

The left-hand corner triangle at the top is about to be completed.

END TRIANGLES

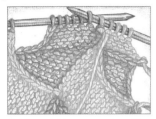

1 After picking up and purling 7 stitches along the side of the LH corner triangle, turn. Knit 8 stitches and turn. P2tog at the beginning of the WS row, and purl to the last stitch. Then, purl the last stitch of the end triangle together with the first stitch of the RS triangle.

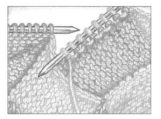

2 When the first end triangle is complete, pick up and purl 7 stitches down the side of the next rectangle—there are 8 stitches on the right-hand needle.

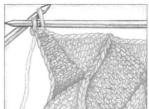

3 Continue to work along the row of rectangles until the last triangle is complete and 2 stitches remain on the right-hand needle. Pass the first stitch over the last stitch and fasten off.

TECHNIQUE

KNITTING BACKWARDS

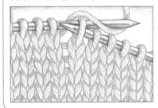

1 With the yarn at the back of the work, insert the tip of the left-hand needle from left to right in the back of the next stitch on the right-hand needle. Wrap the yarn over the top of the left-hand needle as shown.

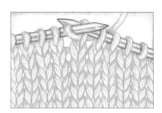

2 Draw the yarn through the stitch with the left-hand needle and let the old stitch slip from the right-hand needle. One backwards stitch complete.

The end triangles are finished to complete the swatch.

Modular Knitting

Modular knitting, also known as **patchwork knitting** or **domino knitting**, is the combination of small knitted geometric shapes into a larger knitted fabric. The basic units, or modules, can be **mitered** squares, triangles, diamonds, or crescents. The modules are formed by a series of increases and decreases. Modules are attached to one another by **picking up stitches** along the side of a previous shape and extended by casting on additional stitches. You also can knit modules individually and sew or crochet them together.

Modular knitting can be used to knit accessories such as hats, shawls, or cowls in addition to sweaters. The method is also used for afghans or knitted bags. Generally the yarns used are fingering weight to worsted weight, and the yarns can be solid, variegated, or self-striping. Different colors can be combined in the same module as well. The yarns should be tightly twisted to show the ridges of garter stitch, which is usually used to construct the modules.

A modular project such as a baby blanket is a handy way to use up stash yarn.

MITERED SQUARES

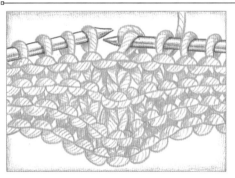

Slip 2 stitches together knitwise.

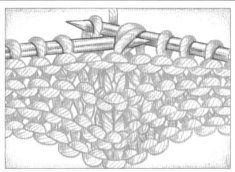

Knit 1, and pass the slipped stitches over the k1.

TECHNIQUE

BASIC MITERED SQUARE

Cast on an odd number of stitches.

Row 1 (WS) Knit through the back loop to the last stitch, purl 1.

Row 2 Slip 1, knit through the back loop to center 3 stitches, slip 2 stitches together as if to knit, knit 1, pass slipped stitches one at a time, over knit stitch (S2KP), knit through back loop to last stitch, purl 1. Repeat rows 1 and 2 until three stitches remain, ending with a right side row.

Last row (WS) Slip 1, p2tog, pass the slipped stitch over. Fasten off or use the remaining stitch to work the next square.

JOINING MITERED SQUARES

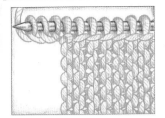
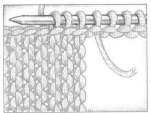
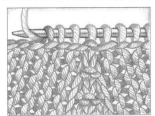

At left edge of square, pick up and knit the required number of stitches along the edge through the back loop only, cast on the remaining stitches using the backwards-loop (or single) cast on. Decrease in the center 3 stitches on the next row to form the miter.

At right edge of square, cast on the required stitches, then pick up and knit the remaining stitches along the edge through the back loop only. Decrease in the center 3 stitches on the next row to form the miter.

Between the two squares, pick up and knit the stitches of the two edges through the back loops. Decrease in the center 3 stitches on the next row to form the miter.

MODULAR SQUARES JOINED WHILE WORKING

2 joined squares

4 joined squares

DIFFERENT PATTERNS WORKED BY MITERING

Ribbed Mitered Square

Seed Stitch Mitered Square

Eyelet Mesh Mitered Square

Reverse Stockinette Mitered Square

TRIANGLES

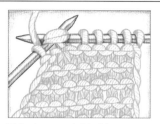

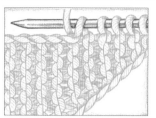

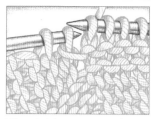

Cast on an odd number of sts. **Next row (WS)** K to last st, p1. **Row 1 (RS)** Sl 1, k to last 3 sts, k2tog, p1. **Row 2** Sl 1, k to last st, p1. Rep rows 1 and 2 until 3 sts rem. **Next row** Sl 1, p2tog. **Next row** Sl 1, p1. **Next row** K2tog.

This shows a right-side row. The first stitch has been slipped. Then knit to the last 3 stitches and knit 2 together, purl 1. Repeat this row to the end of the triangle.

To work another triangle, pick up stitches through the front loop on a wrong-side row.

When joining two triangles, slip the last stitch of the wrong-side row to the left-hand needle to k2tog.

JOINING TRIANGLES TO MITERED SQUARES TO FILL IN DIAMONDS

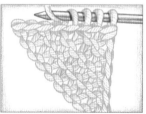

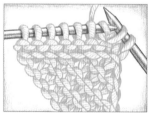

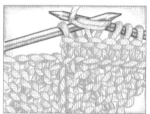

1 With the RS facing, pick up and knit stitches through the back loop along the left edge of the diamond.

2 Slip the first stitch, knit to the last st, purl 1. Then, turn, slip 1, SKP, knit to the last stitch, purl 1.

3 With RS facing, pick up and k stitches along right edge of diamond. Decrease with k2tog at ends of right-side rows. When both triangles are complete, work a diamond by picking up stitches along both inside edges of triangles and working as for square on page 59.

Center-Out Knitting

Geometric shapes, such as squares, circles, hexagons, octagons, and other polygons, can be knit from **the center out** to make pieces that can be used alone or assembled into larger items. These usually are knit by casting on a few stitches on **double-pointed needles** and then increasing until the piece is as large as desired. You also can work on two circular needles or use the magic loop method, as you would for any other small-circumference project. These shapes, also called **medallions**, are designed to form a flat fabric. If you increase too often, the shape will have a ruffled edge; if you increase too few times, the piece will curve in on itself. The placement of the increases may cause geometric units to radiate straight out from the center or increases paired with decreases may form spirals.

Medallion knitting became popular in the eighteenth and nineteenth centuries, when the medallions were used as doilies and for home décor items, such as antimacassars and tablecloths. They were knit using very fine cotton thread. Center-out motifs are used today for blankets, throws, pillows, bags, dishcloths, and other nonwearable items. They also may be used as components in knitted toys. Many shawls such as circular shawls and square shawls are based on center-out motifs, and center-out motifs may be incorporated into garments, such as sweaters or the tops of hats. The yarns used for modern center-out motifs range from cobweb and lace yarn to heavier weights, such as worsted or Aran. The heavier weights are suitable for blankets and hats. Center-out motifs can be constructed using lace stitch patterns, stockinette or garter stitch, or textured stitches. They can be worked in colors: The tops of Fair Isle berets have the same type of colorwork as similarly stranded sweaters. The type of increase affects the final appearance of the fabric. Increases such as make one (M1) or knit front and back (kfb) will shape closed stitch patterns, whereas increases using yarn overs will create a lacy look.

Counterpanes, or coverlets, are constructed from many separate geometric motifs that are sewn together individually or in strips. They may combine more than one shape, and many of the separate units are knit from the center out, although they need not be. Some are knitted flat and then joined so that they form a motif that has a center point.

Other motifs, such as stars or flowers, begin with a center-out construction and are finished by picking up stitches and knitting the points of the star or the petals of the flower. These also can be used as embellishments on other garments or on their own, as in star-shaped baby blankets.

Center-out motifs may be embellished by the addition of borders or crocheted edgings.

Center-out shapes begin with circular cast ons.

ADJUSTABLE RING CAST ON

Adjustable ring made with a crochet hook, also known as Emily Ocker's cast on.

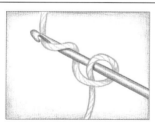

1 Make a ring with the working yarn crossed over the tail. *With crochet hook, draw a loop through the ring.

2 Yarn over hook and draw through the loop to complete the single crochet (sc) (2 sts are on the hook). Repeat from * in step 1 until the number of stitches to cast on is on the crochet hook.

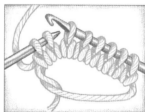

3 Divide the stitches on double-pointed or circular knitting needles to begin the project. When the first round is complete, pull on the tail to close the ring.

ADJUSTABLE RING CAST ON

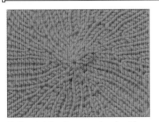

Adjustable ring worked with double-pointed needles.

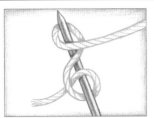

1 Make a ring with the working yarn crossed over the tail. *Insert double-pointed or circular needle point in the ring and wrap working yarn around needle from front to back to front to form loop as shown.

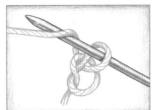

2 Draw a loop through the ring. Wrap yarn around needle and draw through loop to form stitch. Repeat from the * in step 1 until all the stitches have been cast on.

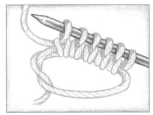

3 Several stitches have been cast on. When the first round is complete, pull on the tail to close the ring.

INVISIBLE CIRCULAR CAST ON

1 Make an overhand knot and hold it with the loop on the left, the tail at the bottom, and the working yarn at the top. Using a double-pointed needle (dpn) smaller than the needle for your project, *wrap the working yarn over the dpn to make a stitch.

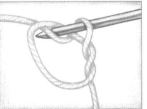

2 Insert the dpn in the ring and draw the working yarn through for the next stitch.

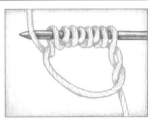

3 Repeat from the * in step 1 until the correct number of stitches has been cast on. When all the stitches have been cast on, pull the tail to close the ring and slide the stitches to the other end of the dpn to begin the round.

PROVISIONAL I-CORD CAST ON

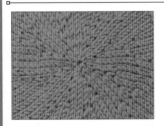

With scrap yarn, make an I-cord with the number of stitches to cast on. Knit the first round in the main color, leaving a long tail.

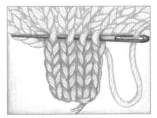

When the medallion is complete, thread the tail through the first round of the main color.

Cut one thread in the last round of scrap yarn and unpick the stitches. Pull the tail to close the hole and weave in the end.

Center-Out Squares

Center-out squares can be knit in two ways. The increases can form diagonal lines that extend from corner to corner, forming four **triangles**, or they can bisect each side, forming four smaller **squares**.

A general rule of thumb for any geometric shape is that the number of stitches to cast on should be twice the number of sides of each shape. For a square, you would then start by casting on eight stitches. To form the square, alternate rounds of increases with rounds of plain knitting (stockinette, garter, or whatever stitch pattern is being used) in which there is no increasing. On each increase round, add eight stitches, in pairs. If you are working on double-pointed needles, it is convenient to place the increases at the beginning and end of each needle. The increases can be yarn overs for an open look or closed increases (knit front and back, make one) for a closed motif. The increases also can be placed so that they swirl out from the center.

Center-out squares are the foundation of many square shawls. The motif is also used for blankets.

INCREASES AT CORNERS

Cast on 2 stitches for each side and divide on 4 double-pointed needles (or place markers to divide in 4 sections). Knit 1 rnd even. Knit 1 rnd and inc in each stitch—16 sts.

Rnd 1 [K1, yo, k to last st, yo, k1] 4 times around.
Rnd 2 Knit. Rep rnds 1 and 2 until the medallion is the desired size. Bind off.

INCREASES IN CENTER

Cast on 2 stitches for each side and divide on 4 double-pointed needles (or place markers to divide in 4 sections). Knit 1 rnd even. Knit 1 rnd and inc in each stitch—16 sts.

Rnd 1 [K1, yo, k to last st, yo, k1] 4 times around.

Rnd 2 Knit. Place marker at center of each section or needle.
Rnd 3 [k to 1 stitch before marker, yo, k1, sl marker, k1 yo, k to end of needle (or section) 4 times around.
Rnd 4 Knit. Rep rnds 3 and 4 until the medallion is the desired size. Bind off.

SWIRL RIGHT

 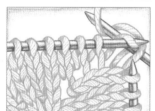

Cast on 8 sts. Knit 1 rnd. Knit 1 rnd and inc in each st—16 sts.
Rnd 1 [K1, yo, k to last st, yo, k1] 4 times around. **Rnd 2** Knit.
Next rnd Increase (yo) after first st and before the yo two rounds below. **Next rnd** Knit.

Work a yo before the yo two rounds below. Work the increase (yo) round every other round until the medallion is the desired size.

SWIRL LEFT

 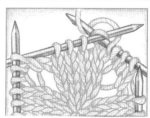

Cast on 8 sts. Knit 1 rnd. Knit 1 rnd and inc in each st—16 sts.
Next rnd [K to end of sts on needle, yo] 4 times around.
Next rnd [K to 1 st after yo on previous round, yo] 4 times around. Repeat this round every round until desired size. Bind off.

Yo after yo on previous round.

Center-Out Circles

Center-out circles can be constructed to have **spirals** or **spokes** radiating from the center. Circles can also be knit using **short-row wedges.**

As for other center-out shapes, the circles with spirals or spokes start by casting on a small number of stitches, usually eight stitches, joined to make a round. The increases are spaced symmetrically from the center out—yarn overs for lacy motifs and closed increases for solid pieces. A round of increases will be separated by rounds of knitting in the pattern stitch.

RADIATING INCREASES

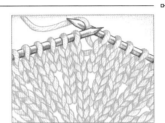

Cast on 8 sts. Join and place marker for beg of round. Knit 1 rnd. **Next rnd** Inc in each st—16 sts. Knit 1 rnd. **Next rnd** *K1, yo; rep from * around—32 sts. Knit 3 rnds. **Next rnd** *K2, yo; rep from * around. Knit 3 rnds. **Next rnd** *K3, yo; rep from * around. Knit 3 rnds. **Next rnd** *K4, yo; rep from * around. Continue

in this manner until piece is the desired size. Bind off. Illustration shows the pattern of the increases.

PI CIRCLE

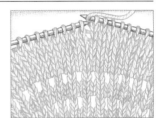

Cast on 8 sts. Join and place marker for beg of rnd. Knit 1 rnd. **Next rnd** Inc in each st—16 sts. Knit 2 rnds. **Next rnd** *K1, yo; rep from * around—32 sts. Knit 4 rnds. **Next rnd** *K1, yo; rep from * around. Knit 8 rnds. **Next rnd** *K1, yo; rep from * around. Knit 16 rnds.

Next rnd *K1, yo; rep from * around. Continue in this way until piece is the desired size. Illustration shows the pattern of increases. Note that the edges are ruffled. Work 2 more rounds even before binding off for a smoother edge.

CIRCLE WITH STAGGERED INCREASES

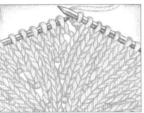

Cast on 8 sts. Join and place marker for beg of round. Knit 1 rnd even here and after every increase rnd. **Next rnd** Kfb in each st—16 sts. **Next rnd** *K1, kfb; rep from * around. **Next rnd** *K2, kfb; rep from * around. **Next rnd** *K3, kfb; rep from * around. **Next rnd** K2, kfb, *K4, kfb; rep from * around.

Next rnd K1, kfb, *k5, kfb; rep from * around. **Next rnd** K5, kfb, *k6, kfb; rep from * around. **Next rnd** K2, kfb, *k7, kfb; rep from * around. **Next rnd** K1, kfb, *k8, kfb; rep from * around. **Next rnd** K6, kfb, *k9, kfb; rep from * around. Cont to desired size. Illustration shows the pattern of the increases.

SHORT-ROW CIRCLE

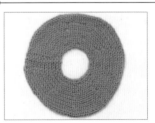
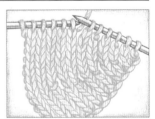

Cast on 12 sts. *Knit 1 row. **Next row** Purl to 2 sts before end of row, turn. Knit to end. **Next row** Purl to 4 sts before end of row, turn. Knit to end. Continue in this manner to 8 sts before end of row, turn. Knit to end. Work desired number of rows (sample

shows 4) over all stitches. Repeat from * until a circle is formed. Sew seam.

The number of rows worked over all stitches determines the size of the center opening.

Illustration shows one repeat complete and a second in progress.

Center-Out Shapes

Several other geometric shapes can be constructed from the center out: **pentagons**, **hexagons**, **septagons**, and **octagons**. These extend the patterns for squares in that the increases (yarn overs or closed increases) can radiate from the center to the points (vertices) of each shape. They can also be positioned to swirl out from the center.

Cast on two stitches for each side of the shape (cast on 10 stitches for a pentagon, cast on 12 stitches for a hexagon, etc). In general, after the cast on, **alternate** rounds of increases with rounds of plain knitting in whatever stitch you are using (most often stockinette or garter stitch).

Some shapes are easier to visualize when using more double-pointed needles, putting the stitches for each side on its own needle. Although less common than squares or circles, these shapes can be used for blankets and tops of hats or be incorporated into sweaters.

CENTER-OUT GEOMETRIC SHAPES

PENTAGON
5 sets of increases, evenly placed, are used to shape the medallion.

HEXAGON
6 sets of increases, evenly placed, are used to shape the medallion.

OCTAGON
8 sets of increases, evenly placed, are used to shape the medallion.

CONSTRUCTION OF A CENTER-OUT STAR OR FLOWER

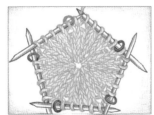
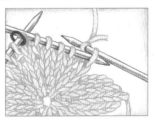

Stars and flowers can be created from the geometric shapes mentioned above. Work the desired shape as described. It will become the center. Shown here is a five-pointed star worked in stockinette stitch.

Use stitch markers to mark your increases. Use one marker in a different color for the beginning of the round. Once your geometric shape (the center) is the desired size and each needle has an even number of sts, work each point separately.

Work each point (sts between a set of markers) in rows as follows:
Row 1 (RS) SKP, k to last 2 sts, k2tog.
Row 2 Purl.
Rep rows 1 and 2 until 2 sts rem, ending with a RS row.

Pass the final SKP over the k2tog to complete. Bind off. Join yarn to next side to work next point.

Brioche Knitting

Knitting with brioche stitches creates a lofty, reversible fabric with pronounced ribs. The **ribs** are formed by **working one stitch and slipping the next**, which divides the piece into **two layers**. In brioche knitting, rather than carrying the working yarn in front or in back of the slipped stitch, the yarn is carried **over** the stitch. You can increase and decrease in brioche knitting, form cables and crossed stitches, and work with color.

Untreated wool yarn is best for brioche knitting because it sticks to itself and keeps the fabric from stretching.

Use needles that are smaller than those recommended on the ball band of the yarn to enhance the rib.

Because the fabric is elastic, cast on and bind off **loosely**. Use a larger needle for casting on than for knitting your piece, or use two needles held together.

Most brioche projects should be lightly steam blocked to relax the stitches, or not blocked at all. For an open, lacy effect, wet block the piece.

Gauge may be more difficult to determine in brioche knitting, and a large swatch will be more accurate than a small one. When you count rows, note that each row is worked twice. Half the stitches were worked in one row and half (those that were slipped in the previous row) are worked in the following row.

You may find other stitch patterns that are formed by knitting into the row below. For example, fisherman's rib uses a different method of working the stitch but has the same end result as brioche stitches.

Designer **Nancy Marchant** developed the terminology for two-color brioche knitting that is referred to in this chapter.

BRIOCHE STITCH

(over an even number of sts)
Set-up row *Yo, sl 1, k1; rep from * to end.
Row 1 *Yo, sl 1, k2tog (sl st and yo of previous row); rep from * to end. Repeat row 1 for brioche stitch.

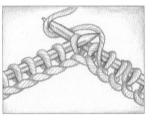

1 In the set-up row, the yarn over has been worked and one stitch has been slipped, the knit stitch is being worked.

2 In row 1 (the pattern row), the yarn over has been worked and the stitch is being slipped.

3 Several rows of row 1 have been repeated, and the yarn over and slipped stitch of the previous row are being knit together.

TWO-COLOR BRIOCHE

Two-color brioche is worked on a circular or double-pointed needle. One color is worked across the row, then the work is moved to the

opposite end of the needle to work the second color from the same side. When the second color has been worked across the row, turn to work the next row with the first color.

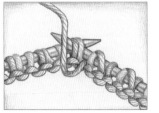

Set-up row 1 With light color, k1, work as for set-up row in one-color brioche st (see above). Slide work to beg of row to work with dark color.

Slip first st, *purl next (dark color) st tog with yo (shown above), sl 1 (shown right), yo; rep from * to last st, with dark yarn in front, slip last light color st.

2 ADVANCED TECHNIQUES

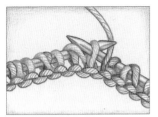

from * to last 2 sts, sl 1, yo, p1. Slide to work with dark color. With dark color, sl 1, k2tog (sl st and yo from previous row), yo, sl 1; rep from * to last st, with dark yarn in front, sl last light color st.

Set-up row 2 With light color, p1, *yo, sl 1, p2tog (sl st and yo from previous row); rep

To work in pat, with light color, knit or purl the selvage sts as they appear, yo and

sl the dark color sts, knit or purl the slip st of previous row (as it appears) tog with yo of previous row (shown is a k2tog). With dark color, sl selvage st and yo and sl light color st, knit or purl slip stitch of previous row (as it appears) tog with yo of previous row.

TWO-COLOR BRIOCHE STITCHES AND BIND OFF

Knit increase on light side To work this inc (which Marchant calls brkyobrk) with light color, k into both strands of knit column st without dropping st from needle, bring working yarn to front between needles, work yo over RH needle, k again into both strands of same knit column st, letting old st drop from LH needle—2 sts inc'd.

Purl increase on light side To work this inc (which Marchant calls brpyobrp), with dark color, p into both strands of purl column st (sl st and yo of previous row) without dropping old st from LH needle, yo, and p into same st again, letting old st drop from LH needle—2 sts inc'd.

Left-leaning knit decrease To work this dec (which Marchant calls brLsl dec), sl next st and its yo knitwise, then with light yarn, k next purl st tog with next knit st and its yo, then pass slipped st and yo over dec'd st—2 sts dec'd.

Right-leaning knit decrease To work this dec (which Marchant calls brRsl dec), with light yarn, sl next st with its yo over knitwise, k next (dark color) purl st and pass slipped sts over knit st, sl resulting dec to LH needle and pass next st with its yo over st just dec'd, place st on RH needle—2 sts dec'd.

Left-leaning purl decrease To work this dec (which Marchant calls brpLsl dec), with dark yarn at front, sl next purl st and its yo purlwise, sl next knit column st to cn, hold to front, sl purl st and yo on LH needle to RH needle, place st from cn on LH needle and p it, pass 2 sets of slipped sts over p st one at a time—2 sts dec'd.

Right-leaning purl decrease To work this dec (called brpRsl dec), with dark yarn, yo and p next purl st with its yo and foll knit column st tog, sl purl st and its yo knitwise to RH needle, place it on LH needle with left leg in front, place dec'd st on LH needle, pass remounted st over it, place dec'd st on RH needle—2 sts dec'd.

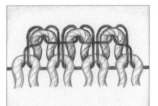

Sewn Italian bind off The sewn Italian bind off works well with brioche stitch and mimics the 2-color Italian cast-on, which is also good for this technique. With yarn needle and matching yarn, follow path of red line as foll: Enter first st purlwise, then knitwise into next (purl column) st, pull yarn through

leaving sts on needle. *Insert yarn needle in front of first st and then purlwise into next knit column st with its yo, pull yarn through, dropping first st from knitting needle. Insert yarn needle through first purl column st again and knitwise into next purl column st, pull yarn through, dropping first st from needle. Rep from * until 3 sts remain. Insert yarn needle into front of first st and purlwise into last knit column stitch with its yo, pull yarn through, dropping first st from needle. Insert yarn needle purlwise through last 2 sts, pull yarn through, dropping sts from needle.

Double Knitting

Showing two sides of one double knit piece.

Double knitting is a method of knitting in which you create a fabric with **two public sides** using two balls of yarn knit on one set of needles. Double-knit fabrics can be knit flat on straight needles or in the round on circular needles or double-pointed needles. The technique is excellent for making very warm blankets, hats, or cowls. When both sides of the work are knit in stockinette, the **double thickness** of the fabric prevents it from curling. When planning your project, keep in mind that you need twice as much yarn as in single-face knitting.

Double knitting is often used with two different color yarns, and the resulting fabric is reversible. Because there is no right or wrong side in double knitting, the side you are working on is described as the **facing side** and the side away from you is the **opposite side**. In each row or round, you alternate knitting stitches from each ball of yarn.

Get started by casting on using one of the methods shown. You need to cast on twice as many stitches as you would for a single fabric. To knit circularly, use any standard method for joining in the round.

CASTING ON WITH 2 COLORS

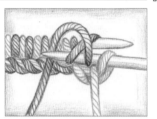

1 Holding 1 strand of each color (A and B) together, cast on the number of stitches for 1 side using preferred cast-on method. *With both strands held to the back, knit 1 with A (facing side stitch).

2 Move both strands to the front between the needles and with B, p1 (opposite side stitch), move both strands to the back between the needles. Repeat from the * in step 1 until all stitches have been worked.

CASTING ON WITH 1 COLOR

1 Using preferred cast-on method, cast on the number of stitches needed for one side. *With both strands held to the back, knit 1 with A but don't drop stitch from needle (facing side stitch).

2 Move both strands to front of work between the needles and with B, purl 1 (opposite side stitch). Move both strands to back of work between the needles. Repeat from * in step 1 until all the stitches have been worked.

KNIT (SHOWING KNIT ON BOTH SIDES OF FABRIC)

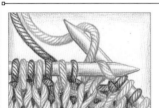

1 Knit on facing side. With both strands held to back, insert needle knitwise in next stitch, wrap yarn for facing side to knit stitch.

2 Purl on opposite side (RS facing). Holding both yarns to front, insert needle purlwise in next stitch, wrap with opposite color and purl.

PURL (SHOWING PURL ON BOTH SIDES OF FABRIC)

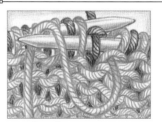

1 Purl on facing side. Holding color for facing side to front and color for opposite side to back, insert needle purlwise in next stitch, wrap with facing color and purl.

2 Knit on opposite side (WS facing to show purl on RS). Holding color for facing side to front and color for opposite side to back, insert needle knitwise in next stitch, wrap with opposite color and knit.

DECREASING

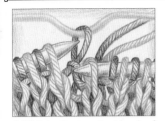   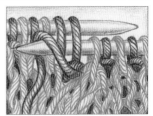

1 With both strands at back of work, slip next (facing) stitch purlwise to the RH needle, place next (opposite) stitch on cable needle, slip next facing stitch purlwise to RH needle.

2 Return stitch from cable needle to LH needle, return the 2 slipped stitches one at a time to the LH needle. Take care not to twist the stitches while returning them to the LH needle.

3 With both strands at back, decrease the facing stitch (k2tog shown).

4 Move both strands to front of work between the needles and decrease the opposite color stitch (p2tog shown).

INCREASING

1 M1 with the color on the facing side: Insert LH needle from front to back under the strand between the last facing stitch worked and the next facing stitch and knit or purl through the back loop with the color indicated in the instructions.

2 M1 with the color on the opposite side: Insert LH needle from front to back under the strand between the last opposite stitch worked and the next opposite stitch and knit or purl through the back loop with the color indicated in the instructions.

BINDING OFF: TWO METHODS

Double Stranded With two colors held together, knit the first facing stitch together with the first opposite stitch, *knit the next facing and opposite stitches together in the same way, pass the first stitch over the second stitch; repeat from the * until all stitches are bound off.

Single Stranded With the facing color, knit the first facing stitch together with the first opposite stitch, *knit the next facing and opposite stitches together in the same way, pass the first stitch over the second stitch; repeat from the * until all stitches are bound off.

Tucks

The tuck (or **welt**) stitch creates **folds** of knitting that are formed when you knit a previous row with your working row. The folds of the tuck project form the right side of the work and can be a decorative addition to garments such as hats and sweaters. Because the folds are doubled, the resulting fabric is very warm.

To knit a tuck stitch, first decide where you would like to position the folded fabric. Then determine how large the tuck should be—that is, how long and how thick you want it. Pull your working needle toward you so that you can peer over it to see the both the right and wrong sides of your piece. Pick up a purl bump from a row below your working row. In general, the stitches picked up should be **four or more rows** below your working row. Put the picked-up purl bump on your needle, and **knit it together** with the stitch

on your working needle. Continue this way until the fold is the desired length. It may help to run a piece of scrap yarn through the stitches on the row to be picked up to help you pick up stitches horizontally.

Tuck stitches can run across a full row of knitting or they can be partial rows. They can be positioned at regular intervals, or they can be staggered to form a decorative pattern. You can create tucks that are thinner at the ends than the middle, or pick up staggered rows to have slanted tucks on the right side of your work. The tucks need not be stockinette stitch. If you plan for the fold, you can incorporate another stitch pattern, such as garter or reverse stockinette, into the tuck. Using intarsia, the tucks can be knit in a color that contrasts with the rest of the piece.

TUCKS

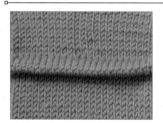

Tuck stitch across the row

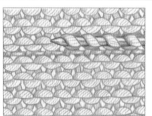

Work in pattern to tuck row. *Thread lifeline to mark row. Work 8 rows more (or until the work folded to back along tuck row is desired depth) end with a WS row. Thread smaller size needle through purl sts on marked row, as shown. Holding working row in front and smaller needle to back, knit 1 stitch from front needle together with 1 stitch from back needle. Work 12 rows in Stockinette stitch or depth before next tuck and rep from *.

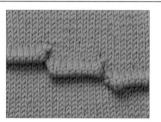

Tuck stitch over partial rows

Holding working row in front and smaller needle to back, knit 1 stitch from front needle together with 1 stitch from back needle, as shown.

Loop Stitch

Loop stitch is a method of working **long loops of yarn** in your piece. The loops may be clustered in an allover pattern or placed along a border. The loops also can be cut to make a **fringe** or tied together in a **bowknot**.

Although loops are typically knitted on every **right-side row** so that they appear on the front of your work, you could form loops on both sides of a fabric. For a dense fabric, knit a loop in every stitch. It is more common, however, to knit a loop in every other stitch. You can stagger the loops on consecutive right-side rows or knit them in vertical rows. The

looped yarn can be single or doubled (wrapped around your thumb twice). You can add color to your work by knitting horizontal stripes of different colors or using variegated or self-striping yarn.

Loop stitches are often used in knitted toys because they represent the fur of an animal—and, in fact, you may see these stitch patterns identified as fur stitch. They can also be used in garments, either in the body or as trim. Items knit in loop stitch require more yarn than those knit in stockinette or textured stitches.

LOOP STITCH

Worked over any number of stitches. Make a loop in every stitch on RS rows. Purl WS rows.

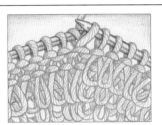

1 With right side facing, knit 1 stitch and leave on needle.

2 Bring yarn to front between needles, wrap around left thumb, bring yarn to back between the needles.

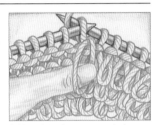

3 Knit 1 in the same stitch.

ALTERNATIVE METHOD, FROM THE WRONG SIDE

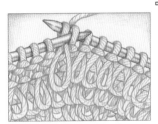

4 Pass the first knit stitch over the second.

This method is worked from the wrong side and is easier for Continental knitters.
1 With WS facing and yarn looped around left index finger, draw both strands of loop through stitch using RH needle and slip from LH needle.

2 Insert LH needle in front loop of double stitch just worked, wrap yarn and knit stitch as usual.

A row of loops can be used along the lower edge and trimmed to create fringe.

Elongated and Drop Stitches

Elongated stitches are created in two ways. The first is to use **a yarn over** and the second is to **wrap** the yarn one or more times around the needle. The pattern instructions will tell you how many wraps you need. On the next row, drop the yarn over or wrap to form the elongated stitch.

Elongated stitches create interesting textures. They work well with variegated and hand-dyed yarns. Elongated stitches are often used in shawls and scarves, but they can be used in sweaters and other garments. Try using different colors for the bands of elongated stitches and stitches of normal size.

The key to using dropped or elongated stitches in a pattern is to start with a platform stitch that places the ladder arising from the dropped stitch where you want it and controls its length. Note that the ladder is about **three times** the width of a normal stitch, and a stitch of this type can also be used to enlarge a garment.

SEAFOAM PATTERN

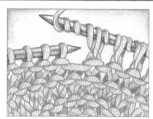

(Multiple of 10 plus 6) **Rows 1 and 2** Knit. **Row 3 (RS)** K6, *(yo) twice, k1, (yo) 3 times, k1, (yo) 4 times, k1, (yo) 3 times, k1, (yo) twice, k6; rep from *. **Row 4** Knit, dropping all yos. **Rows 5 and 6** Knit. **Row 7** K1; rep from * in row 3, end last rep k1 instead of k6. **Row 8** Knit. Rep rows 4–8.

Yarn is wrapped for (yo) 3 times.

On the wrong side, knit, dropping all yos.

Knit 1 on wrong side before and after knitting into the multiple yo.

INDIAN CROSS STITCH

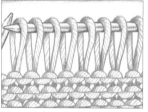

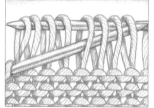

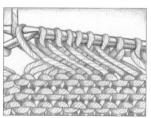

(Multiple of 8 sts) **Rows 1–4** Knit. **Row 5 (RS)** K1, knit to last st wrapping 4 times for each st, k1. **Row 6** See illustrations at right. **Rows 7–10** Knit. **Row 11** Rep row 5. **Row 12** Sl 4 sts dropping extra wraps, cross 2 over 2 as for 4-st cross in row 6, then rep steps 1–3 in row 6 to last 4 sts, cross 2 over 2. Rep rows 1–12 for Indian Cross St.

(Row 6) 1 With the yarn at back, slip 8 stitches, dropping extra wraps.

2 Insert left-hand needle from front into first 4 slipped stitches.

3 Pass the first 4 stitches over the second 4 stitches, return the 8 stitches to the left-hand needle and knit them in this position.

ELONGATED STITCH

With RS facing, insert needle to knit and wrap the yarn twice around the needle.

Draw the 2 wraps through the stitch.

On the next row, knit, dropping the extra wraps.

ELONGATED CROSS GARTER STITCH

One row of elongated cross garter stitch.

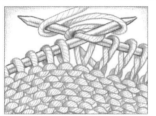

1 With WS (purl side) facing and yarn in back, insert RH needle as if to knit, wrap working yarn from front to back around RH needle, then from back to front around LH needle, and from back to front and over top of RH needle.

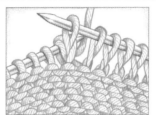

2 Draw RH needle through, bringing strand nearest needle tip behind front strand and through stitch, dropping old stitch and extra wraps from needles.

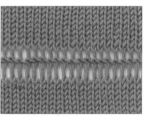

Two rows of elongated crossed garter stitch.

ELONGATED STITCH

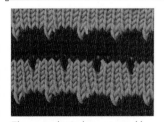

Elongated stitches created by pulling a new stitch through a stitch from several rows below.

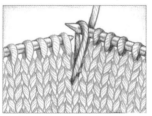

With contrasting color and yarn at back, insert the right-hand needle from front to back through the designated stitch, wrap the yarn knitwise and draw the loop through as shown, knit the loop together with the corresponding stitch.

TECHNIQUE

CONDO KNITTING

Condo knitting uses two needles of different sizes, one needle three to five sizes larger than the other. The stitches knit with the larger needle are more open than those knit from the smaller needle and result in a pattern with horizontal bands of loose and tight stitches. This method can be used with most yarn weights, variegated or hand-dyed yarns, and textured or novelty yarns. It is a good technique for scarves, but can also be used to make lacy sweaters.

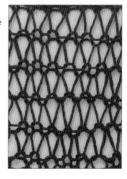

BASIC LADDER

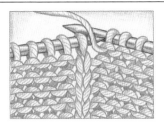
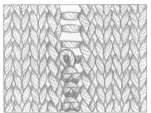

Keep the sides of the ladder firm by knitting the stitches on each side through the back loops. Purling the stitch to be dropped makes it easier to identify the stitch as you work. The illustration shows knitting through the back loop.

Work a yarn over in the last row before dropping the stitch. Knit the yarn over through the back loop when binding off.

Let the stitch drop all the way down. Use your hands to help unravel it if necessary.

PLACED LADDER IN RIBBED FABRIC

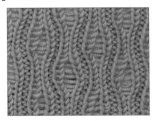

Placed ladders are created by working a yarn over where the bottom of the ladder will be. After working the number of rows desired, drop the stitch. The ladder will stop at the yarn over.

DROPPED STITCH BETWEEN CABLE

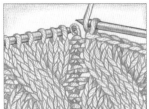

Ladders can be used to set off a cable. The ladder will spread laterally, so 1 dropped st on each side is enough for a dramatic effect. Drop the sts before binding off.

DECORATIVE LADDER

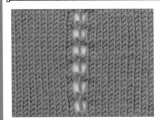
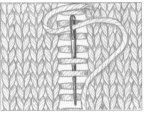
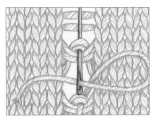

Ladders can be manipulated when the knitting is complete to create a decorative pattern. In the example, a stitch has been dropped over a multiple of 4 rows.

1 Drop the stitch to form the ladder. Thread a yarn needle with matching yarn. Working from bottom up, insert needle from top to bottom over 2 strands and under 2 strands.

2 Twist the needle up to cross the strands and pull the yarn through. Continue to work in this manner through the next group of 4 strands.

2 ADVANCED TECHNIQUES

Understanding Instructions

Understanding Garment Knitting Instructions

Knitting instructions for garments may vary in style, but essentially all follow a basic order and sequence and use the same standard abbreviations and terms. Some of the **terminology** and **abbreviations** may seem confusing at first, especially if you have never worked from knitting instructions, but they are actually logical and simple to use once you are familiar with them. This chapter covers size **selection,** project or **skill levels,** the meaning of knitted **measurements,** the selection **of materials,** and the use of a **gauge swatch.** Later, abbreviations, symbols, and special terms are explained. Even if you plan to design your own garments, you will find this chapter helpful.

Before beginning to knit from knitting instructions, **read** them carefully from start to finish. Look at any special notes, pattern stitches, or materials needed to complete your project. Once you have a general idea of what the instructions entail, you will know if the design suits your technical ability and personal style. Use the **project level symbols** to determine if it's within your expertise. If you are a beginner, choose styles with simple patterns and shaping until you have enough experience to tackle more complicated projects.

SIZES

Knitting instructions are generally written in more than one size. The smallest is given first and appears outside of the parentheses. The larger sizes are given inside the parentheses in ascending order. As you read the instructions, your size will be in the **same position** throughout. For example, if your size is third in the sequence, subsequent figures for your size—indicating yarn amounts, number of stitches to be cast on, and so on—will always appear third in the sequence. If only one number is given, it applies to all sizes. It's a good idea to **highlight** your size to simplify reading the pattern as you work.

Sizes are expressed as standard garment sizes based on standard body measurements. It's important to note that these sizes reflect **actual body measurements** and not the finished measurements of the sweater. The following sections on finished measurements and reading schematics will help you determine the right fit.

KNITTED MEASUREMENTS

Knitted measurements are the **dimensions** of the garment after all the pieces have been knit and sewn together. These measurements, along with the schematic drawing, will help you to decide which size to select. The range of knitted measurements varies from sweater to sweater. If a sweater has simple shaping and a flexible stitch pattern, it will accommodate a wider range of sizes than a sweater with complicated shaping or with large pattern repeats that cannot be broken up.

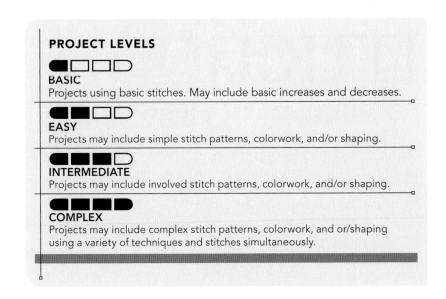

PROJECT LEVELS

BASIC
Projects using basic stitches. May include basic increases and decreases.

EASY
Projects may include simple stitch patterns, colorwork, and/or shaping.

INTERMEDIATE
Projects may include involved stitch patterns, colorwork, and/or shaping.

COMPLEX
Projects may include complex stitch patterns, colorwork, and or/shaping using a variety of techniques and stitches simultaneously.

Schematics

A schematic is a **drawn-to-scale representation** of the finished pieces of a garment that frequently accompanies knitting instructions. Although the format of schematics may vary depending on their source, all have diagrams corresponding to each piece you'll be knitting, such as the fronts, backs, and sleeves of a sweater. Schematics show the dimensions of the garment's pieces **before** they are sewn together or finished. The schematic will also indicate in parentheses or brackets the measurements for different sizes. Schematics help you to assess the garment's fit and to determine the best size for you. They are also useful in making alterations.

Schematics provide much useful information. In addition to the **sizing** information, they also indicate how the garment is **constructed.** For example, you can see at a glance if the garment is to be knit flat or in the round, or if it requires a combination of methods, as when the body is knitted flat but the sleeves are picked up and knitted in the round.

Some schematics for flat knitting show full body pieces; however, when the front and back have similar shapes, only one schematic is given for both pieces. For cardigans, typically the back and only one of the front pieces are shown. In some instructions, only half of each piece is shown.

Carefully check the **measurements** on a schematic. Some instructions will have drawings that show overall measurements, as in the total length of the garment, and others give incremental measurements. Often schematics have both sets of measures. For example, in the schematic shown below, the measurements on the left-hand side of the back show the total measurement from hem to shoulder. The measurements on the right-hand side of the back show incremental measurements between the dots. There is one measure for the ribbing, another for the distance above the ribbing to the armhole, and a third for the depth of the armhole.

In reading the pattern instructions, compare the finished bust/chest size measurement to the figure on the schematic that shows the width of the piece. For pullovers, this figure is usually **half** of the finished bust/chest measurement. To calculate the finished measurement of a cardigan, add the back width, double the width of the front piece, and add the width of one front band.

The sleeve schematic tells you the kind of sleeve used. You can easily determine if the sleeve is a raglan, a drop shoulder, or a fitted sleeve. The schematic shown below is of a fitted sleeve. The figures tell you the length of the sleeve and the component measurements: depth of ribbing, length from cuff to armhole, and depth of sleeve cap. The horizontal lines show you the size of the cuff and the widest width of the sleeve under the armhole.

The schematic drawing on the left shows the entire **back** piece of a cardigan. The numbers along the side indicate the measurement of each section between the dots. The schematic in the middle shows the **right front** piece of the cardigan with the numbers along the side representing incremental measurements beginning at the lower edge to the dots.

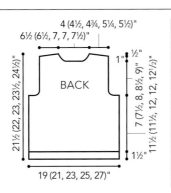

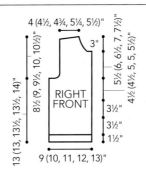

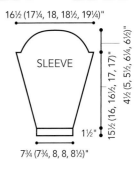

MATERIALS

All knitting instructions provide a list of materials and tools. Read carefully to determine what you will need.

Knowing as much as possible about the yarn suggested in the instructions is helpful whether you plan to use it or a substitute. The instructions will specify the **amount** needed. It is wise to buy a little extra. Be sure each ball has the same **dye lot** number to ensure consistent color. (The dye lot of a yarn is given on the ball band and signifies the "bath" in which that particular ball was dyed.) The **weight** of the yarn appears in ounces or grams or sometimes both. When using a substitute yarn, information about the **length** of the yarn in yards or meters is essential. Make sure the total required amount of the substitute yarn equals the total yardage or meters of the original yarn.

The **color name and number** of the yarn are also listed. Some instructions give a generic color rather than the specific color name printed on the ball band of the yarn. If more than one yarn or color is given, it is usually identified by a letter or letters shown in parentheses after the color. When only two colors are given, they are often referred to as **MC (main color)** and **CC (contrasting color).** When more than two yarns or colors are given, they are most likely expressed as A, B, C, and so on. The same letters will be used to identify these colors in chart keys. Other information about the yarn such as its type, fiber content, and weight is sometimes included and is valuable for substitution.

Other than yarn, the next most important information given in your instructions is the suggested **needle size**. Needles may be expressed in American or metric sizing or sometimes in both. If a special needle length is required, as for a project worked on a circular needle, it will also be noted. If you can't get the proper gauge using the needles suggested, try other sizes until you obtain the correct gauge.

SEAMLESS SCHEMATICS

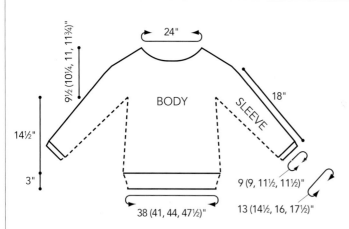

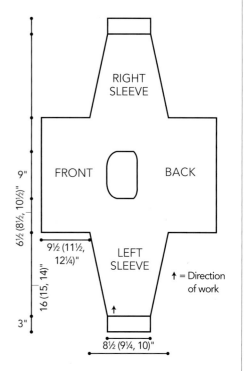

The schematic on page 77 shows a typical schematic for a sweater that is knit flat in pieces and is assembled by seaming. Schematics can represent other construction methods as well. The schematic above represents a sweater **knit in the round.** The dashed lines show the outline of the garment, but they indicate that there is no seam. This sweater is knit from the neck down in the round. The sleeves are picked up and also knit in the round from shoulder to cuff. The curved arrows at the neck, wrists, and bottom show that this is a circular sweater and the numbers are the total measure for the circular piece. Other sweaters may be **knit in one piece,** and the schematic for such a garment will indicate that. In the schematic on the right, the body of the garment is knit starting at the left sleeve.

Gauge

Gauge (also called tension) is the **number of stitches and rows per inch,** based on the size of a knitted stitch. The size of a stitch will vary depending on the yarn, the size of your needles, and the way you control the yarn.

Most knitters control the yarn **tension** by weaving it through their fingers. Each knitter has a different way of controlling the yarn, which can further vary depending on the type of yarn and needles used. Because no two knitters work alike, one knitter may have to use a different needle size (even as much as two or three times larger or smaller) than another to obtain the same gauge.

Another factor that affects gauge is **yarn substitution.** A different yarn can alter the gauge as well as produce a differ-

ent texture. Gauges using the same quality yarns may differ from color to color. For example, a black yarn can have a different gauge than the same type of yarn in white.

Even the type of needle that you use can affect the gauge. You may obtain a slightly different gauge using metal needles than you would with either wood or plastic ones. Be sure to use the same needles for your swatch as for your project.

Make sure that you use the same type of yarn, color, and needles throughout your project.

If you do not achieve exact gauge, you will alter the size and texture of your finished garment. It is imperative to **check your gauge** before beginning every project.

NEEDLE SIZE AND GAUGE

Each swatch was made in stockinette stitch with the **same number of stitches and rows,** but using three different needle sizes, from smaller to larger. The smaller the needle, the smaller the swatch; the larger the needle, the larger the swatch.

PATTERN STITCH AND GAUGE

Here are three different **pattern stitches** that were made using the same needle size and the same number of stitches and rows, and resulted in three different finished sizes.

HOW TO CHECK AND MEASURE GAUGE

It is easiest to measure stitches on a flat, even swatch. You may need to **steam or wet block** your swatch after taking it off the needles, unless the finishing instructions say not to block. Pin the damp swatch on a flat surface, such as an ironing board, and do not stretch it.

When the swatch is thoroughly dry, **measure the gauge** with a measuring tape or stitch gauge. Be sure to count the stitches carefully, because a variation of even half a stitch will make a significant difference in your finished piece.

On certain fabrics, such as ribs, you may have to stretch the fabric slightly to obtain an accurate gauge.

Your gauge may change from your swatch to your knitted piece because your style of knitting may be different when you have only a few stitches on the needle. **Check your knitting** after working 5 or 6 inches (12 or 15 cm) to be sure the gauge is accurate. If it has changed, you will have to knit the piece again using the next size needle, measuring again after several inches.

IMPORTANCE OF ROW GAUGE

Some knitters believe that the row gauge is not as essential as the stitch gauge. This is not true. In shaping pieces, such as sleeves, if you work the increases given in the instructions without getting proper row gauge, you may alter the length.

When you work a sweater from a full body chart, you must work the **exact number of rows** on the chart. If you do not have

the correct row gauge, your finished piece will either be too long or too short.

Some sweaters are worked from side to side. In this case, the rows determine the width, making the row gauge essential for proper fit.

MEASURING GAUGE

You can measure your gauge swatch between selvage stitches using a **measuring tape,** as the first two photos show. Or you can use a **stitch gauge** in the center of your swatch and count the stitches and rows inside the 2-inch (5-cm) right angle opening, as shown in the third photo.

Gauge Swatch for Knitting in the Round

The procedure for making an accurate gauge swatch when knitting in the round differs from that for flat knitting. When you knit stockinette in the round, you are always knitting and never purling. Most knitters purl more tightly or more loosely than they knit, and the difference affects the number of stitches and rows per inch or centimeter in their work when knitting flat. To make a swatch that will represent a fabric knitted circularly, you must **knit every row** and not purl to mimic the knit-only stitches in your work.

A simple, flat method used to create a gauge swatch for circular knitting is shown below.

As with a flat swatch, you can add extra stitches at the edges to make it easier to measure your swatch. A **double-pointed needle** that is long enough to hold 4 inches (10 cm) worth of stitches or a circular needle with a relatively short cable helps to make swatching in the round easier. You should, however, use the same brand of needle for the swatch as for the finished project because there can be slight differences in needle size across brands.

You will be left with a flat swatch that was knit with the **right side** facing you and that is **always knit,** and not purled. **Block** the swatch as you would for a gauge swatch knitted flat and then evaluate it as you would for a flat swatch. If you are not getting gauge, adjust your needle size and try again.

CIRCULAR GAUGE SWATCH

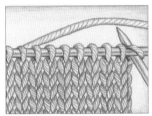

To knit a gauge swatch for circular knitting, use two double-pointed needles. Knit one row and slide the stitches to the **opposite end** of the needle to knit the next row from the right side. Pull the working yarn **very loosely across the back** of the work.

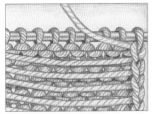

The floats lie loosely on the wrong side of the swatch. **Cut the floats** at the center and block the swatch before measuring the gauge.

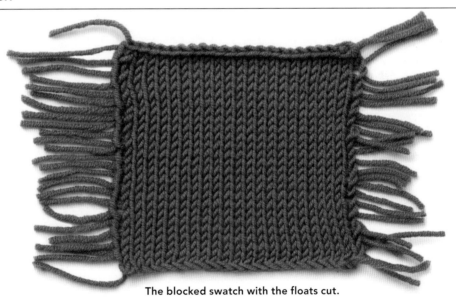

The blocked swatch with the floats cut.

TIP

USES FOR GAUGE SWATCHES

Not only do gauge swatches help ensure the success of your projects, they can have many other useful purposes. Here are some suggestions:

- Carry them with you when buying buttons or other notions for the project.
- Use them to practice borders, buttonholes, embroidery, and finishes.
- Sew squares together to make an afghan or blanket.
- Put swatches in a notebook to keep for future reference.

Counting Rows

Unless you are knitting a simple rectangle in which you cast on a certain number of stitches and bind off when it is long enough or when you've run out of yarn, you will have to count at least some rows in your project. Sweater instructions typically ask you to increase or decrease after knitting a certain number of rows to shape sleeves, waistlines, and necklines. You may also need to count rows to shape hat crowns, sock toes, and mitten tops. On textured stitch motifs, you may have to purl after knitting a set number of rows or manipulate stitches in some other way, and cable crosses occur on specified rows. To be sure you've followed the stitch pattern or instructions correctly or to check your work after knitting for a while, it is important to know how to count rows.

Illustrations of counting garter stitch, stockinette stitch,

and cable stitches appear below. No matter which method you use, **do not count the cast-on row,** but **do include the row of stitches on your needle** because those stitches have been knit (or purled). These rules and the descriptions below apply equally to rounds of circular knitting.

Many needle gauges have openings to help you count rows, but you need to know how to interpret what you see through the window that you position over your work. These are set up so that the Vs of stockinette stitch form a column that is easy to count.

There are other ways to keep track of your rows that do not require counting. You can use row counters and add removable markers at the end of specific numbers of rows. If you have two identical pieces, such as sleeves, you can knit them at the same time.

COUNTING GARTER STITCH ROWS

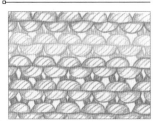

When working in garter stitch every ridge is formed by **two knit rows.**

COUNTING STOCKINETTE STITCH ROWS

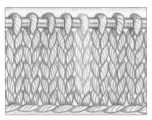

The knit stitch forms a V shape. Skipping the cast-on row and counting the stitch on the needle, **count the Vs** in a single column all the way up the work.

COUNTING ROWS BETWEEN CABLES

Use **two needles** to determine how many rows you have worked between cable crosses. Slide one needle through the opening made by twisting the stitches. Slide a second needle through the next opening. Skip the stitch directly on top of the top needle and count the stitch on top of the lower needle.

COUNTING ROWS BETWEEN CABLES

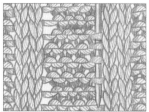

Turn the work to the **wrong side.** Slide a needle through the running strand between the stitches in the cable panel and the stitches along the cable panel, beginning with the first row above the cable cross and ending with the row in the next cable cross.

Knitting Abbreviations Explained

A

ALT: alternate; alternately

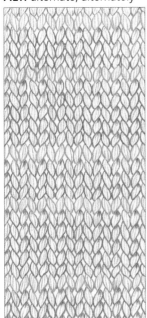

Alternate increases or decreases are used when shaping pieces to create an even slant. For example, in the illustration above, the yellow rows highlight every 4th and 6th row. This means the first increase or decrease is worked on the 4th row. 5 rows are worked even and then the stitches are increased or decreased again on the next row (the 6th row after the 1st increase or decrease, or the 10th row from the beginning). Therefore every 10 rows you work 2 sets of increases or decreases.

APPROX: approximately

B

BC: back cross; back cable (See cable.)

BEG: begin; begins; beginning

BO: bind off

C

C: cable; cross
A cable (also called cross) is formed by using an extra needle, usually a cable needle or double-pointed needle, to hold stitches to be crossed either to the front (which crosses them to the left), or to the back (which crosses them to the right). The cable crossing is generally worked on the right side of the work. The extra needle should be thinner than those you are working with to avoid stretching the stitches. After you have worked the cable, be sure to pull the yarn firmly before working the next stitch to prevent gaps in your work.

CC: contrasting color.
When two colors are used, the contrasting color is the yarn that is used as an accent.

CH: chain

CM: centimeter(s)

CN: cable needle

CO: cast on

CONT: continue; continuing

D

DC: double crochet

DEC(S): decrease(s); decreasing

DEC'D: decreased

DK: double knitting weight yarn

DP; DPN:
double-pointed needles

F

FC: front cross (See cable.)

FOLL: follow; follows; following

G

G: gram

H

HDC: half double crochet

I

IN: inch; inches

INC(S): increase(s); increasing

INC'D: increased

K

K: knit

K1-B: knit stitch in row below

KFB: knit into the front and back of a stitch

KFBF: knit through front, back, and front of stitch

K TBL: knit through back loop

K2TOG: knit 2 together

L

LC: left cross (See cable.)

LH: left-hand

LP(S): loop(s)

LT: left twist

M

M: meter(s)

MB: make bobble
A bobble is a three-dimensional stitch made by working multiple increases in 1 stitch, sometimes working a few rows, and then decreasing back to 1 stitch.

MC: main color
When two or more colors are used, the main color is the yarn that is dominant.

MM: millimeter(s)

M1: make one

M1 P-ST: Make one purl stitch

M1L: make one left

M1R: make one right

O

OZ: ounce

P

P: purl

PAT(S): pattern(s)

P1-B: purl stitch in the row below

PFB: purl into the front and back of a stitch

PM: place marker

PSSO: pass the slipped stitch over

P TBL: purl through back loop

P2TOG: purl 2 together

Crochet Abbreviations Explained

B

BL or BLO: back loop or back loop only

BO: bobble

BP: back post

BPDC: back post double crochet

BPHDC: back post half double crochet

BPSC: back post single crochet

BPTR: back post treble crochet

BPDTR: back post double treble crochet

C

CH: refers to chain or space previously made, e.g., ch-1 space

CH SP: chain space

CL: cluster

D

DC: double crochet (UK: treble crochet–tr)

DC2TOG: double crochet 2 stitches together

DTR: double treble crochet (UK: triple treble crochet–trtr)

E

EDC: extended double crochet

EHDC: extended half double crochet

ESC: extended single crochet

ETR: extended treble crochet

F

FL or FLO: front loop or front loop only

FP: front post

FPHDC: front post half double crochet

FPDC: front post double crochet

FPDTR: front post double treble crochet

FPSC: front post single crochet

FPTR: front post treble crochet

H

HDC: half double crochet (UK: half treble crochet—htr)

HDC2TOG: half double crochet 2 stitches together

M

M: marker

P

PC: popcorn stitch

PREV: previous

PS or PUFF: puff stitch

S

SC: single crochet (UK: double crochet–dc)

SC2TOG: single crochet 2 stitches together

SH: shell

SK: skip

SL ST: slip stitch (UK: ss)

SM or SL M: slip marker

SP: space

T

TCH OR T-CH: turning chain

TR: treble crochet (UK: double treble–dtr)

TR2TOG: treble crochet 2 stitches together

TRTR: triple treble crochet

Y

YOH: yarn over hook

R

RC: right cross (See cable.)

REM: remain(s); remaining

REP: repeat

REV ST ST: reverse stockinette stitch

RH: right-hand

RND(S): round(s)

RS: right side

RT: right twist

S

SC: single crochet

SK: skip

SKP: slip 1, knit 1, pass the slipped stitch over

S2KP: slip 2, knit 1, pass the slipped stitch over

SK2P: slip 1, knit 2 together, pass the slipped stitch over

SL: slip

SL ST: slip stitch

SM: slip marker

SP(S): space(s)

SSK: slip, slip, knit decrease

SSP: slip, slip, purl decrease

ST(S): stitch(es)

ST ST: stockinette stitch

T

TBL: through back loop

T-CH: turning chain

TOG: together

TR: treble

W

WS: wrong side

W&T: wrap and turn (see page 139)

WYIB: with yarn in back

WYIF: with yarn in front

Y

YB: yarn to the back

YF: yarn to the front (or forward)

YFON: yarn forward and over needle

YFRN: yarn forward and round needle

YO: yarn over
A yarn over is a decorative increase made by wrapping the yarn around the needle. There are various ways to make a yarn over depending on where it is placed. (see page 85)

YO TWICE: yarn over 2 times

YON: yarn over needle

YRN: yarn round needle

Between two knit stitches

Bring the yarn from the back of the work to the front between the two needles. Knit the next stitch, bringing the yarn to the back over the right needle as shown.

Between a knit and a purl stitch

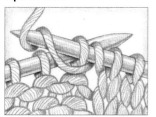

Bring the yarn from the back to the front between the two needles, then to the back over the right needle and to the front again as shown. Purl the next stitch.

Between two purl stitches

Leave the yarn at the front of the work. Bring the yarn to the back over the right needle and to the front again as shown. Purl the next stitch.

At the beginning of a knit row

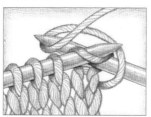

Keep the yarn at the front of the work. Insert the right needle knitwise into the first stitch on the left needle. Bring the yarn over the right needle to the back and knit the next stitch, holding the yarn over with your thumb if necessary.

At the beginning of a purl row

To work a yarn over at the beginning of a purl row, keep the yarn at the back of the work. Insert the right needle purlwise into the first stitch on the left needle. Purl the stitch.

Multiple yarn overs

1 In multiple yarn overs (2 or more), wrap the yarn around the needle as for a single yarn over, then wrap the yarn around the needle once more (or as many times as indicated). Work the next stitch on the left needle.

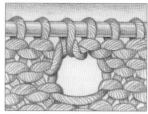

2 Alternate knitting and purling into the multiple yarn over on the subsequent row, always knitting the last stitch on a purl row and purling the last stitch on a knit row.

Between a purl and a knit stitch

Leave the yarn at the front of the work. Knit the next stitch, bringing the yarn to the back over the right needle as shown.

Knitting Terminology

A

ABOVE MARKERS:
Knitting worked after the point where stitch markers have been placed.

ABOVE RIB:
Knitting worked after the last row of ribbing.

AFTER...NUMBER OF ROWS HAVE BEEN WORKED:
Continue working as instructed after completing the designated number of rows.

ALONG NECK:
Generally used when picking up stitches at an unshaped, or straight, neck edge.

AROUND NECK:
Generally used when picking up stitches at a shaped, or curved, neck edge.

AS ESTABLISHED:
Continue to work the pattern as it has been set up.

AS FOLL:
Work the instructions that follow.

AS FOR BACK (FRONT):
Work in the same way as the back (or the front).

AS IF TO KNIT:
Insert the needle or wrap the yarn as if you were knitting.

AS IF TO PURL:
Insert the needle or wrap the yarn as if you were purling.

AT SAME TIME:
Work the instructions that immediately follow this term simultaneously with those that immediately precede it.

ATTACH:
Join a new strand of yarn.

B

BEG AND END AS INDICATED:
Used when working with charts. Begin the row of knitting at the point on the chart that is indicated for your size by an arrow or straight line and the term "beg" (beginning). Continue working the chart as instructed, knitting the last stitch at the point indicated by another arrow or straight line and the term "end."

BIND OFF...STS AT BEG OF NEXT...ROWS:
Often used in armhole and shoulder shaping. Stitches are almost always bound off at the beginning of a row. Therefore, after binding off the designated number of stitches, work to the end of the row, turn the work, and bind off the same number of stitches at the beginning of the next designated number of rows.

BIND OFF CENTER...STS:
Determine the center stitches and place markers on either side of the designated number of center stitches, if desired, on the needles. Work the next row to the first marker, join a new ball of yarn, and bind off the center stitches, then work to the end of the row with the new ball of yarn.

BIND OFF FROM EACH NECK EDGE:
A phrase used when both sides of the inside neck edge are shaped simultaneously after binding off the center stitches.

BIND OFF IN RIB (OR PAT):
Bind off stitches as they appear. That is, knit the knit stitches and purl the purl stitches as you bind them off.

BIND OFF LOOSELY:
Do not pull the yarn too tightly when binding off. Or use a needle one size larger on the bind-off row.

BIND OFF REM STS EACH SIDE:
A phrase usually used for the remaining stitches of each shoulder after shaping a neck. After you have completed all the shaping, bind off the stitches that remain on one side, then bind off the remaining stitches on the other side.

BLOCK PIECES:
The process of laying flat completed pieces of knitting to even and smooth the stitches and to give them their permanent shape.

BODY OF SWEATER IS WORKED IN ONE PIECE TO UNDERARM:
A term used when using a circular needle to knit a sweater with no side seams up to the underarm.

BOTH SIDES AT ONCE:
A term used after an opening has been made on a row, such as for a neck shaping, When stitches have been bound off and you have two separate pieces on one needle, work both sides simultaneously with separate balls of yarn. That is, work one row on the first side, then work the corresponding row on the second side with the second ball of yarn. Then turn the work.

C

CAP SHAPING:
The shaped part of the sleeve above the armhole, which will fit into the armhole of the sweater.

CARRY YARN LOOSELY ACROSS BACK OF WORK:
In color knitting, let the yarn not in use span loosely across the wrong side of the work until you need to use it again.

CARRY YARN UP THE SIDE OF WORK:
When using more than one color, carry the unused colors along the edge of the work. Do not cut.

CAST ON...STS AT BEG OF NEXT...ROWS:
When adding two or more stitches at the edges of a piece, cast on the designated number of stitches before beginning the row, work the cast-on stitches, then work to the end of the row. Turn the work and cast on the same number of stitches at the beginning of the next row.

CAST ON...STS OVER BOUND-OFF STS:
Often refers to making buttonholes. Work to where the stitches from the previous row were bound off. Cast on the specified number of stitches, then work to the end of the row.

CENTER BACK (FRONT) NECK:
The point that marks the center of the back (or front) neck.

CHANGE TO SMALLER (LARGER) NEEDLES:
Proceed with the work using smaller (or larger) needles than those used previously.

CONT IN PAT:
Continue to work the pattern as previously described.

CONT IN THIS WAY (MANNER):
Continue to work the instructions as previously described.

D

DIRECTIONS ARE FOR SMALLEST (SMALLER) SIZE, WITH LARGER SIZES IN PARENTHESES:
Many knitting instructions are written for more than one size. Usually, the number referring to the smallest (smaller) size is the number before the parentheses. The numbers indicating larger sizes appear inside the parentheses in ascending order.

DISCONTINUE PAT:
Stop working the pattern stitch immediately preceding and continue as directed.

DO NOT PRESS:
Do not use an iron to press or steam the knitted fabric.

DO NOT TURN WORK:
Keep the work facing in the same direction as the row you have just completed.

E

EACH END (SIDE):
Work designated stitches at both the beginning and the end of a row.

EASING IN ANY FULLNESS:
In seaming, gather in any extra fabric evenly.

END LAST REP:
After completing a full repeat of a pattern and not enough stitches remain to complete another repeat, end the pattern repeat as directed.

END WITH A RS (WS) ROW:
The last row worked is a right-side (wrong-side) row.

EVERY OTHER ROW:
When shaping, work one row between each increase or decrease row.

EVERY FOURTH, SIXTH…ROW:
When shaping, work 3, 5… rows between the increase or decrease rows.

F

FASTEN OFF:
When binding off, cut the yarn leaving a long tail, then pull the yarn through the last loop on the needle to finish the piece and prevent unraveling.

FINISHED BUST:
The circumference of a garment at the bustline after garment is completed.

FINISHED BUST (BUTTONED):
A phrase usually used for cardigans or jackets to indicate the circumference at the bustline after the garment is completed and the fronts are buttoned.

FROM BEG:
A phrase used when measuring from the cast-on edge of the piece or beginning of the knitted piece.

FULL-FASHIONED:
A phrase that means deliberately showing increases or decreases worked a few stitches in from the edge.

G

GAUGE:
The number of stitches and rows per inch (centimeter).

GRAFTING:
Joining two edges together that have not been bound off, resulting in an invisible seam.

H

HOLD TO FRONT (BACK) OF WORK:
A phrase usually referring to stitches placed on a cable needle that are held to the front (or the back) of the work as it faces you.

I

INC…STS EVENLY ACROSS ROW:
Increase the stitches at even intervals across the row.

INC STS INTO PAT:
When increasing, work the added stitches into the established pattern.

IN SAME WAY (MANNER):
Repeat the process that was previously described.

IT IS ESSENTIAL TO GET PROPER ROW GAUGE:
When instructions are written for a specific number of rows (such as in garments with large motifs), you must obtain the specified row gauge to get the correct length.

J

JOIN: When used in circular knitting, the process of uniting the first and last stitch of a round. Or, joining separate sections to be continued in one piece.

JOIN A SECOND BALL (SKEIN) OF YARN:
A phrase used when dividing the work into two sections (such as for placket or neck shaping), where each section is worked with a separate ball (or skein) of yarn.

JOIN, TAKING CARE NOT TO TWIST STS:
When casting on in circular knitting, join the first and the last cast-on stitch to form a circle, making sure that the stitches are not twisted on the needle.

K

K THE KNIT STS AND P THE PURL STS (AS THEY APPEAR):
A phrase used when a pattern of knit and purl stitches has been established and will continue for a determined length (such as ribbing). Work the stitches as they appear: Knit the knit stitches and purl the purl stitches.

K THE PURL STS AND P THE KNIT STS:
A phrase used when a pattern of knit and purl stitches will alternate on the following row or rows (such as in a seed stitch pattern). Work the stitches opposite to how they appear: Purl the knit stitches and knit the purl stitches.

KEEP CAREFUL COUNT OF ROWS:
Advice usually given with intricate patterns or shaping in which the row count is important. Keep track either by writing down each row as you complete it or by using a row counter.

KEEPING TO PAT (OR MAINTAINING PAT):
A term used when new instructions are given (such as shaping), but the established pattern must be continued.

KITCHENER STITCH:
A method of grafting two live edges together.

KNITWISE (OR AS IF TO KNIT):
Insert the needle into the stitch and/or wrap the yarn as if you were going to knit it.

L

LOWER EDGE:
The bottom edge of the piece, usually the cast-on edge.

M

MATCHING COLORS:
Work the stitches in the same color as on the previous row.

MULTIPLE OF...STS:
Used when working a pattern. The total number of stitches should be divisible by the number of stitches in one pattern repeat.

MULTIPLE OF...STS PLUS...:
Used when working a pattern. The total number of stitches should be divisible by the number of stitches in one pattern repeat, plus the additional stitches (added only once).

N

NEXT ROW (RS), OR (WS):
The row following the one just worked will be a right-side (or wrong-side) row.

O

ON ALL FOLL ROWS OR RNDS:
A direction that applies to all the rows that follow the row just worked.

P

PICK UP AND K:
Used to refer to pulling up loops of working yarn through stitches and rows of a finished edge with the stated knitting needles and a ball of yarn to begin an edge or a new piece.

PIECE MEASURES APPROX:
A term used when a specified number of rows must be worked, as in shaping or pattern work. The piece should measure the stated amount within ¼ inch (6 mm) if you have the correct row gauge.

PLACE MARKER(S):
Slide a stitch marker either onto the needle (where it is slipped every row) or attach to a stitch, where it remains as a guide.

PLACE STITCHES ON A HOLDER:
Slip the stitches from the needle to a stitch holder or thread them on a length of scrap yarn for later use.

PREPARATION ROW:
A row that sets up the stitch pattern but is not part of the pattern repeat.

PULL UP A LOOP:
Often used in crochet, this phrase in knitting signifies drawing a new stitch (or loop) through the knit fabric.

PURLWISE (OR AS IF TO PURL):
Insert the needle into the stitch and/or wrap the yarn as if you were going to purl it.

R

REP FROM * TO * OR REP BETWEEN *S:
Repeat the instructions that fall between the two asterisks.

REP FROM * AROUND:
In circular knitting, repeat the instructions that begin at the asterisk, ending at the joining.

REP FROM *, END...:
Repeat the instructions that begin at the asterisk as many times as you can work full repeats of the pattern, then end the row as directed.

REP FROM * TO END:
Repeat the instructions that begin at the asterisk, ending the row with a full repeat of the pattern.

REP FROM...ROW:
Repeat the pattern rows previously worked, beginning with the row specified.

REP INC (OR DEC):
Repeat the increase (or decrease) previously described.

REP...TIMES MORE:
Repeat a direction the designated number of times (not counting the first time you work it).

REVERSE PAT PLACEMENT:
A term used for garments such as cardigans, mittens, and gloves where the right and left pieces have symmetrical patterns. Generally, the instructions for only one piece are given, and you must work patterns for the second piece in the opposite order.

REVERSING SHAPING:
A phrase used for garments such as cardigans where shaping for the right and left fronts is identical, but reversed. The instructions for only one piece are given, and you must work the shaping for the second piece on the opposite edge.

RIGHT SIDE (OR RS):
Refers to the surface of the work that will face outside when the garment is worn.

ROUND:
A circular row of stitches.

ROW:
A horizontal line of stitches formed by transferring all the stitches from one needle to the other.

ROW 2 AND ALL WS (EVEN-NUMBERED) ROWS:
A phrase used when all the wrong-side or even-numbered rows are worked the same.

RUNNING STRAND:
The horizontal strand between two stitches.

S

SAME AS:
Follow the instructions given in another section or piece of the garment.

SAME LENGTH AS:
A term used when two or more pieces of a garment are equal in length, and the measurement of one has already been given.

SCHEMATIC:
A scale drawing showing specific measurements of all the pieces of a garment before they are sewn together and finished.

SELVAGE ST:
An extra stitch (or stitches) at the edge of a piece used either to make seaming easier or as a decorative finish.

SET IN SLEEVES:
Sew the sleeves into the armholes

SEW SHOULDER SEAM, INCLUDING NECKBAND:
A phrase used when seaming one shoulder before working a neckband. After the neckband is completed, sew the open shoulder seam along with the side edges of the neckband.

SEW TOP OF SLEEVES BETWEEN MARKERS:
A phrase generally used when the garment has no armhole shaping (such as for drop shoulders), and markers must be used to denote the depth of the armhole. Center the sleeve at the shoulder seam, with the ends of the sleeve top at the markers, and sew it to the front and back of the garment.

SHORT ROW:
A technique, generally used in shaping, or color work, to add rows in one segment of a piece without decreasing the number of stitches on the needle.

SHAPING:
Using increases, decreases, or short rows to alter the measurements of a piece.

SIDE TO SIDE:
When a piece is worked horizontally from side seam to side seam instead of vertically.

SLEEVE WIDTH AT UPPER ARM:
The measurement of the finished sleeve at its widest point, which fits around the widest part of the arm.

SLIGHTLY STRETCHED:
A term often used when measuring stitch patterns that tend to pull in, such as ribbing or cables. A more accurate gauge of the pattern is obtained when the stitches are pulled apart slightly.

SLIP MARKER:
To keep the stitch marker in the same position from one row to the next, transfer it from one needle to the other as you work each row.

SLIP MARKER AT BEG OF EVERY RND:
In circular knitting, slip the marker from one needle to the other every time you begin a new round.

SLIP STS TO A HOLDER:
Transfer the stitches from the needle to a stitch holder.

SWATCH:
A sample of knitting used to measure the gauge or to try out a stitch or colorwork pattern before knitting the garment.

SWEATER IS WORKED IN ONE PIECE:
Work all the parts of a sweater—the front, back and sleeves—as one piece.

SWEATER IS WORKED IN TWO PIECES:
Work the front half of the sweater (including the front half of the sleeves) in one piece and the back half in another.

T
THROUGH BOTH (ALL) THICKNESSES:
A phrase usually used in seaming when working through two pieces of fabric at one time.

THROUGH...ROW (ROUND):
Work up to and include the designated row.

TO...ROW (ROUND):
Work up to but do not include the specified row.

TOTAL LENGTH:
The length of a garment, after finishing, from the highest point of the shoulder to the lowest edge.

TURNING:
The process of switching your knitted piece from right side to wrong side or vice versa to work a new or partial row.

TURNING RIDGE:
A row of raised stitches (often purl stitches on stockinette stitch) that indicates where the piece will fold in or out, as for a hem.

TWIST YARNS ON WS TO PREVENT HOLES:
A term used in colorwork when changing from one color to the next across a row. Twist the old and the new yarns around each other to prevent a hole in your work.

U
USE A SEPARATE BOBBIN FOR EACH BLOCK OF COLOR:
When working intarsia (large color block patterns), where the yarn cannot be carried across large areas of color, use a bobbin for each separate block of color.

W
WEAVE IN ENDS:
In finishing, loose ends must be worked in so that they will not unravel.

WEAVE OR TWIST YARNS NOT IN USE:
In stranded knitting, when you must carry yarns for more than a few stitches, weave or twist yarns that are not being used around the working yarn to avoid long, loose floats.

WHEN ARMHOLE MEASURES:
This phrase is used to denote the point in a sweater at which the neck or shoulder shaping begins, and it is measured from the beginning of the armhole shaping.

WIDTH FROM SLEEVE EDGE (CUFF) TO SLEEVE EDGE (CUFF):
When the body and sleeves of a sweater are knit in one piece, this is the measurement from the edge of one sleeve, across the shoulder and neck edges, to the edge of the second sleeve.

WITH RIGHT (WRONG) SIDES TOGETHER (FACING):
Placing two pieces so that the right (wrong) sides are facing each other.

WITH RS FACING:
The right side of the work must be facing you and the wrong side facing away from you.

WITH WS FACING:
The wrong side of the work must be facing you and the right side facing away from you.

WORK ACROSS STS ON HOLDER:
Work the stitches directly from the stitch holder, or transfer the stitches from the holder to a knitting needle and then work them.

WORK BACK AND FORTH IN ROWS:
When knitting on a circular needle, turn the work at the end of every row instead of joining it and working in rounds.

WORK BUTTONHOLES OPPOSITE MARKERS:
When markers for buttons have been placed on the button band, work the buttonholes opposite these markers on the other band so that they will correspond to the buttons.

WORK EVEN (STRAIGHT):
Continue in the established pattern without working any shaping.

WORKING IN PAT:
Follow the instructions for the pattern, whether written or charted.

WORK IN ROUNDS:
In circular knitting, the process of working a piece in which

the ends have been joined and that has no seam.

WORKING NEEDLE:
The needle being used to make new stitches.

WORKING YARN:
The yarn being used to make new stitches.

WORK REP OF CHART... TIMES:
When working a pattern from a chart, work the stitches in the repeat as many times as designated.

WORK TO CORRESPOND:
A phrase used when instructions are given for one piece, and a similar second piece must be made to match.

WORK TO END:
Work the established pattern to the end of the row.

WORK TO...STS BEFORE CENTER:
Work the row to a specified number of stitches before the center of the row, which is generally indicated by a stitch marker.

WORK TO LAST...STS:
Work across the row until the specified number of stitches remains on the left needle.

WORK UNTIL...STS FROM BIND OFF (OR ON RH NEEDLE):
After binding off, work until the specified number of stitches remains on the right needle.

WRONG SIDE (OR WS):
Usually refers to the surface of the work that will face inside when the garment is worn.

Symbols

Symbols are a universal form of knitting instructions. Instead of writing out a stitch pattern with words and abbreviations, symbols are used.

Each symbol **represents the stitch** as it appears on the right side of the work. For example, the symbol for a knit stitch is an empty box and the symbol for a purl stitch is a horizontal line. On right-side rows, you work the stitches as they appear on the chart—knitting the empty boxes and purling the horizontal lines. When reading wrong-side rows, work the opposite of what is shown; that is, purl the empty boxes and knit the horizontal lines.

In charts, **each square represents one stitch** and **each line of squares equals one row**. The rows are read from bottom to top. Usually, the odd-numbered rows are listed on the right-hand side of the chart. Unless otherwise stated, these are right-side rows and are read horizontally from right to left. The numbers on the left-hand side of the chart are wrong-side rows, and these rows are read from left to right. If you are working in the round, you would read all the rows from right to left.

Sometimes only a single repeat of the pattern is charted. But if the pattern is complex, more than one repeat will be shown so that you can see how the finished motif will look. Heavy or colored lines are usually drawn through the entire chart to **indicate the repeat**. These lines are the equivalent of an asterisk (*) or brackets [ ] used in written instructions.

CHART SYMBOLS

SELVAGE OR EDGE STITCH

K ON RS, P ON WS Knit on RS, purl on WS (stockinette stitch).

P ON RS, K ON RS Purl on RS, knit on WS (reverse stockinette stitch).

YO Yarn over

YO TWICE Wrap yarn over needle twice.

K1TBL ON RS, P1TBL ON WS Knit stitch through back loop on RS; purl stitch through the back loop on WS.

P1TBL ON RS, K1TBL ON WS Purl stitch through back loop on RS; knit stitch through back loop on WS.

SL 1 With yarn in back, slip stitch *purlwise* on RS; with yarn in front, slip stitch *purlwise* on WS.

SL 1 With yarn in front, slip stitch *purlwise* on RS; with yarn in back, slip stitch *purlwise* on WS.

K1-B Knit stitch in row below on RS; purl stitch in row below on WS.

P1-B Purl stitch in row below on RS; knit stitch in row below on WS.

M1 Make one stitch as follows: On RS, insert left needle from front to back under horizontal strand between stitch just worked and next stitch on left needle. Knit this strand through the back loop. On WS, insert left needle from back to front under strand as before and purl it through back loop.

M1-P ST Make one stitch as follows: On RS, insert left needle from back to front under horizontal strand between stitch just worked and next stitch on left needle and purl it through back loop. On WS, insert left needle from front to back under strand as before. Knit this strand through the back loop.

M1-OPEN Make one stitch to form an eyelet as follows: on the RS, insert left needle from front to back under horizontal strand between stitch just worked and next stitch on left needle. Knit this strand. On WS, insert left needle from back to front under strand as before and purl it.

KFB Knit front and back: Increase 1 stitch to the right as follows: knit in front then in back of stitch on RS; purl in back then in front on WS.

RL-INC Right-leaning inc: Increase 1 stitch to the right as follows: with right needle, pick up next stitch on left needle in row below. Place loop on left needle and knit it.

LL-INC Left-leaning inc: Increase 1 stitch to the left as follows: with left needle, pick up next stitch on right needle one row below and knit it.

INC 3 STS Increase 3 stitches in 2 as follows: insert right needle knitwise into next two stitches on left needle. Knit one, purl one, knit one. Drop loops off left needle.

K2TOG ON RS, P2TOG ON WS Knit two stitches together on RS; purl two stitches together on WS.

SKP ON RS, SPP ON WS Slip one stitch, knit next stitch and pass slip stitch over knit stitch on RS; slip one stitch, purl one stitch, then pass slip stitch over purl stitch on WS.

SSK ON RS, SSP ON WS Slip next two stitches knitwise, insert tip of left needle into fronts of these two stitches and knit them together on RS; Slip next two stitches knitwise, slip these two stitches back to left needle without twisting them and purl them together through the back loops on WS.

P2TOG ON RS, K2TOG ON WS Purl two stitches together on RS; knit two stitches together on WS.

P2TOGTBL ON RS, K2TOG TBL ON WS Purl two stitches together through the back loops, on RS; knit two stitches together through back loops on WS.

K3TOG ON RS, P3TOG ON WS Knit three stitches together on RS; purl three stitches together on WS.

P3TOG ON RS, K3TOG ON WS Purl three stitches together on RS; knit three stitches together on WS.

SK2P On RS, slip one stitch, knit two stitches together. Pass slipped stitch over two stitches knit together. On WS, slip two stitches to right needle as if knitting two together. Slip next stitch knitwise. Slip all stitches to left needle without twisting them. Purl these three stitches together through back loops.

S2KP On RS, slip two sts knitwise onto RH needle one at a time, k next st, then pass both slipped sts over the k st.

K4TOG ON RS, P4TOG ON WS, Knit four stitches together on RS; purl four stitches together on WS.

MAKE BOBBLE (K1, p1, k1, p1, k1) in the same st, making 5 sts from one; then pass the 4th, 3rd, 2nd and 1st over the last st made. Or as instructed.

CAST ON ONE STITCH

BIND OFF ONE STITCH

NO STITCH A placeholder in the chart, marking a stitch that has been decreased out of, or has yet to be increased into, the pattern. The use of this symbol helps to keep the stitches lined up and easier to read. Just skip that no stitch square(s) and work the next charted stitch.

2-ST RBC 2-st right back cable: Slip 1 st to cn and hold to back of work, k1tbl, k1 from cn.

2-ST LBC 2-st left back cable: Slip 1 st to cn and hold to front of work, k1, k1tbl from cn.

3-ST RPC 3-stitch right purl cable: Slip 2 sts to cn and hold to back of work, k1, then p2 from cn.

3-ST LPC 3-stitch left purl cable: Slip 1 st to cn and hold to front of work, p2, then k1 from cn.

3-ST RPC 3-stitch right purl cable: Slip 2 sts to cn and hold to back of work, k1, then p1, k1 from cn.

3-ST LPC Slip 1 st to cn and hold to front of work, k1, p1, then k1 from cn.

4-ST RPC 4-stitch right purl cable: Sl 2 sts to cn and hold to back of work, k2, then k1, p1 from cn.

4-ST LPC 4-stitch left purl cable: Sl 2 sts to cn and hold to front of work, p1, k1, then k2 from cn.

4-ST WRAP Wyib sl 4, wyif sl same 4 sts to LH needle, wyib sl same 4 sts.

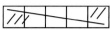

5-ST LC 5-stitch left cable: Sl 3 sts to cn and hold to front of work, k2, k3 from cn.

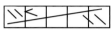

5-ST RPC 5-stitch right purl cable: Sl 3 sts to cn and hold to back of work, k2, then p1, k2 from cn.

5-ST RPC 5-stitch right purl cable: Slip 1 st to cn and hold to back of work, k4, then p1 from cn.

5-ST LPC Slip 4 sts to cn and hold to front of work, p1, k4 from cn.

6-ST RPC 6-stitch right purl cable: Sl 3 sts to cn and hold to back of work, k3, then p3 from cn.

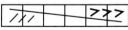

6-ST LPC 6-stitch left purl cable: Sl 3 sts to cn and hold to front of work, p3, then k3 from cn.

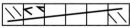

6-ST RPC 6 stitch right purl cable: Sl 4 sts to cn and hold to back of work, k2, then p2, k2 from cn.

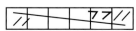

6-ST LPC 6-stitch left purl cable: Sl 2 sts to cn and hold to front of work, k2, p2, then k2 from cn.

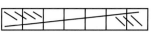

7-ST RC 7-stitch right cable: Sl 4 sts to cn and hold to back of work, k3, then k4 from cn.

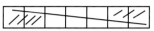

7-ST LC 7-stitch left cable: Sl 4 sts to cn and hold to front of work, k3, then k4 from cn.

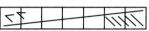

7-ST RPC 7-stitch right purl cable: Sl 2 sts to cn and hold to back of work, k5, then p2 from cn.

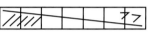

7-ST LPC 7-stitch left purl cable: Sl 5 sts to cn and hold to front of work, p2, then k5 from cn.

8-ST RC 8-stitch right cable: Sl 4 sts to cn and hold to back of work, k4, then k4 from cn.

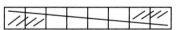

8-ST LC 8-stitch left cable: Sl 4 sts to cn and hold to front, k4, then k4 from cn.

8-ST RPC 8-stitch right purl cable: Sl 4 sts to cn and hold to back, k4, then p4 from cn.

8-ST LPC 8-stitch left purl cable: Sl 4 sts to cn and hold to front of work, p4, then k4 from cn.

UNUSUAL AND ALTERNATIVE SYMBOLS

K ON RS, P ON WS

RT Knit 2nd stitch without dropping it from left needle, knit first stitch and drop both stitches together. This symbol can also be used for a k2tog.

LT Insert needle from back of work in back loop of second stitch, knit 2nd stitch without dropping it from left needle, knit first stitch and drop both stitches together. This symbol can also be used for a left-leaning decrease such as SKP.

K2TOG TBL Knit 2 together through the back loop.

SSSK Slip 3 stitches, one at a time, to the right-hand needle, insert left-hand needle in front loops and knit the 3 stitches together to decrease 2 stitches. This symbol is useful if another left-leaning double decrease is used in the same chart.

Remove the beginning of round marker, slip next stitch purlwise to right-hand needle, replace marker.

Pick up or hide short-row wraps in this round.

Loop left after binding off.

Drop stitch.

K2TOG ON RS This symbol is used over two boxes when it is practical to keep the stitches lined up in the chart. It is likely that there will be a compensating increase in the next row.

P2TOG ON RS This symbol is used over two boxes when it is practical to keep the stitches lined up in the chart. It is likely that there will be a compensating increase in the next row.

S2KP Slip 2 stitches as if to knit 2 together, knit next stitch, then pass both slipped sts over the knit st. This symbol is used over three boxes when it is practical to keep those boxes in the chart.

3-ST RT *Skip first 2 stitches on left-hand needle and insert right-hand needle purlwise into 3rd stitch, from front of row. Pass this stitch over the first 2 stitches and drop it off the left-hand needle.* K1, yo, k2.

3-ST RT DEC Work between *s of 3-st RT, k2—1 st decreased.

Knit 3 stitches, with tip of left needle, pass first stitch over last 2 stitches and off needle.

K1, YO, K1 in same stitch. This symbol has also been used for yo, slip 1.

4-ST EYELET RC Slip 2 stitches to cable needle and hold to back, yo, SKP, yo, SKP from cable needle.

4-ST EYELET LC Slip 2 stitches to cable needle and hold to front, yo, SKP, yo, SKP from cable needle.

Wrap 4 stitches 5 times.

SSK using CC.

K2TOG using MC.

AB Add bead.

Multiple decrease worked over 2 rows. RS row: ssk, k1, k2tog. WS row: p3tog—5 stitches decreased to 1.

yo twice, on WS row drop extra wrap.

yo twice

ON WS K1, p1 in double yo.

4-st wrap: Wyib sl 4, wyif sl same 4 sts to LH needle, wyib sl same 4 sts.

Correcting Errors

Correcting Errors

Common errors encountered when knitting include stitches that are **backwards, unwanted, dropped,** or **incomplete**. Check your work often because it is easier to correct mistakes soon after you've made them.

If you have worked only a row or two beyond an error, you can work back to it stitch by stitch.

If you discover an error after working many more rows, unravel to the mistake and rework from that point. You may be able to drop individual stitches above the error and unravel only those back to the mistake, instead of unraveling several complete rows.

To **unravel**, use a contrasting yarn or stitch marker to mark the row with the error. Remove the knitting needle and pull out the stitches to that row. When working an intricate stitch pattern, keep track of the number of rows you unravel so that you won't lose your place.

After unraveling, put the stitches back onto a smaller needle—it will be easier to slip the needle into the loops. Make sure that the stitches are not backwards as you return them to the needle. Work the stitches with the correct needle size.

Certain novelty yarns and mohair are not easy to unravel. You may want to use scissors to carefully free the hairs of fuzzy yarns as you unravel.

TWISTED STITCHES: KNIT AND PURL

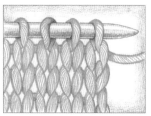

A twisted or backwards stitch is created either by wrapping the yarn incorrectly on the previous row or by dropping a stitch and returning it to the needle backwards.

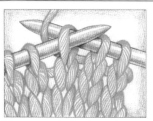

To correct the backwards knit stitch, knit it through the back loop.

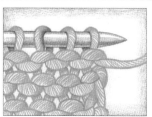

A backwards purl stitch looks different from a regular purl stitch in that the back loop is nearer the tip of the needle than the front loop.

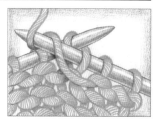

To correct the backwards purl stitch, purl it through the back loop.

PICKING UP A DROPPED KNIT STITCH

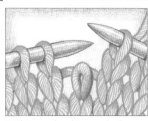

1 This method is used when a knit stitch has dropped only one row. Work to where the stitch was dropped. Be sure that the loose strand is behind the dropped stitch.

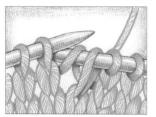

2 Insert the right needle from front to back into the dropped stitch and under the loose horizontal strand behind.

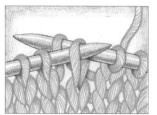

3 Insert the left needle from the back into the dropped stitch on the right needle, and pull this stitch over the loose strand.

4 Transfer this newly made stitch back to the left needle by inserting the left needle from front to back into the stitch and slipping it off the right needle.

PICKING UP A DROPPED PURL STITCH

 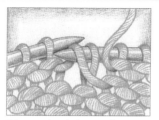 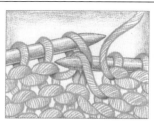 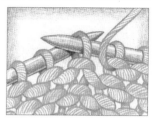

1 This method is used when a purl stitch has been dropped only one row. Work to the dropped purl stitch. Be sure that the loose horizontal strand is in front of the dropped stitch.

2 Insert the right needle from back to front into the dropped stitch, and then under the loose horizontal strand.

3 With the left needle, lift the dropped stitch over the horizontal strand and off the right needle.

4 Transfer the newly made purl stitch back to the left needle by inserting the left needle from front to back into the stitch and slipping it off the right needle.

PICKING UP A RUNNING KNIT AND PURL STITCH

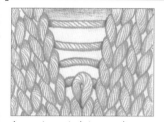 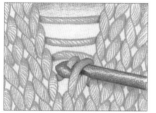 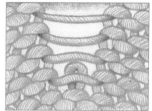 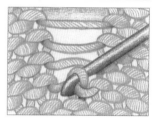

A running stitch is one that has dropped more than one row. It is easiest to pick it up with a crochet hook. For a knit stitch, be sure the loose horizontal strands are in back of the dropped stitch.

Insert the hook into the stitch from front to back. Catch the first horizontal strand and pull it through. Continue up until you have worked all the strands. Place the newest stitch on the left needle, making sure it is not backwards.

Before picking up a dropped purl stitch several rows below, be sure that the loose horizontal strands are in front of the stitch.

Insert the hook into the stitch from back to front. Pull the loose strand through the stitch. Continue up until you have worked all the strands. Place the newest stitch on the left needle, making sure it is not backwards.

INCOMPLETE KNIT AND PURL STITCHES

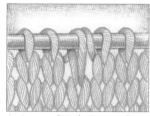 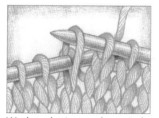 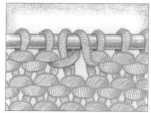 

An incomplete knit or purl stitch is one where the yarn is wrapped around the needle but not pulled through the stitch. The illustration above shows an incomplete stitch from the previous purl row.

Work to the incomplete stitch. Insert the right needle from back to front into the stitch on the left needle and pull it over the strand and off the needle.

This illustration shows an incomplete stitch from the previous knit row.

Insert the right needle into the stitch on the left needle and pull it over the strand and off the needle.

AN EXTRA STITCH AT THE EDGE

If you bring the yarn back over the top of the needle at the beginning of the **knit row,** the first stitch will have two loops instead of one, as shown.

To avoid creating this extra stitch, keep the yarn under the needle when taking it to the back to knit the first stitch.

At the beginning of a **purl row,** if the yarn is at the back, and then brought to the front under the needle, the first stitch will have two loops instead of one, as shown.

To avoid making these two loops, the yarn should be at the front before you purl the first stitch.

UNRAVELING STITCH BY STITCH

Knit stitches Keep the yarn at the back. Insert the left needle into the stitch from front to back one row below the stitch on right needle. Drop the stitch and pull the yarn to undo it.

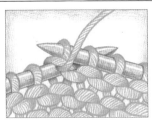

Purl stitches Keep the yarn at the front. Insert the left needle from front to back into the stitch one row below the stitch on the right needle. Drop the stitch and pull the yarn to undo it.

UNRAVELING ROWS

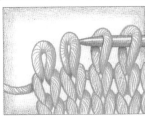

If you need to unravel one or more rows, you must put the stitches back onto the needle correctly. With working yarn at left side, insert a smaller needle from back to front into each stitch across the row.

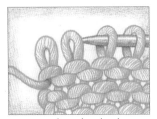

To put purl stitches back on the needle after unraveling them, first make sure the working yarn is at the left side. Insert a smaller needle from back to front into each stitch across the row.

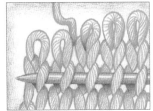

If concerned about dropping stitches, weave the right needle under the first loop and over the second loop of each knit stitch in the row. Pull working yarn to unravel all stitches above needle.

You can also use this method with purl stitches. Insert the needle under the first loop and over the second loop of each purl stitch along the entire row. Pull the working yarn to unravel all the stitches.

ADDING LIFELINES

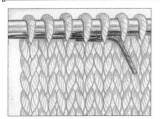

Pull a strand of contrasting yarn through each stitch on the needle. If an error is found, drop down to the lifeline to avoid ripping out the whole piece.

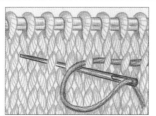

1 If a mistake is discovered and you did not add a lifeline, thread a yarn needle with a contrasting yarn and pull it through a completed row a few rows below the error you want to fix.

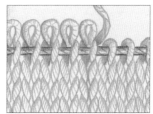

2 Once the lifeline has been threaded through the knitting, rip out the rows to the lifeline.

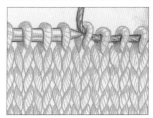

3 Slide the knitting needle from left to right through the stitches, while carefully removing the lifeline.

CORRECTING A BASIC CABLE

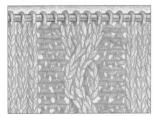

The 2nd cross of this cable goes the wrong way.

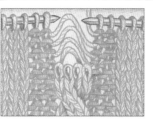

1 Work in pattern to the cable panel. When you come to the stitches above the ones with the error, slide the left-hand needle out of the stitches and let them unravel to the row below the row that needs to be fixed.

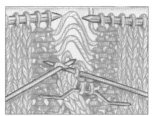

2 Place first two cable sts on cable needle, hold to front. Place 3rd and 4th cable sts on a thin dpn. With 2nd thin dpn, knit 3rd and 4th cable sts with float from first row of dropped sts. Knit first two sts from cable needle with the same float.

3 After knitting the stitches from the cable needle, use thin dpn to knit rest of cable panel, using the floats created by the dropped stitches in each row. Use the float in the same row as the stitches on either side of the cable panel.

CORRECTING A CABLE BY CUTTING

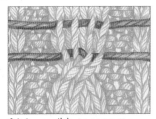

1 It is possible to correct a cable without ripping out any stitches. Thread a contrast yarn in the row below the cable row and another one in the row above the cable cross, as shown.

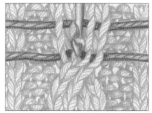

Use a crochet hook to pick out the running thread between the two center stitches of the cable panel.

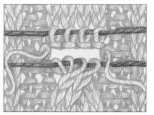

Snip the yarn and unravel the stitches between the two rows of stitches on contrast threads. Rearrange the stitches forming the cable to fix the mistake. Graft the stitches together.

The cable after it has been corrected and grafted. The graft is shown in a contrast color for clarity.

CORRECTING A RUNNING (OR DROPPED) STITCH IN GARTER STITCH

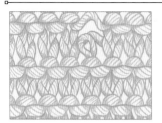

Determine if the stitch to be picked up is a knit or purl.

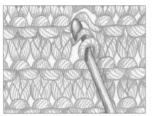

If the first dropped stitch is a knit stitch, insert the crochet hook from front to back into the dropped stitch. Catch the first horizontal strand and pull it through.

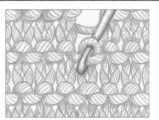

If the stitch to be picked up is a purl, insert the crochet hook from back to front and pull up the stitch.

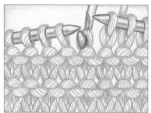

Alternate knits and purls until the last stitch is worked up. Use the crochet hook to place it on the left-hand needle, ready to be knit.

MENDING A HOLE

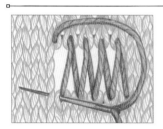

To mend a hole in knitted fabric, use a yarn as close as possible to the yarn used in the item. A contrast color is used here for clarity. Thread the yarn through the bottom and top stitches of the hole, making the stitch length equal to the number of rows to be worked into the hole.

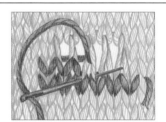

Weave stitches as for duplicate stitch around the long strands.

DARNING

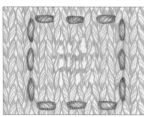

1 To darn a worn spot in a knitted fabric, use a yarn as close as possible to the yarn used in the project. A contrast color is used here for clarity. Stabilize the area around the worn stitches with a running stitch.

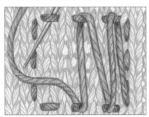

2 Thread the yarn vertically through the top and bottom running stitches.

3 Weave the yarn in and out of the vertical strands.

4 A woven patch covers and strengthens the worn fabric.

Finishing

Introduction to Blocking

Blocking is the process of wetting, pressing, or steaming finished knit pieces to give them their permanent **size and shape**. You should give this process as much care and attention as you do to knitting the pieces.

Water or steam is an essential element in the blocking process. You can wet block by submerging the pieces in water or by spraying them, or you can steam press them with an iron or hand-held steamer.

Most pieces of knitting should be blocked **before seaming**. As you knit, the edges of the pieces may roll and become uneven, especially in stitch patterns such as stockinette. Blocking the pieces will flatten and smooth out the edges. Blocking also evens out the stitches.

In addition, you can lightly steam seams from the wrong side once they are sewn.

The only times you would block a completed sweater is when making a circular garment or when washing a sweater after wearing it.

Your decisions about how to block your pieces will depend on the **content of the yarn** and the type of **stitch pattern**. Understanding the properties of the yarns you used will help you decide how to block. Always read the ball band carefully before you proceed. It will often give you important information about the care of the yarn.

5 FINISHING

PREPARARTION

Before you begin to block your pieces, you should have all your equipment as well as a **schematic** drawing or the written finished measurements on hand. It is especially important to know half the finished bust/chest and length measurements as well as the sleeve width at the upper arm. If these measurements are not given, you can easily calculate them by dividing the number of stitches or rows by the stitch or row gauge for 1 inch (2.5 cm). For example, if your bust/chest is 100 stitches and the stitch gauge for 1 inch is 5 stitches, the piece should measures 20 inches (50 cm) at the bust/chest.

TECHNIQUE

WEAVING IN ENDS

The first step in finishing a project is hiding the ends and tails left when beginning and ending a new ball of yarn. When a piece is finished, weave the ends in and out of the stitches on the wrong side of the work. Thread a **yarn needle** or use a **crochet hook**, and work the ends into the stitches, taking care not to distort the stitches and checking to make sure that the yarn cannot be seen from the right side of the work. Try to hide them in a place that will be discreet, such as into a seam or close to an edge. Weave approximately three inches, working in 2 different directions. If you are working with a bulky yarn, split the plies and work them in separately. After the piece has been blocked and is dry, **trim** the excess close to the surface of the fabric.

SUPPLIES

TOOLS FOR BLOCKING

- Large, flat, padded surface
- Rustproof pins
- Tape measure
- Spray bottle with cool water
- Steam iron or hand-held steamer
- Pressing cloth
- Towels
- Blocking wires (optional)

Pin the piece evenly as shown.

Blocking

It's a good idea to block pieces **right side up** so that you can see the results as you work.

To **pin**, begin at key areas such as the shoulders, the bust/chest just below the armhole, and at the lower-edge points. Keep all the pieces straight and even as you pin them, smoothing them from the center out. You may want to mark the center of each piece at its widest point. Measure from this center point, placing the first crucial pins. Make sure the width and length measurements are accurate before you place pins at closer intervals. Insert the pins at a **slight angle**, approximately 1 inch (2.5 cm) apart. The pins should be close enough together so that you don't leave marks or create scalloped edges when the pieces are dry. Do not pin ribbed areas that are intended to pull in (see photo on page 102).

If you have two matching pieces such as cardigan fronts or sleeves, you block them side by side to ensure that the measurements of both pieces are accurate. Block one piece first and then use a large piece of brown paper or non-woven interfacing to trace around it. Block the matching piece on the tracing. Or you can block the pieces one on top of the other. When the pieces are partially dry, remove the top one to allow for faster drying. To block a piece that has blouson areas above a tighter rib, pin it to a curved cushion, because it is impossible to lay the piece completely flat.

WET BLOCKING

Wet blocking is done without steaming or pressing. You can either completely **submerge** the pieces in cool water before laying them on your blocking surface, or you can first pin the pieces down and then use a **spray bottle** to wet them thoroughly. You may find that it is slightly easier to work with dry pieces and dampen them once the pinning is complete. This method works especially well to shorten the drying time for heavy garments. No single method is correct; it really depends on your personal preference. Always allow the pieces to **dry completely** before beginning to seam them.

STEAM PRESSING

You can steam press with an iron or a hand-held steamer. The important elements in blocking are heat and moisture, not the pressure of the iron, so take care when pressing. If you use an iron, **never place it directly onto your knitted piece.** Hold it above the piece and slowly work over the entire area. Let the steam dampen each piece completely.

It is a good idea to use a **pressing cloth** between the iron and the knitted piece to protect the surface from intense heat and to keep it clean. You can steam press either by using a dry pressing cloth with a steam iron or a wet pressing cloth with a dry iron.

Set the temperature of your iron carefully. Cottons can stand warmer temperatures than wools. Synthetics may need a very cool iron setting. Be especially careful with synthetic blends, as the wrong type of blocking or steaming could permanently damage the fibers.

PRESSING GUIDE

Because fibers react differently to heat, it is best to know what to expect before you press or steam them. Just remember that there are many combinations of fibers, and you should choose a process that is compatible with all the fibers in your yarn. If you are unsure about the fiber content of your yarn, test your gauge swatch before you block your sweater pieces.

- **Angora:** Wet block by spraying.
- **Cotton:** Wet block or warm/hot steam press.
- **Linen:** Wet block or warm/hot steam press.
- **Metallics:** Do not block.
- **Mohair:** Wet block by spraying.
- **Novelties (highly textured):** Do not block.
- **Synthetics:** Carefully follow instructions on ball band—usually wet block by spraying, do not press.
- **Wool and all animal fibers (alpaca, camel hair, cashmere):** Wet block or warm steam press.
- **Wool blends:** Wet block by spraying, do not press unless tested.

Seaming

You can choose from many types of seaming techniques, depending on your personal preference. Each method has its own characteristics and may require different tools.

Use your **knitting yarn** to sew the pieces together, unless it is a novelty or untwisted roving yarn. In that case, sew the seams with a smooth, firm yarn in a compatible color. Be sure that it has the same washability as your knitting yarn.

Block your pieces before you sew them together to make the edges smoother and easier to seam. **Pin or baste the seams** before final seaming. Try the garment on and make sure that it fits properly.

Attach any small items, such as pockets or embroidery, before seaming, as it is easier to work with one piece than the entire garment.

Most knitters follow this sequence when seaming a garment: Sew one or both **shoulder seams**, depending on the type of garment and the method you'll use to add any neckband. Sew the sleeves to the body, and then sew the **side and sleeve seams**.

As you seam, try to keep an even tension. Pull the yarn firmly as you go but not so tightly that the edges will pucker.

Do not use too long a piece of yarn when seaming—no more than 18 inches (46 cm). The constant friction of the yarn through the knitting can cause the yarn to weaken.

Be sure to keep the seam in a neat, straight line. Always insert your needle or hook in the same place along the edges. If necessary, run a contrasting thread through the stitches or rows to help you see the line more clearly.

If the two pieces you are seaming are slightly different lengths, you can compensate by picking up two rows or stitches on the longer side every few inches. This can only work if the difference is ½ inch (1.5 cm) or less. If it is any more than that, you must rework one of the pieces.

Any edges that will be turned back, such as cuffs or a turtleneck, should be seamed from the **wrong side** so that the seam will not show when the edge is turned.

HOW TO BEGIN SEAMING

If you have left a long tail from your cast-on row, you can use this strand to begin sewing. To make a neat join at the lower edge with no gap, use the technique shown here. Thread the strand into a yarn needle. With the right sides of both pieces facing you, insert the yarn needle from back to front into the corner stitch of the piece without the tail. Making a figure eight with the yarn, insert the needle from back to front into the stitch with the cast-on tail. Tighten to close the gap.

MATTRESS STITCH ON STOCKINETTE STITCH

This invisible vertical seam is worked from the **right side** and is used to join two edges row by row. It hides the uneven selvage stitches at the edge of a row and creates an invisible seam, making it appear that the knitting is continuous.

The finished vertical seam on stockinette stitch.

Insert the yarn needle under the horizontal bar between the first and second stitches. Insert the needle into the corresponding bar on the other piece. Continue alternating from side to side.

MATTRESS STITCH ON REVERSE STOCKINETTE STITCH

As with stockinette stitch, this invisible seam is worked from the **right side, row by row,** but instead of working into the horizontal strand between stitches, you work **into the stitch** itself. Alternate working into the top loop on one side with the bottom loop on the other side.

The finished vertical seam on reverse stockinette stitch.

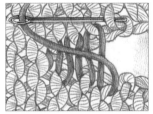

Working into the stitches inside the edge, insert the yarn needle into the top loop on one side, then in the bottom loop of the corresponding stitch on the other side. Continue to alternate in this way.

MATTRESS STITCH ON GARTER STITCH

This invisible seam is worked on garter stitch. It is similar to the seam worked on reverse stockinette stitch in that you **alternate** working into the top and bottom loops of the stitches.

The finished vertical seam on garter stitch.

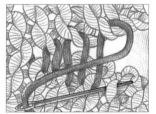

Insert the yarn needle into the top loop on one side, then in the bottom loop of the corresponding stitch on the other side. Continue to alternate in this way.

INVISIBLE HORIZONTAL SEAM

This seam is used to join two **bound-off edges,** such as shoulder seams, and is worked stitch by stitch. You must have the same number of stitches on each piece. Pull the yarn tightly enough to hide the bound-off edges. The finished seam resembles a row of knit stitches.

The finished horizontal seam on stockinette stitch.

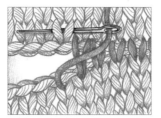

With the bound-off edges together, lined up stitch for stitch, insert the yarn needle under a stitch inside the bound-off edge of one side and then under the corresponding stitch on the other side.

INVISIBLE VERTICAL TO HORIZONTAL SEAM

This seam is used to join **bound-off stitches to rows,** as in sewing the top of a sleeve to an armhole edge. Because there are usually more rows per inch (2.5 cm) than stitches, occasionally pick up two horizontal bars on the piece with rows for every stitch on the bound-off piece.

The finished vertical to horizontal seam on stockinette stitch.

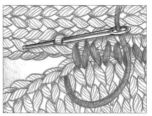

Insert the yarn needle under a stitch inside the bound-off edge of the vertical piece. Insert the needle under one or two horizontal bars between the first and second stitches of the horizontal piece.

TECHNIQUE

BASTING

Some knitters use basting as a seaming technique. However, it is unattractive and is not recommended for finished seams. Basting is best used as a **preliminary step** to seaming. Baste the pieces together with a contrasting yarn, try on the garment, then remove the basting yarn and seam the pieces together. Baste close to the edge, so the basted seam allowance is as similar as possible to that of the finished garment. Use a yarn needle and yarn that is heavy enough to hold the pieces together. Do not use sewing thread, as it can easily break when you try on the sweater.

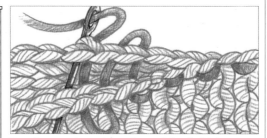

Run the yarn in and out through both thicknesses.

BACKSTITCH

This is a strong seam that is worked from the **wrong side** and creates a **seam allowance.** Because it is not worked at the edge of the fabric, it can be used to take in fullness. The seam allowance should not exceed ³⁄₈ inch (1 cm).

The finished backstitch on stockinette stitch.

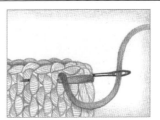

1 With the right sides of the pieces facing each other, secure the seam by taking the needle twice around the edges from back to front. Bring the needle up about ¼ inch (.5 cm) from the point where the yarn last emerged, as shown.

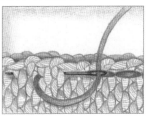

2 In one motion, insert the needle into the point where the yarn emerged from the previous stitch and back up approximately ¼ inch (.5 cm) ahead of the emerging yarn. Pull the yarn through. Repeat this step, keeping the stitches straight and even.

OVERCASTING

This seam is usually worked from the wrong side, but it can also be worked from the right side with a thick yarn in a contrasting color to create an **exposed decorative, cordlike seam.**

The finished overcast seam on stockinette stitch.

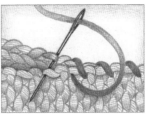

With the right sides of the pieces facing each other and the bumps lined up, insert the needle from back to front through the strands at the edges of the pieces between the knots. Repeat this step.

EDGE-TO-EDGE SEAM

The edge-to-edge seam, being flat, is perfect for **reversible garments.** It is worked at the very edge of the piece. Because it is not a strong seam, it is best used with lightweight yarns.

The finished edge-to-edge seam on stockinette stitch.

The finished edge-to-edge seam on reverse stockinette stitch.

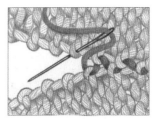

With the purl sides facing you and the edges of the pieces together, insert the yarn needle into the bump on one side, then into the corresponding bump on the other side.

Grafting or Kitchener Stitch

Grafting, also called **Kitchener stitch**, joins two **open edges** stitch by stitch using a yarn needle. The grafted edges resemble a row of stitches and leave no seam. This makes grafting a useful technique when a seam is undesirable, such as on mittens, hoods that may fold over, and the toes of socks.

You must follow the **path** of the stitches with the yarn needle. Therefore, grafting is most easily worked on simple stitch patterns such as stockinette, reverse stockinette, or garter stitch, which have been worked in flat, smooth yarns, making the stitches clearly visible.

You should graft stitches together while they are still on the knitting needle, slipping a few stitches off at a time as you work, or slipping each stitch singly. The needles should point in the same direction when the wrong sides of your work are placed together. To do this, you will need to work one row less on one needle or reverse one of the needles.

When grafting garter stitch, make sure the purl stitches of the front piece face the knit stitches of the back piece.

GRAFTING ON STOCKINETTE STITCH

A grafted seam on stockinette stitch.

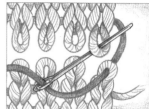

1 Insert the yarn needle purlwise into the first stitch on the front piece, then knitwise into the first stitch on the back piece. Draw the yarn through.

GRAFTING ON GARTER STITCH

A grafted seam on garter stitch.

1 Insert the yarn needle purlwise into the first stitch on the front piece, then purlwise into the first stitch on the back piece. Draw the yarn through.

GRAFTING ON KNIT ONE, PURL ONE RIBBING

A grafted seam on knit 1, purl 1 ribbing. You will need four double-pointed needles or a circular needle for this technique.

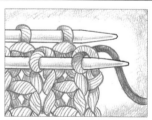

1 Separate the knit stitches from the purl stitches on each ribbed piece by slipping the knit stitches onto one needle and the purl stitches onto a second needle.

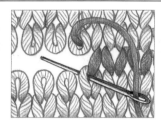

2 Insert the yarn needle knitwise into the first stitch on the front piece again. Draw the yarn through.

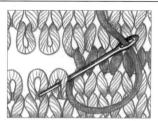

3 Insert the yarn needle purlwise into the next stitch on the front piece. Draw the yarn through.

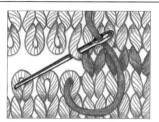

4 Insert the yarn needle purlwise into the first stitch on the back piece again. Draw the yarn through.

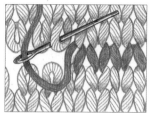

5 Insert the yarn needle knitwise into the next stitch on the back piece. Draw the yarn through. Repeat steps 2 through 5.

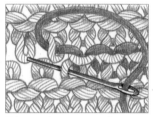

2 Insert the yarn needle knitwise into the first stitch on the front piece again. Draw the yarn through.

3 Insert the yarn needle purlwise into the next stitch on the front piece. Draw the yarn through.

4 Insert the yarn needle knitwise into the first stitch on the back piece again. Draw the yarn through.

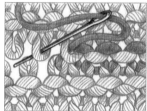

5 Insert the yarn needle purlwise into the next stitch on the back piece. Draw the yarn through. Repeat steps 2 through 5.

2 Graft all the knit stitches on one side of the piece as shown.

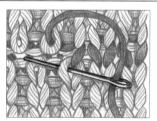

3 Turn the work. Graft all the knit stitches on the other side.

OPEN STITCHES TO EDGE

A finished seam showing open stitches grafted to rows on stockinette stitch.

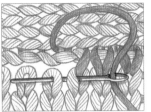

When grafting open stitches to rows, you must compensate for the difference in stitch and row gauge by occasionally picking up two horizontal bars for every stitch.

A finished seam showing open stitches grafted to rows on reverse stockinette stitch.

When grafting open stitches to rows in reverse stockinette stitch, pick up the loop of the purl stitch inside the edge, as shown.

OPEN STITCHES TO BOUND-OFF STITCHES

A finished seam showing open stitches grafted to bound-off stitches on stockinette stitch.

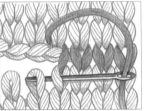

When grafting open stitches to bound-off stitches, insert the yarn needle under the stitch inside the bound-off edge and then into the corresponding stitch on the open edge.

A finished seam showing open stitches grafted to bound-off stitches on reverse stockinette stitch.

When grafting open stitches to bound-off stitches on reverse stockinette stitch, pick up two vertical strands just inside the bound-off edge, as shown.

TECHNIQUE

JOINING KNIT ONE, PURL ONE RIBBING

When joining ribbing with a purl stitch at each edge, insert the yarn needle under the horizontal bar in the center of a knit stitch on each side.

When joining ribbing with a knit stitch at each edge, use the bottom loop of the purl stitch on one side and the top loop of the corresponding purl stitch on the other side.

When joining purl and knit stitch edges, skip the knit stitch and join two purl stitches as above.

SLIP-STITCH CROCHET

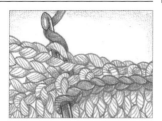

This seam can be worked any distance from the edge.

With RS tog, insert crochet hook through both thicknesses. Catch yarn and draw a loop through. *Insert hook again. Draw loop through both thicknesses and loop on hook. Repeat from *, keeping sts straight and even.

SINGLE CROCHET

The single crochet seam is worked on the right side of the work, forming a decorative, raised seam.

Insert hook into inside loop of a bound-off stitch from each piece. Catch yarn and pull a loop through. *Pull up a loop through next two bound-off sts, then catch yarn and pull it through both loops on hook. Repeat from the *.

TWO-NEEDLE CROCHET

This seam is worked by using a **crochet hook** to join two pieces that are still on the knitting needles.

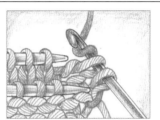

1 With the right sides of the pieces facing each other, insert the hook knitwise into the first stitch on both needles and slip them from the needles. Wrap the yarn around the hook as shown.

2 Pull the yarn through both loops on the hook. *With the hook, slip the next stitch from both needles. You now have three loops on the hook. Wrap the yarn around the hook as shown.

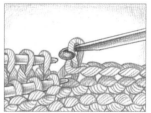

3 Pull the yarn through all three loops. You now have one loop on the hook. Repeat from the *.

BIND-OFF SEAM

This is a finished bind-off seam on stockinette stitch. The seam is worked from the wrong side with the stitches still on the knitting needles. This creates a very **firm, inelastic** seam.

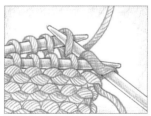

1 *Insert a third needle knitwise into the first stitch on the front needle, then purlwise into the first stitch on the back needle and slip them off. Pull the first stitch over the 2nd stitch. Repeat from the * to the end of the row.

2 Turn the work. Slip the first two stitches purlwise. *Pull the first stitch over the second. Slip the next stitch purlwise. Repeat from the * until all the stitches have been worked. Fasten off the last stitch.

Picking Up Stitches

When you add any type of border, such as a neckband, to finished pieces, you generally pick up stitches along the edge. It is important that you do so **evenly** to make a smooth join between the edge and the border.

The neatest way to pick up stitches is to do it from the **right side** of the work. It is also important to actually **make knit stitches** on a knitting needle with a separate strand of yarn rather than picking up a strand from the edge of the piece itself, which will stretch and distort the edge.

Begin picking up by attaching the yarn to the edge of the piece, or simply start picking up, holding the end to make sure that the stitches do not unravel.

You can use a straight or circular knitting needle or a crochet hook to pick up stitches. Be sure that it is **one or two sizes smaller** than the needles used for the main body. The smaller size is easier to insert into the fabric and will not stretch the work. After picking up, change to the needle size used for the edging.

If the instructions do not tell you how many stitches to pick up, measure the total edge and multiply that figure by the stitch gauge of the edging to be added. To determine the gauge of the edging, pick up and add the edging to your gauge swatch or make a separate piece using the pattern stitch for the edging. If you have already used the edging in the main body of the sweater, measure your gauge from that.

Along **a shaped edge**, such as a neck, make sure you pick up inside the edge so as not to create any holes.

If you are making **a band** in a different color from the main piece, pick up stitches with the main color, then change the color on the first row.

If you change the size of the sweater from the instructions, make sure you **adjust** the number of stitches picked up accordingly.

When you pick up stitches on a long piece, such as the entire outside edge of a cardigan, there may be too many stitches to fit on a straight, single-pointed needle. Divide the edge in half, working first along the right front to the center back neck and then from the center back neck along the left front. Then seam your edging at the **back neck**. Alternatively, all of your stitches may fit on a long circular needle.

When picking up for a neckband on a pullover with a single-pointed needle, **sew one shoulder seam**. Pick up the stitches required, work the edging, then sew the second shoulder seam and the side of the neckband. If using circular or double-pointed needles, sew both shoulder seams, pick up the required stitches, join, and work the edging in rounds.

TIP

MARKING AN EDGE FOR PICKING UP STITCHES

Stitches must be picked up evenly so that the band will not flare or pull in. Place pins, markers, or yarn, as shown, every 2 inches (5 cm) and pick up the same number of stitches between each pair of markers.

If you know the number of stitches to be picked up, divide this by the number of sections to determine how many stitches to pick up in each one.

HORIZONTAL EDGE WITH KNITTING NEEDLE

Stitches picked up along a bound-off edge.

1 Insert the knitting needle into the center of the first stitch in the row below the bound-off edge. Wrap the yarn knitwise around the needle.

2 Draw the yarn through. You have picked up one stitch. Continue to pick up one stitch in each stitch along the bound-off edge.

VERTICAL EDGE WITH KNITTING NEEDLE

Stitches picked up along a side edge.

1 Insert the knitting needle into the corner stitch of the first row, one stitch in from the side edge. Wrap the yarn around the needle knitwise.

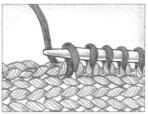

2 Draw the yarn through. You have picked up 1 stitch. Continue to pick up stitches along the edge. Occasionally skip one row to keep the edge from flaring.

SHAPED EDGE WITH KNITTING NEEDLE

Stitches picked up along a curved edge.

Pick up stitches neatly just inside the shaped edge, following the curve and hiding the jagged selvage.

Stitches picked up along a diagonal edge.

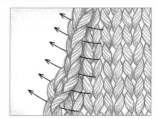

Pick up stitches one stitch in from the shaped edge, keeping them in a straight line.

PICKING UP ALONG A V-NECKLINE

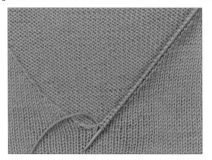

The stitches for this neckband are picked up around the V-neck using straight needles. Leave the right shoulder seam unsewn and begin picking up stitches at the right back neck. Work the neckband back and forth.

The stitches for this neckband are picked up around the V-neck using a circular needle. Sew both shoulders and begin picking up stitches at the right back neck. Place a marker and join the piece.

The stitches for this neckband are picked up around the V-neck using double-pointed needles. Sew both shoulders and begin picking up stitches at the right back neck. Use one needle for the back and one needle for each front. Place a marker and join the piece.

PICKING UP STITCHES WITH A CROCHET HOOK

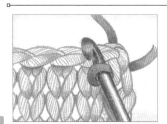

1 Insert the crochet hook from front to back into the center of the first stitch one row below the bound-off edge. Catch the yarn and pull a loop through.

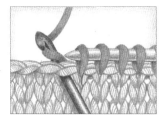

2 Slip the loop onto the knitting needle, being sure it is not twisted. Continue to pick up one stitch in each stitch along the bound-off edge.

TECHNIQUE

THE NUMBER OF STITCHES TO PICK UP

If **the correct** number of stitches are picked up, the finished edge will be straight and even.

If **too few stitches** are picked up, the finished edge will pull in.

If **too many stitches** are picked up, the finished edge will flare out.

Attaching Separate Pieces and Hemming

ATTACHING

You can make separate pieces, such as collars or elaborate edgings, and attach them later. Because these seams often follow a curve, it is important to keep the stitches even.

When you sew the open stitches of a border to the finished edge of a garment, place the open stitches on a **contrasting yarn** or circular needle to keep them from unraveling. Remove the contrasting yarn or needle a few stitches at a time while seaming.

HEMMING

When securing a knitted-in hem, your stitching should leave no visible line on the right side of your garment.

Fold the hem to the wrong side (along the turning ridge, if applicable), and carefully pin it in a straight line. Do not pull the yarn tightly or the work will pucker.

You can hem with various types of stitches. The **whip stitch** is best used on medium or lightweight yarns. It creates a neat and firm seam. The **stitch-by-stitch** method is good for bulky yarns, as you eliminate a bulky cast-on edge by grafting open stitches to the back of the work.

SLIP STITCH A POCKET

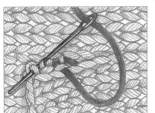

When attaching a separate piece, such as a patch pocket, to the knitted fabric, pick up the horizontal bar in the center of a stitch from the fabric, then the horizontal bar one stitch in from the pocket edge. Draw the yarn through.

WHIP STITCH ON A HEM

Fold the hem to the wrong side, being sure that the stitches are straight. Insert the needle into a stitch on the wrong side of the fabric and then into the cast-on edge of the hem. Draw the yarn through.

HERRINGBONE STITCH ON A HEM

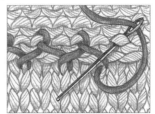

Working from left to right, attach the yarn to the upper left corner of the hem. Tack the cast-on edge of the hem to the fabric using the herringbone stitch as shown.

SLIP STITCHING LIVE STITCHES FOR A DOUBLED NECKBAND

You can join the live stitches of a neckband by slip stitching them to the neck edge from the wrong side.

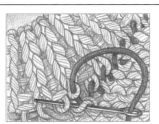

Slip stitch If working a doubled neckband, pick up the stitches along the neck edge, then work the neckband to twice the desired depth. Do not bind off the stitches, but fold the band to the wrong side and slip stitch the open stitches to the fabric.

FINISHING A HEM STITCH BY STITCH

A finished stockinette stitch hem worked stitch by stitch, shown on the right side.

A finished stockinette stitch hem worked stitch by stitch, shown on the wrong side. Use a provisional cast on for the hem.

1 Graft the open cast-on stitches of the hem to the reverse stockinette side of the fabric, matching stitch for stitch.

2 On the fabric, follow the line of the purl stitches.

KNITTED-IN BAND ON THE RIGHT-HAND SIDE

A knit 1, purl 1 ribbed band worked along the slip-stitch selvage of a stockinette stitch piece.

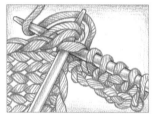

1 Cast on and *rib one row of the band to the last stitch (a knit stitch) leaving it on the left needle. Insert the left needle under the first selvage stitch on the main piece and knit it together with the stitch on the left needle.

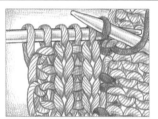

2 Turn the work and slip the first stitch purlwise with the yarn in the front, rib to the end. Repeat from the *.

KNITTED-IN BAND ON THE LEFT-HAND SIDE

A knit 1, purl 1 ribbed band worked along the slip-stitch selvage of a stockinette stitch piece.

1 *Work to the last stitch of the band (a purl stitch). With the yarn in front, slip the last stitch purlwise. Turn the band. With the yarn in back, insert the left needle into the first selvage stitch on the main piece and knit it together with the slipped stitch.

2 Leave the stitch on the right needle and rib to the end of the row. Repeat from the *.

Cleaning

CLEANING AND STORING KNITS

Proper care is just as important to the life of your knit garments as the way you knit them in the first place. Take time to do it carefully. Because different fibers need different types of care, it is helpful to save information from the yarn's ball band or to sew a care label into your knit garments.

PREPARING TO CLEAN

Prepare your garment for cleaning by removing any non-washable trims and making necessary repairs. To help cardigans keep their shape, baste the pockets and buttonholes closed. Check the garment for stains. You can highlight them by circling the stain with a contrasting yarn or thread.

To make sure that your sweater will have the same measurements once it is cleaned, draw a rough schematic with key measurements such as the body length and width, shoulder width, and sleeve length and width.

HAND WASHING

You can hand wash many fibers if you do so properly, avoiding felting or shrinkage. The water temperature should be cool or lukewarm and be the same temperature both in the washing and rinsing stages. Wash one garment at a time in a large sink or tub and change the water after each piece.

Dissolve soap flakes, a mild detergent, a specialty woolwash in the water before adding the knits. Use hot water if the soap doesn't easily dissolve, but let the water cool down before washing. Lay the knits flat and work the soap into the fabric by gently pressing it up and down. Do not twist, swirl, or rub the knit. Let the garment soak a short time.

MACHINE WASHING

Take care before machine washing a knit. Begin by reading the yarn label. Yarns labeled superwash can be machine washed. Use a delicate synthetic or gentle wash cycle with cold water. Just as for hand washing, you can use warm water to dissolve the soap, allowing the water to cool before you add the garments.

RINSING

You may need to rinse your garment several times to remove the soap residue, if you did not use a no-rinse woolwash. The water should be clear on the last rinse.

Squeeze out any excess water without wringing the garment. Press it against the tub or sink to remove water. Avoid stretching the garment as you lift it out by supporting it with both hands.

DRYING AND BLOCKING

Dry your knits as quickly as possible. If left damp, they may mildew. This is true with cotton fibers, especially heavy ones.

To further remove water, neatly roll the garment in a terry-cloth towel. You may want to repeat this process several times. You can also wrap the garment carefully in a towel and place it inside a washing machine. Use the spinning cycle to remove excess water.

All knits should be **dried flat** on an absorbent towel. As the garment dries, turn it over. Avoid drying pieces in direct sunlight or heat.

Using the measurements from your schematic drawing, reshape your garment, pinning if necessary. Smooth the pieces out to prevent wrinkles.

Machine dry your garment only at a low or delicate setting and remove it immediately from the machine. Check the progress of your garment as it dries. It's a good idea to test a knit swatch before you dry the whole garment. You can remove it before it is completely dry and lay it flat to air dry.

LONG-LASTING SWEATERS

Experiment with the **gauge swatch** if you're in doubt about how to wash and care for a sweater. A ruined swatch can be reknit for further experimenting, but a ruined sweater will be gone forever.

• Wool sweaters do not show soil readily. **Spot clean** with a mild solution of soap and water rather than washing the sweater frequently. This treatment also prevents wool sweaters from becoming deeply soiled, which is when they are most difficult to clean.

• Make your own **care labels** with the fiber content and a code, such as MW for machine washable. Use labeling tape and an indelible pen to make the labels, then sew labels into finished sweaters.

• Prepare for **repairs**. Make a reeling from your sweater's yarn. Attach it to a seam or tack it on when washing your sweater to ensure that the color quality of the extra yarn is the same as your sweater.

• Keep a **notebook** for finished knitting projects. File each project's yarn label and gauge swatch, and make notes for accurate care instructions. This becomes a reference when it's time to clean your sweaters.

Folding and Storing

Check for stains and needed repairs before you put your knits away. They should be stored folded and clean. In addition, you should always store knits **flat** and as loosely as possible.

If you are storing sweaters for the season, pack them loosely in tissue paper to allow the air to circulate. You may want to add tissue at the necks to keep them in shape. Divide your sweaters into two groups when storing—those that need moth prevention and those that don't. Moths are attracted to dirt, oils, and animal proteins. Yarns such as cotton and synthetics will not be damaged by moths. Take special care of sweaters with lanolin and natural oils, because they are especially attractive to moths.

After dry cleaning a sweater, remove if from the plastic bag. Air it out before storage so the sweater harbors no chemical fumes.

STANDARD SWEATER

1 With the sweater face down, fold the front toward the back.

2 Fold the sleeve down, then fold the other side in the same way.

3 Fold the sweater in half.

BULKY SWEATER

1 With the sweater face down, fold back one sleeve, then the other.

2 Fold the turtleneck down.

3 Fold the sweater in half.

Designing

Taking Body Measurements

When designing your very own garments, you must begin with an accurate set of body measurements. Below are the most important measurements and the location of the body where they are taken. You may find it easier and more accurate to have someone measure you.

1 BUST/CHEST

Measure around the **fullest part of the bust**. Don't let the tape measure slip down on the back. The bust measurement is the beginning point in determining how much **ease** to add or subtract. The ease determines the fit of a garment, from very close fitting to oversized.

2 WAIST AND HIPS

To help you find your **natural waistline**, tie a piece of string around your waist and let it fall naturally. The waist should be measured **loosely** for a better fit. Wrap the tape measure around your waist over the string and move it from side to side, allowing it to settle. Measure the hip at the **widest point** below the waist.

3 CROSSBACK

The crossback includes **the two shoulders and the neck width**. It should be measured across the back from the tip of one shoulder bone to the other. This measurement is important when you create garments that should fit well at the shoulders, such as those with set-in sleeves.

4 WIDTH AT UPPER ARM

The upper arm is measured around the arm at its **widest** point.

5 WRIST

The wrist is measured just **above the hand**. Some sweaters have a generous amount of ease above the cuff; other, more fitted sweaters may have a tight measurement above the cuff. The width of the sleeve at the lowest edge should be wide enough to go over the hand with a closed fist.

6 BACK NECK TO WAIST

This is determined by measuring from the **bone at the base of the back of your neck to the waist**. If you want the lower edge of the sweater to fall below the hips, measure from waist to the lower edge and add this amount to the measurement.

7 ONE SHOULDER

This should be measured from the **center back neck to the point where the arm joins the body**. This measurement is used most often in conjunction with the crossback measurement.

8 CENTER BACK NECK TO WRIST

Take this measurement from the **bone in the center of the back of your neck to the wrist bone** with your arm extended, or to the point you want your sleeve cuff to end. This determines the finished sleeve length.

9 FRONT NECK TO WAIST

Measure from the **shoulder over the fullest part of the bust to the waist**. This measurement is particularly helpful if the bustline is full, otherwise the back neck to waist measurement, which is slightly easier to take, is adequate.

10 WAIST TO UNDERARM

This is measured **from the waistline** to approximately 1 inch (2.5 cm) before the actual underarm. This measurement will help you decide where to begin the armhole shaping of your sweater.

11 NECK WIDTH

Measure **around the neck** at its fullest point. The neck width of the finished garment is larger than this measurement to accommodate the size of your head.

12 WRIST TO UNDERARM

Measure from the wrist bone **along the underside of your arm**, with your elbow slightly bent, to approximately 1 inch (2.5 cm) before your underarm. This measurement is used to determine the sleeve length for a set-in sleeve.

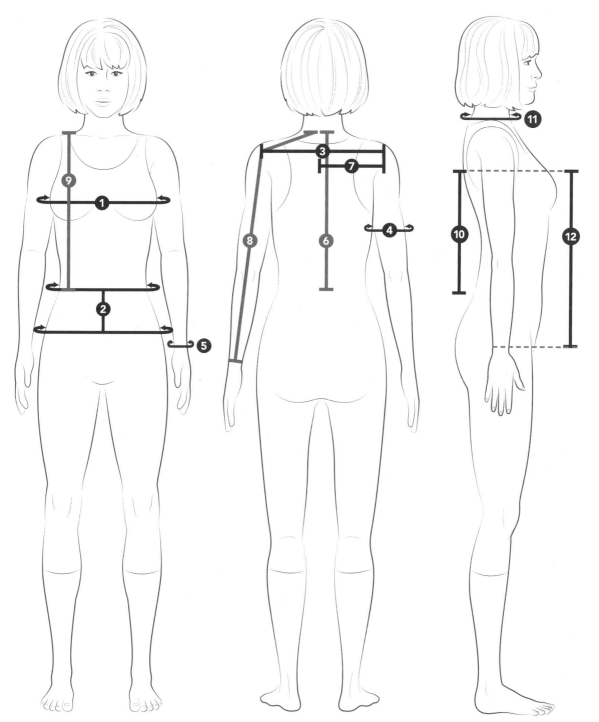

Standard Body Measurements

When designing a garment for yourself or a specific person, it is best to use actual body measurements. When you do not have access to the measurements of the intended recipient or are designing for a general audience, use the standard body measurements found in the following charts.

When using these charts, remember that these reflect actual body measurements, not the knitted measurements of the garment. Adjust the knitted measurements of the garment for the desired fit and ease (see page 124).

MEN

SIZES	SMALL	MEDIUM	LARGE	X-LARGE	2X
Chest	34–36" 86–91.5 cm	38–40" 196.5–101.5 cm	42–44" 106.5–111.5 cm	46–48" 117–122 cm	50–52" 127–132 cm
Center Back (Neck to Wrist)	32–32½" 81–82.5 cm	33–33½" 83.5–85 cm	34–34½" 86.5–87.5 cm	35–35½" 89–90 cm	36–36½" 91.5–92.5 cm
Back Hip Length	23–24" 58.5–61 cm	25–26" 63.5–66 cm	26–27" 66–68.5 cm	28" 71 cm	29" 73.5 cm
Cross Back (Shoulder to Shoulder)	15½–16" 39.5–40.5 cm	16½–17" 42–43 cm	17½–18" 44.5–45.5 cm	18–18½" 45.5–47cm	19–20" 48–51 cm
Arm Length to Underarm	18" 45.5 cm	18½" 47 cm	19½" 49.5 cm	20" 50.5 cm	20½" 52 cm
Upper Arm	12" 30.5 cm	13" 33 cm	15" 38 cm	15½" 39.5 cm	16½" 42 cm
Armhole Depth	8½–9" 21.5–23 cm	9–9½" 23–24 cm	9½–10" 24–25.5 cm	10–10½" 25.5–26 cm	11" 28 cm
Waist	28–30" 71–76 cm	32–34" 81.5–86.5 cm	36–38" 91.5–96.5 cm	42–44" 106.5–112 cm	46–48" 117–122 cm
Hips	35–37" 89–94 cm	39–41" 99–104 cm	43–45" 109–114 cm	47–49" 119–124.5 cm	51–53" 129–134 cm

WOMEN

SIZES	X-SMALL	SMALL	MEDIUM	LARGE
Bust	28–30" 71–76 cm	32–34" 81–86 cm	36–38" 91.5–96.5 cm	40–42" 101.5–106.5 cm
Center Back (Neck to Wrist)	26–26½" 66–68.5 cm	27–27½" 68.5–70 cm	28–28½" 71–72.5 cm	29–29½" 73.5–75 cm
Back Waist Length	16½" 42 cm	17" 43 cm	17¼" 43.5 cm	17½" 44.5 cm
Cross Back (Shoulder to Shoulder)	14–14½" 35.5–37 cm	14½–15" 37–38 cm	15½–16" 39.5–40.5 cm	16½–17" 42–43 cm
Arm Length to Underarm	16½" 42 cm	17" 43 cm	17" 43 cm	17½" 44.5 cm
Upper Arm	9¾" 25 cm	10¼" 26 cm	11" 28 cm	12" 30.5 cm
Armhole Depth	6–6½" 15.5–16.5 cm	6½–7" 16.5–17.5 cm	7–7½" 17.5–19 cm	7½–8" 19–20.5 cm
Waist	23–24" 58.5–61 cm	25–26½" 63.5–67.5 cm	28–30" 71–76 cm	32–34" 81.5–86.5cm
Hips	33–34" 83.5–86 cm	35–36" 89–91.5 cm	38–40" 96.5–101.5 cm	42–44" 106.5–111.5 cm

WOMEN PLUS

SIZES	1X	2X	3X	4X	5X
Bust	44–46" 111.5–117 cm	48–50" 122–127 cm	52–54" 132–137 cm	56–58" 142–147 cm	60–62" 152–158 cm
Center Back (Neck to Wrist)	29–29½" 73.5–75 cm	30–30½" 76.5–77.5 cm	30½–31" 77.5–79 cm	31½–32" 80–81.5 cm	31½–32" 80–81.5 cm
Back Waist Length	17¾" 45 cm	18" 45.5 cm	18" 45.5 cm	18½" 47 cm	18½" 47 cm
Cross Back (Shoulder to Shoulder)	17½" 44.5 cm	18" 45.5 cm	18" 45.5 cm	18½" 47cm	18½" 47 cm
Arm Length to Underarm	17½" 44.5 cm	18" 45.5 cm	18" 45.5 cm	18½" 47 cm	18½" 47 cm
Upper Arm	13½" 34.5 cm	15½" 39.5 cm	17" 43 cm	18½" 47 cm	19½" 49.5 cm
Armhole Depth	8–8½" 20.5–21.5 cm	8½–9" 21.5–23 cm	9–9½" 23–24 cm	9½–10" 24–25.5 cm	10–10½" 25.5–26.5 cm
Waist	36–38" 91.5–96.5 cm	40–42" 101.5–106.5 cm	44–45" 111.5–114 cm	46–47" 116.5–119 cm	49–50" 124–127 cm
Hips	46–48" 116.5–122 cm	52–53" 132–134.5 cm	54–55" 137–139.5 cm	56–57" 142–144.5 cm	61–62" 155–157 cm

YOUTH

SIZES	12	14	16
Chest	30" 76 cm	31½" 80 cm	32½" 82.5 cm
Center Back (Neck to Wrist)	26" 66 cm	27" 68.5 cm	28" 71 cm
Back Waist Length	15" 38 cm	15½" 39.5 cm	16" 40.5 cm
Cross Back (Shoulder to Shoulder)	12" 30.5 cm	12¼" 31 cm	13" 33 cm
Arm Length to Underarm	15" 38 cm	16" 40.5 cm	16½" 42 cm
Upper Arm	9" 23 cm	9¼" 23.5 cm	9½" 24 cm
Armhole Depth	6½" 16.5 cm	7" 17.5 cm	7½" 19 cm
Waist	25" 63.5 cm	26½" 67.5 cm	27½" 69.5 cm
Hips	31½" 80 cm	33" 83.5 cm	35½" 90 cm

CHILDREN

SIZES	2	4	6	8	10
Chest	21" 53 cm	23" 58.5cm	25" 63.5 cm	26½" 67 cm	28" 71 cm
Center Back (Neck to Wrist)	18" 45.5 cm	19½" 49.5 cm	20½" 52 cm	22" 56 cm	24" 61 cm
Back Waist Length	8½" 21.5 cm	9½" 24 cm	10½" 26.5 cm	12½" 31.5 cm	14" 35.5 cm
Cross Back (Shoulder to Shoulder)	9¼" 23.5 cm	9¾" 25 cm	10¼" 26 cm	10¾" 27 cm	11¼" 28.5 cm
Arm Length to Underarm	8½" 21.5 cm	10½" 26.5 cm	11½" 29 cm	12½" 31.5 cm	13½" 34.5 cm
Upper Arm	7" 18 cm	7½" 19 cm	8" 20.5 cm	8½" 21.5 cm	8¾" 22 cm
Armhole Depth	4¼" 10.5 cm	4¾" 12 cm	5" 12.5 cm	5½" 14 cm	6" 15.5 cm
Waist	21" 53.5 cm	21½" 54.5 cm	22½" 57 cm	23½" 59.5 cm	24½" 62 cm
Hips	22" 56 cm	23½" 59.5 cm	25" 63.5 cm	28" 71 cm	29½" 75 cm

Standard Head Measurements

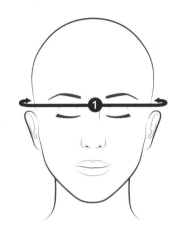

1 HEAD CIRCUMFERENCE
2 HAT HEIGHT

HOW TO MEASURE A HEAD

To measure a head for a hat, use a tape measure placed across the forehead and measure around the **circumference** of the head. The measuring tape should be snug to get an accurate value. To determine the hat height, place the measuring tape at the **top of the crown** and measure to the desired length. Approximate sizes are listed in the table.

STANDARD HEAD MEASUREMENTS

AGE	HEAD CIRCUMFERENCE	HAT HEIGHT
Newborn	13–15" 33–38 cm	5" 13 cm
Baby, 3–6 months	15" 38 cm	6" 16 cm
Baby, 6–12 months	16" 40.5 cm	7" 18 cm
Toddler, 1–3 years	17" 43 cm	8" 20.5 cm
Child, 3–10 years	18" 46 cm	8½" 22 cm
Teen	20" 51 cm	10" 25 cm
Adult Woman	22" 56 cm	11" 28 cm
Adult Man	23" 58.5 cm	11½" 29.5 cm

Standard Hand Measurements

HOW TO MEASURE HAND DIMENSIONS

To determine hand circumference, measure around the fullest part of the knuckle area, keeping the tape level. The hand should be open and fingers slightly spread, as shown.

1 HAND CIRCUMFERENCE

2 LENGTH OF HAND ABOVE CUFF

3 WRIST CIRCUMFERENCE

4 THUMB LENGTH

5 GUSSET LENGTH

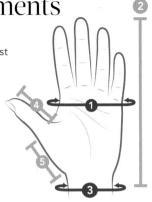

STANDARD HAND MEASUREMENTS

SIZES	Child, 2–4 years	Child, 4–6 years	Child, 6–8 years	Child Large, Woman's Small	Woman's Medium	Woman's Large, Man's Small	Man's Medium	Man's Large
Hand Circumference	5" / 13 cm	6" / 16 cm	6½" / 16.5 cm	7" / 18 cm	7½" / 19 cm	8" / 20.5 cm	8½" / 21.5 cm	9" / 23 cm
Hand Length (Above Cuff)	4" / 10 cm	4¾" / 12 cm	5¼ / 13.5 cm	6" / 16 cm	6½" / 16.5 cm	7½" / 19 cm	7¾" / 20 cm	8½" / 21.5 cm
Thumb Length	¾" / 2 cm	1" / 2.5 cm	1¼" / 3 cm	1¼" / 3 cm	1½" / 4 cm	1¾" / 4.5 cm	2" / 5 cm	2" / 5 cm
Thumb Opening	1¾" / 4.5 cm	2" / 5 cm	2" / 5 cm	2¼" / 6 cm	2½" / 6.5 cm	2¾" / 7 cm	3" / 8 cm	3¼" / 8.5 cm
Mitten Top Length	1" / 2.5 cm	1¼" / 3 cm	1¼" / 3 cm	1½" / 4 cm	1½" / 4 cm	1¾" / 4.5 cm	1¾" / 4.5 cm	2" / 5 cm
Glove Wrist to Little Finger	-----	2¾" / 7 cm	3" / 8 cm	3¼" / 8.5 cm	3½" / 9 cm	3¾" / 9.5 cm	4¼" / 11 cm	4½" / 11.5 cm
Glove Wrist to Glove Ring to Middle Index Finger	-----	3" / 8 cm	3¼" / 8.5 cm	3½" / 9 cm	3¾" / 9.5 cm	4" / 10 cm	4¾" / 12 cm	5" / 13 cm
Little Finger Length	-----	1½" / 4 cm	1½" / 4 cm	1¾" / 4.5 cm	1¾" / 4.5 cm	2" / 5 cm	2¼" / 6 cm	2½" / 6.5 cm
Ring and Index Finger Length	-----	1¾" / 4.5 cm	2" / 5 cm	2¼" / 6 cm	2½" / 6.5 cm	2¾" / 7 cm	3" / 8 cm	3¼" / 8.5 cm
Middle Finger Length	-----	2" / 5 cm	2¼" / 6 cm	2½" / 6.5 cm	2¾" / 7 cm	3" / 8 cm	3¼" / 8.5 cm	3½" / 9 cm

Standard Foot Measurements

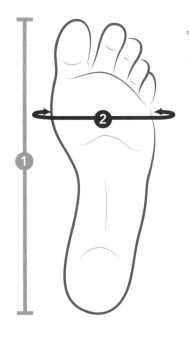

MEASURING THE FOOT

1 FOOT LENGTH

2 FOOT CIRCUMFERENCE

STANDARD FOOT MEASUREMENTS

U.S. Shoe Size	Foot Circumference	Foot Length
Child		
0–4	4½" 11 cm	4" 10 cm
4–8	5½" 14 cm	5" 13 cm
7–11	6" 15.5 cm	6" 15.5 cm
10–2	6½" 16.5 cm	7½" 19 cm
2–6	7" 18 cm	8" 20.5 cm
Women		
3–6	7" 18 cm	9" 23 cm
6–9	8" 20.5 cm	10" 25.5 cm
8–12	9" 23 cm	11" 28 cm
Men		
6–8	7" 18 cm	9½" 24 cm
8½–10	8" 20.5 cm	10½" 26.5 cm
10½–12	9" 23 cm	11" 28 cm
12½–14	10" 25.5 cm	11½" 29 cm

Selvages

The selvage (or selvedge) of knit fabric is an **edge** formed by changing the stitch pattern at the **beginning and end of every row**. This stabilizes the fabric and prepares it for seaming or creates a finished edge on pieces that will have no further finishing.

You can add selvage stitches to existing patterns or when designing your own garments. Be sure to add them to the total stitch count. Usually a selvage is one stitch, but it can be two or more. Multiple-stitch selvages are often used to prevent curling on pieces that are not seamed, such as scarves.

Selvage stitches form a firm edge that is helpful when working openwork patterns that tend to widen or when working with slippery yarns, such as silk, that have a tendency to lose their shape.

Selvage stitches can be used to avoid interrupting colorwork or stitch patterns with a seam. The selvage stitches serve as the **seam allowance** and disappear when the pieces are sewn.

Some selvages, such as garter or slip-stitch selvages, can help you keep track of rows. The ridges or chains created on every other row make it easy to count the rows.

Work all increases and decreases **inside** selvage edges. When you shape a piece by binding off stitches, the selvage stitch is also bound off. Establish it again on the first row that is worked even. Always measure inside selvage edges.

ONE-STITCH SELVAGES

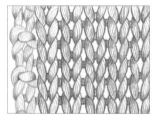

Garter stitch selvage (left side) This selvage is best worked on stockinette stitch fabrics and is the easiest selvage for beginners.

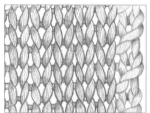

Garter stitch selvage (right side) The selvage looks slightly different on the right edge as shown here. Work left and right edges as follows: **Row 1:** Knit 1, work to the last stitch, knit 1. Repeat this row.

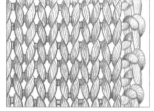

Reverse stockinette stitch selvage Suitable for stockinette stitch, this is easy for beginners. Work both sides as follows: **Row 1 (right side):** Purl 1, work to the last stitch, purl 1. **Row 2:** Knit 1, work to the last stitch, knit 1. Repeat these 2 rows.

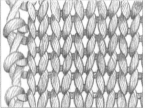

Slip garter stitch selvage (left side) This selvage is similar to the garter stitch selvage, only firmer. It is ideal for patterns that tend to spread laterally. The left side shown above differs slightly from the right side.

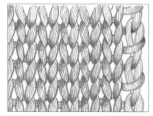

Slip garter stitch selvage (right side) Work both sides of the slip garter stitch selvage as follows: **Row 1:** Slip the first stitch knitwise, work to the last stitch, knit 1. Repeat this row.

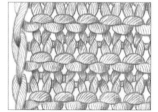

Chain stitch selvage This selvage is for garter stitch and is worked as follows: **Row 1:** With the yarn in front, slip the first stitch purlwise, with the yarn in back, knit to the end. Repeat this row.

SLIP-STITCH SELVAGES

This method has three variations. All of them make a chain stitch edge, with each chain loop representing two rows. Use it when you must later pick up stitches.

English method
Row 1 (right side): Slip the first stitch knitwise, work to the last stitch, slip the last stitch knitwise.
Row 2: Purl 1, work to the last stitch, purl 1.
Repeat these 2 rows.

French method
Row 1 (right side): Slip the first stitch knitwise, work to the last stitch, knit 1.
Row 2: Slip the 1st stitch purlwise, work to the last stitch, purl 1.
Repeat these 2 rows.

German method
Row 1 (right side): Knit the first stitch, work to the last stitch. With the yarn in back, slip the last stitch purlwise.
Row 2: Purl the first stitch, work to the last stitch. With the yarn in front, slip the last stitch purlwise.
Repeat these 2 rows.

TWO-STITCH SELVAGES

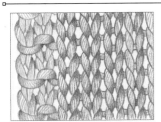

Double garter stitch selvage
This is ideal for free-standing edges, such as scarves, and is worked as follows:
Row 1: Slip the first stitch knitwise through the back loop, knit the second stitch, work to the last two stitches, knit 2. Repeat this row.

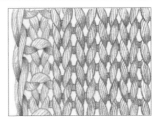

Chain garter stitch selvage
This selvage is good for patterns with more depth, such as double knits.

Work the chain garter stitch selvage as follows:
Row 1 (right side): With the yarn in back, slip the first stitch knitwise. With the yarn in front, purl the next stitch. Work to last 2 stitches, purl the next stitch, slip the last stitch knitwise with the yarn in back.
Row 2: Purl 2, work to the last 2 stitches, purl 2.
Repeat these 2 rows.

DECORATIVE SELVAGES

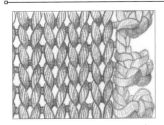

Beaded picot selvage Work this decorative alternative to a simple selvage as follows:
Row 1: Cast on 2 or 3 stitches (as desired). Bind off these stitches, work to the end. On next row, repeat row 1. Repeat these 2 rows as desired.

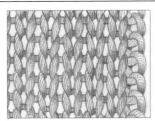

Picot selvage This makes a delicate trim on baby garments and shawls. It can also be used as a buttonloop for small buttons.
The picot selvage is worked as follows:

Row 1 (right side): Bring the yarn over the right needle and knit the first 2 stitches together. Work to the last 2 stitches, slip these 2 stitches knitwise with the left needle and pass the first stitch over the second stitch.
Row 2: Bring the yarn over the right needle from front to back and to the front again and purl 2, work to the last 2 stitches, purl 2.
Repeat these 2 rows.

Ribbing

The **elastic property** of ribbing allows it to grip at key areas, such as the wrists and the waist. When designing, you must plan every aspect of the ribbing carefully, including how much it pulls in, how it is cast on, how it is seamed, and the type of pattern you are using.

To make ribbing more elastic, work it on a needle that is one or two sizes smaller than the needle you will use for the main part of the garment. It may be necessary to use an even smaller needle with less-resilient yarns.

The number of stitches cast on for the ribbing is not always the same as for the body of the piece. Generally, if you want the ribbing **to pull in**, you cast on fewer rib stitches than you will use for the main body. If you want a **relaxed rib** (one that doesn't pull in at all), cast on the same or nearly the same number of stitches. In some cases, you might cast on more stitches for the ribbing than for the main body, such as when the stitch used above the ribbing has a very loose gauge. If you want to see the effect the ribbing will have on the main body stitch, work a large swatch of the ribbing and the pattern stitch together.

Many **stitch patterns** other than knit and purl stitches can be used for ribbing. For example, you could use stitches such as mock cables alone or in combination with knit and purl stitches. Ribbing can also be worked in two or more colors in vertical stripes (called corrugated ribbing) or horizontal stripes.

You can use a basic cast on for ribbing or choose one that will enhance its look, such as the Channel Islands or the tubular cast on. Because the cast-on edge looks different on each side, plan which will be the right side of the work. Use the same side for each piece so that when you sew them together, their edges will match perfectly.

To make your ribbing match at the seams, you must begin and end with the correct stitch. In knit one, purl one ribbing, begin and end with a knit stitch on right-side rows and sew one-half of a knit stitch from each side to make one full knit stitch. On knit two, purl two ribbing, you can begin and end with either two knits or two purls and sew in a whole stitch on each side. When working in the round, you must have an exact multiple of stitches to keep a continuous ribbing.

MEASURING RIBBING GAUGE

When you lay the ribbed piece flat without stretching it, it will look like the piece pictured above. When taking the gauge, don't forget to count the purl stitches, which tend to disappear between the knit stitches.

Unless otherwise stated, you should measure your ribbing **slightly stretched**. Just pull the ribbing apart slightly to measure the gauge.

When ribbing is measured stretched (sometimes called **relaxed ribbing**), it must be pulled apart even more than the slightly stretched piece. If the ribbing is to remain in this state, it should be wet blocked or steamed.

MEASURING RIBBING LENGTH

If you are knitting on two straight needles, measure the ribbing when you have knit halfway through a row. If the stitches are bunched together on one needle, the piece will measure longer than it actually is. If knitting circularly, spread out the stitches on the cable and measure.

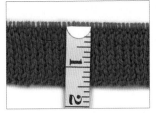

The ribbing above is approximately 1½ inches (4 cm) long when measured with the stitches quite close together on one needle.

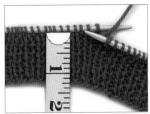

To measure more accurately, work to the center of a row and lay the piece flat. Notice that the ribbing now measures 1¼ inches (3 cm).

INCREASING ABOVE THE RIBBING

When the ribbing pattern continues up to become part of the body pattern, each increase on the last row of the ribbing must be placed carefully. Work a swatch before beginning your piece to determine the best placement.

A knit two, purl two ribbing can be worked into a knit four, purl two pattern by increasing one stitch on either side of the two knit stitches on the last row of ribbing.

You can work a mock cable and a knit one, purl two ribbing pattern into a four-stitch cable with a knit three, purl two ribbing by adding one stitch on either side of the mock cable and the knit stitch.

DIFFERENCES IN RIBBING

There is a visible difference in the way knit one, purl one ribbing pulls in compared to knit two, purl two ribbing.

The knit two, purl two ribbing shown above pulls in more than a knit one, purl one ribbing (left) over the same number of stitches.

The depth of the ribbing also affects how much it pulls in. This is especially important to know when you work with fibers that are not resilient, such as cotton. Using a deeper ribbing with cotton yarns is a good idea.

The deeper ribbing (above) pulls in more than the shorter ribbing (left) over the same number of stitches.

Bands, Borders, and Edges

Bands, borders, and edges are used to complete garments and to cover and flatten raw edges on knit pieces that have a tendency to curl. Bands and borders are usually wider than edges; they are used to give **stability** to pieces. Edges, such as those in lace patterns, are often used to add a decorative touch.

The classic ribbing stitch is often used for bands, but you can use other stitch patterns. Choose those that don't **curl**, such as garter or seed stitch, except when curling is desired or for folded bands.

You can work a band at the same time as the piece, but for a firmer edge, work it **separately** on smaller needles.

You can either pick up stitches to work a separate band or apply the band once the piece is complete. Prepare pieces for picked-up bands by adding selvage stitches on the edges. For picked-up bands, be sure to have the correct number of stitches. Too few stitches will make the band pull in; too many will cause it to wobble or ruffle. Check the band gauge on your knit swatch.

You can make bands and borders of single or double thickness. They are usually not more than 1 to 2 inches wide, so that they remain stable. Bands can also be reinforced with ribbon or tape to keep them firm.

RIBBED BANDS

Ribbed bands are **flexible** and **elastic**, which makes them perfect for areas that are intended to grip. They can be simple knit one, purl one or knit two, purl two ribbing or some of the other variations shown here.

Horizontal
This band, more elastic then a vertical one, is often used on cardigan or jacket fronts. It is the easiest type of band to work, but requires careful attention to make sure that you pick up the correct number of stitches for an even, flat edge.

Vertical
For an unbroken line, you can work vertical bands from ribbing stitches left on a holder after the lower edge is complete. Once beginning the band, add a selvage stitch for seaming.

To attach the vertical band, pin it along the edge as you work, without stretching it. Then either bind off the stitches or leave them on a holder to work the neckband. Sew the band in place.

Purl three, knit one ribbing (a multiple of 4 stitches plus 3 extra)
Row 1 (right side): *Purl 3, knit 1; repeat from the *, end purl 3.
Row 2: *Knit 3, purl 1; repeat from the *, end knit 3.
Repeat these 2 rows.

Stockinette/garter stitch ribbing (a multiple of 4 stitches plus 2 extra)
Row 1 (right side): Knit.
Row 2: *Purl 2, knit 2; repeat from the *, end purl 2.
Repeat these 2 rows.

Stockinette/seed stitch ribbing (a multiple of 4 stitches plus 2 extra)
Row 1 (right side): *Knit 2, purl 1, knit 1; repeat from the *, end knit 2.
Row 2: *Purl 2, knit 1, purl 1; repeat from the *, end purl 2.
Repeat these 2 rows.

STOCKINETTE STITCH BANDS

Doubled on a curve
This band is picked up and worked with a **turning ridge**. It works best with lighter-weight yarns. To keep the curved edges flat, decrease stitches on every knit row up to the turning ridge, then increase to correspond on the second half.

Picot band
An odd number of stitches is picked up for this double band. Work the picot row on the right side as follows: *Knit 2 together, yarn over; repeat from the *, end knit 1. Work the inside band to the same depth as the outside.

Bias band
This band is worked separately and then sewn onto the piece. Increase 1 stitch at the beginning of each right-side row and decrease one stitch at the end of the same row.

Outside rolled band
Pick up the stitches from the right side along the edge. Beginning with a purl row, work in stockinette stitch for about 4 or 5 rows or as desired. Bind off with a larger needle. The purl side rolls to the outside (right side).

Inside rolled band
Pick up the stitches from the right side along the edge. Beginning with a knit row, work in stockinette stitch for about 4 or 5 rows or as desired. Bind off with a larger needle. The purl side rolls to the inside (wrong side).

KNIT-IN BORDERS

The advantage of knit-in borders is that your piece is complete once you have finished the knitting. The best stitches are those that **lie flat**, such as ribbing, seed stitch, or the bias edge shown here. Avoid working stitches that may differ in row gauge from your piece, such as stockinette with garter stitch. When working bands in contrasting colors, twist yarns on the wrong side to prevent holes.

Ribbing on a curve
To shape an armhole and make the band at the same time, rib 2 stitches, then decrease 1 stitch. On right-side rows, keep increasing 1 stitch at the edge (in rib) and decreasing inside the ribbing edge until the armhole is shaped and the desired stitches are in the rib pattern.

Seed stitch
This is a good choice for a border on a stockinette stitch body because it has the same row gauge as stockinette stitch. Also, a seed stitch pattern makes a nice flat edge.

Bias
Leave this stockinette stitch band flat or fold it in half to the inside and sew it in place. On right-side rows, slip the first stitch knitwise, work a make-one increase, work to the last 2 stitches of the band, knit 2 together. On wrong-side rows, purl all border stitches.

GARTER STITCH BORDERS WITH CORNERS

These borders, ideal for jackets, shawls, or blankets, are worked separately. Because corners are wider at the outer edge, you decrease on **either side of a central stitch** at each corner. To determine number of stitches to cast on, measure all side edges and multiply this number by stitch gauge. Then find the required number of decreases by multiplying the band width by the row gauge. Add the number of decreases (for each corner) to find the number of stitches to cast on.

Knit corner Cast on and mark each corner. Knit to 2 stitches before the corner, knit 2 together, knit the corner stitch, knit 2 together through the back loops. On wrong-side rows, purl the corner stitches and knit the remaining stitches.

Eyelet corner Cast on and mark each corner. Work to 3 stitches before the corner, knit 3 together, yarn over, knit the corner stitch, yarn over, knit 3 together through the back loops. On wrong-side rows, purl the corner stitch and knit all the others.

MISCELLANEOUS BANDS

Garter stitch band Work this band by picking up 2 stitches for every 3 rows along a straight edge. Knit every row. To bind off, use the decrease bind off.

Pick up and knit border This border makes a good firm narrow edge and is sometimes called "mock crochet." Pick up the stitches and then bind them off on the next row. Or knit 1 row and then bind off.

Held miter band Cast on stitches to desired width, plus width of band. Work 1 stitch less on each row, placing it on a holder. When reaching the desired band depth, work the piece, leaving the stitches on a holder for the mitered edge.

Pick up stitches along the side edge. On right side rows, knit a band stitch with a holder stitch, then work a make-one increase. On wrong-side rows, work to the last stitch, make 1, work the last stitch together with the next holder stitch.

TECHNIQUE

OPEN CHAIN CAST ON

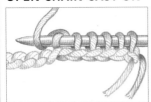

1 Use this cast on to **later add a band.** Chain the number of stitches above the rib in contrasting yarn. With main-color yarn, pick up 1 stitch in the back bump of each chain.

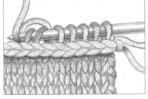

2 After the piece is complete, work band with a smaller needle and pick up the main-color loops under the chain, working 2 loops together as shown, if decreasing is desired.

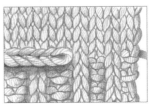

3 When the band is complete, remove the chain from the piece.

Hems

A hem or facing is an edge that **folds under** to keep the knitting from curling or stretching. Horizontal or vertical hems can replace ribbing. A hem allows pieces to hang properly and is ideal for edges that do not hug the body. Hems can be used for the lower edges of knit garments or the necklines and front edges of cardigans and coats.

A hem can also be used to form a **casing** for elastic such as at the top of a skirt. It can be worked at the same time as the piece or picked up after it is complete.

The edge of the hem can be **sharp (turning ridge)** or **rounded (without turning ridge)**. The folded part of the hem should be knit in a smooth stitch such as stockinette,

regardless of the stitch pattern used for the piece, and it should be worked on a needle **at least one size smaller** —possibly even two or three sizes smaller—than the needles used for the main body. You may have to increase or decrease stitches once the hem is complete, depending on the gauge of the stitch pattern above the hem. Try a small sample before you begin. Hems are not ideal to use with openwork patterns because the folded area will show through when viewed from the right side.

The folded edge should be sewn to the garment as invisibly as possible with whip stitch or blind stitch, or grafted stitch by stitch.

TURNING RIDGES

A turning ridge is used to create a clean line that makes a neat edge when the hem is sewn in place. All ridges are made after the hem is the desired depth, whether they are at the lower or the upper edge. The piece worked before (at the lower edge) or after (at the upper edge) is the hem.

Purl A ridge is formed by knitting the stitches through the back loops on the WS, thus forming a purl ridge on the RS of the work. On the following RS row, begin the body pattern.

Picot This ridge is worked over an even number of stitches. Work picot row on the RS as follows: K1, *k2tog, yo; rep from * to last st, k1.

Slip stitch This ridge is worked over an odd number of stitches. Work the slip-stitch row on the RS as follows: K1, *wyif sl 1, k1; rep from * to end.

KNIT-IN HEM

To reduce bulk, the cast-on edge is worked together with stitches on the needle so that sewing is not necessary. This hem can be worked with any basic cast on or with an open cast on.

This knit-in hem was worked using a long-tail cast on. Stitches were picked up along the cast-on row and placed on a spare needle. It should be noted that a knit-in hem is not easy to unravel if alterations must be made.

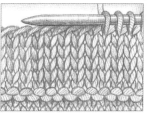

1 Work hem to desired depth and then make a turning ridge. Work main piece until it is same depth as hem, end with a WS row. Using spare needle and separate yarn, pick up and k 1 loop from cast-on edge for each stitch on main needle.

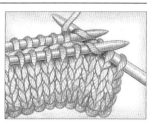

2 Cut extra yarn. Then fold up hem and *knit 1 stitch from spare needle together with 1 stitch from main piece; rep from * to end. Continue in pattern, beginning with a WS row.

VERTICAL FACINGS

These facings are ideal for tailored jacket and cardigan fronts. When the facing is to be picked up later, make a selvage stitch at the edge to aid in picking up stitches. Steam or wet block the pieces carefully before stitching the facing in place.

Garter stitch A simple facing can be made by using garter stitch as a turning ridge. On every row, knit the turning ridge stitch.

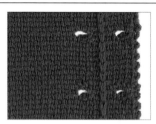

Slip stitch For a cardigan front, a band can be worked with double buttonholes. Work the slip stitch turning ridge by slipping the stitch purlwise on RS rows and purling it on WS rows. Fold band and reinforce buttonholes through both thicknesses.

Picked-up After the piece is worked, pick up three stitches for every four rows along the edge and work the desired depth. Stitches can be bound off as shown or sewn down stitch by stitch.

MITERED-FACING AND HEM

When making a garment with a horizontal hem and vertical facing, you can reduce bulk and create a smooth edge by making edges that meet but don't overlap. To do this, calculate the number of rows in the hem depth. Divide this in half and reduce the number of stitches you cast on by the result (about 1 inch).

After casting on, work the hem by increasing one stitch every other row until all the stitches are added back. Make a turning ridge. For the front facing, increase 1 stitch every other row, adding 1 stitch for the front turning ridge.

On this mitered edge, increase 1 st every other row 4 times before making the purl turning ridge, then make the facing by increasing 1 st every other row plus 1 st for the garter st turning ridge. Sew hem and facing, matching corners.

CURVED FACINGS

Inside curve A picked-up hem that curves to the inside, such as the neck edge shown, must be increased as it is worked to make the curve larger.

After sts are picked up along neck edge, knit 1 row on WS as turning ridge. As you make the facing, work increases at the points where the curving takes place. You may wish to place a marker at these points.

Outside curve A picked-up hem, such as the lower edge of a cardigan, has an outside curve and needs decreases to make the curve smaller.

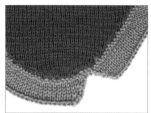

After the stitches are picked up along the curve, knit 1 row on the wrong side as a turning ridge. Decrease evenly along the most curved part of the edge as you work the facing.

Patch Pockets

Pockets can be decorative or functional, and they can be integral to the design of a garment. The most common types are **patch**, **horizontal inset**, and **vertical inset**. Pocket size should be proportional to the garment; for example, don't apply a tiny pocket to a bulky jacket.

The average size of a woman's pocket is 5–6½ inches wide by 5–7½ inches deep. For a man's pocket, add 1 inch and for a child's pocket, subtract 1 inch or more.

Place the pocket at a level that is comfortable for your hands. The easiest way is to check an existing sweater.

On a woman's sweater, the lower edge of a horizontal or patch pocket should be no farther than 21–22 inches from the shoulder and approximately 2½–4 inches from the center front edge. Vertical or side seam pockets are easier to wear in cropped sweaters.

To add pockets, decide what type of pocket and edging, placement, and whether it should contrast or match your sweater's yarn and pattern. Calculate the number of stitches and rows needed for the pocket. Don't forget to add a little extra yarn to the amount required for the garment.

PATCH POCKET OPTIONS

Simple square or rectangular patch pockets are easiest to make. You can also work patch pockets in contrasting stitch patterns, colors, or other shapes such as circles or triangles.

It is essential to work neatly. Apply pocket subtly with a nearly invisible stitch or boldly using a contrasting color in blanket stitch. Pockets in non-curling stitches, such as garter or seed stitch, are easiest to apply. For a neater edge, add a slip-stitch selvage to side edges.

Simple pocket Patch pockets should be applied to firmly knit pieces in stable yarns that can support the extra weight of the pocket. For easier application, place the pocket directly above the rib or hem. This gives you a straight line along the lower edge.

Simple with a cable A patch pocket can be made with a center cable that goes over the body cable. Line up the pocket cable over the body cable and sew in place.

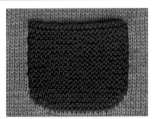

Curved lower edge For this pocket, cast on the desired number of stitches, less four to six depending on the pocket size and yarn. *Work one row even. Cast on 1 stitch at each end of the next row. Repeat from the * to add back the 4–6 stitches.

APPLYING A PATCH POCKET

Block or press the pocket. Measure it and outline an area the same size on the garment, using a contrasting yarn in basting stitch. Pin pocket over the area before applying. Then overcast the pocket in place.

Another method of applying a patch pocket is to run a needle in and out of one-half of every other row along both vertical edges of the pocket and one-half of every stitch along the lower edge of the pocket.

Pin the pocket in place in the center of the needles and, using the overcast stitch, sew one stitch from the needle, and one stitch from the pocket.

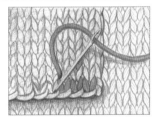

To make a neater, nearly invisible pocket seam, use duplicate stitch along the edges through the pocket and the body piece as shown.

Inset Pockets

Inset pockets, the most common type, are inconspicuous. They can be made with a **horizontal**, **vertical**, or **slanted opening**. Although the ways to make this pocket vary, they all have the same basic elements.

The **lining** of the inset pocket is usually made before the piece is begun.

Inset pockets can be made with a border that is knit in or added later, normally ¾–1½ inches. A disadvantage of the knit-in border is that it may be too loose if the needle is the same size as the body.

To make an added border, you can bind off the stitches or place them on a holder until you are ready to work the edge. To create a firmer edge on a ribbing border, bind off all the stitches knitwise.

HORIZONTAL INSET POCKETS: VERSION A

   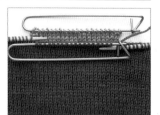

The horizontal inset pocket is one of the most frequently used methods for adding a pocket. You must first make a pocket lining, which is usually attached from the wrong side of the work.

1 On the right side, work to the pocket placement and bind off to prepare for adding the pocket lining. The pocket edge is worked after the piece is complete.

2 On the next row, work the lining over the place where the stitches were bound off. For a neater join, add 2 extra stitches to the lining and work them together with the first and last stitches of the piece.

Another method of joining the lining in one row is to place the stitches on a holder. With the right side of the lining facing the wrong side of the piece, work the stitches of the lining, then work to the end of the row.

HORIZONTAL INSET POCKETS: VERSION B

 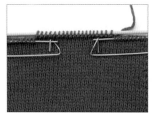 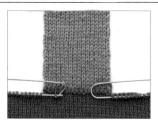 

This inset pocket has an attached double lining that is worked in a strip and rejoined to the piece. The sides of the pocket are sewn later and the pocket lining hangs free.

1 To begin this horizontal pocket on the right side, work to the pocket opening, then place these stitches on a holder. Purl across the stitches for the opening to make a turning ridge and place the remaining stitches on a holder.

2 Continue in stockinette stitch on the pocket lining for approximately 8" (20 cm), ending with a knit row. Fold the pocket lining in half and work the stitches from the second holder to the end of the row.

3 To rejoin the lining to the body, work to the pocket lining on the next row. Work across the stitches of the pocket lining. Slip the remaining stitches to a knitting needle and work to the end of the row. Sew sides of pocket lining and work the edging.

Short-Row Shaping

Short rows are partial rows of knitting used to shape or curve sections or to compensate for patterns with different row gauges. The result is that one side or section has more rows than the other, but no stitches are decreased. This technique is sometimes called **turning** because the work is turned within the row. Short rows can be worked on one or both sides of the piece at the same time.

When working with patterns of varying row gauges, short rows can be used to add rows to the shorter sections, allowing the finished piece to lie flat.

In pattern instructions, the short-row shaping method you're likely to find is **wrap and turn**. The other methods shown produce the same result.

Short-row shaping can also be used for darts, back necks on circular yokes, hats, and medallions with circular pieces, and sock heels.

When you add an extra row into the knit piece, you must make a smooth transition between the edge where one row is worked and the edge that has the extra row. Use one of the methods shown here.

WRAPPING STITCHES (KNIT SIDE)

1 To prevent holes in the pieces and create a smooth transition, wrap a knit stitch as follows: With the yarn in back, slip the next stitch purlwise.

2 Move the yarn between the needles to the front of the work.

3 Slip the same stitch back to the left needle. Turn the work, bringing the yarn to the purl side between the needles. One stitch is wrapped.

4 When you have completed all the short rows, you must hide the wraps. Work to just before the wrapped stitch. Insert the right needle under the wrap and knitwise into the wrapped stitch. Knit them together.

WRAPPING STITCHES (PURL SIDE)

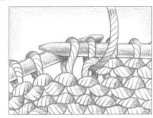 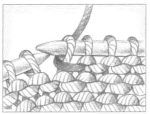 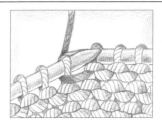 

1 To prevent holes in the piece and create a smooth transition, wrap a purl stitch as follows: With the yarn at the front, slip the next stitch purlwise.

2 Move the yarn between the needles to the back of the work.

3 Slip the same stitch back to the left needle. Turn the work, bringing the yarn back to the purl side between the needles. One stitch is wrapped.

4 After working the short rows, you must hide the wraps. Work to just before the wrapped stitch. Insert the right needle from behind into the back loop of the wrap and place it on the left needle as shown. Purl it together with the stitch on the left needle.

JAPANESE METHOD (KNIT SIDE)

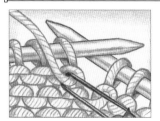

Set-up Knit to the turning point and turn. Place a coil-less safety pin around the working yarn and snug it up against the work. Purl to the end of the row.

1 Knit to the first turn and pull on the marker to create a loop. Place the loop on the left-hand needle.

2 Knit the loop together with the next stitch on the needle and remove the safety pin.

JAPANESE METHOD (PURL SIDE)

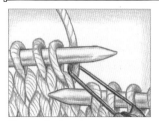

Set-up Purl to the next turning point and turn. Place a coil-less safety pin around the working yarn and snug it up against the work. Knit to the end of the row.

1 Purl to the first turn and pull on the marker to create a loop. Place the loop on the right-hand needle. Slip the next stitch knitwise to the left-hand needle.

2 Place both loops on the left-hand needle and purl them together through the back loops.

YARN OVER METHOD (KNIT SIDE)

Set-up Knit to the turning point and turn. Wrap the working yarn over the right-hand needle, from front to back, and purl to the next turning point.

1 Knit to the yarn over on the left-hand needle.

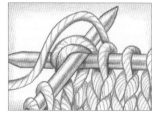

2 Knit the yarn over together with the next stitch on the left-hand needle.

YARN OVER METHOD (PURL SIDE)

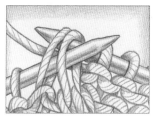

Set-up Purl to the turning point. Turn. Wrap the yarn around the right-hand needle from back to front, and knit to the next turning point.

1 Purl to the yarn over on the left-hand needle. With the yarn in back, slip the yarn over to the right hand needle and slip the next stitch on the left-hand needle knitwise.

2 Place both stitches back on the right-hand needle and purl them together through the back loops.

DOUBLE-STITCH SHORT ROW (KNIT SIDE)

1 Work to the turning point and after a knit stitch, turn. Slip the first stitch on the left-hand needle purlwise.

2 Bring the yarn to the back of the work over the top of the needle and pull it tightly so that both legs of the stitch in the row below are on the needle, creating a double stitch. Work to the end of the row.

3 Work to the double stitch and knit the two loops together.

DOUBLE-STITCH SHORT ROW (PURL SIDE)

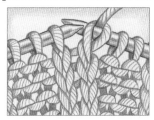

1 Work to the turning point and after a purl stitch, turn. Work steps 1 and 2 as for the knit side.

2 Work to the double stitch and purl the two loops together.

Buttonholes

TWO-ROW HORIZONTAL BUTTONHOLE

The two-row buttonhole is made by **binding off** a number of stitches on one row and **casting them on again** on the next. The last stitch bound off is part of the left side of the buttonhole. The backwards loop cast-on makes the neatest edge for the upper part of the buttonhole. Some versions have techniques to strengthen the corners. All the horizontal buttonholes shown are worked over four stitches.

Simple two-row buttonhole
This buttonhole is frequently used in knitting instructions.

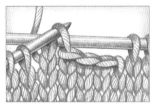

1 Row 1: Work to placement of buttonhole. K2, with left needle, pull 1 st over other st, *k1, pull 2nd st over the k1; rep from * twice more. Four stitches are bound off.

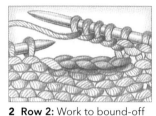

2 Row 2: Work to bound-off sts and cast on 4 sts using backwards loop cast-on method.
On next row, work these sts through the back loops to tighten them.

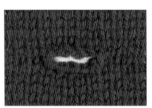

VERSION A Row 1: Work as for simple two-row. **Row 2:** Work to within 1 st of bound-off sts, kfb, then cast on 3 stitches (the bound-off stitches less one) with backwards loop cast-on method.

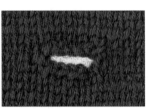

VERSION B Row 1: Bind off 3 sts. Slip last st to left needle and knit it together with next st. **Row 2:** At bound-off sts, cast on 5 sts. **Row 3:** Work to 1 st before extra cast-on st, k2tog.

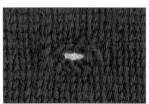

VERSION C Row 1: Work as for simple two-row. **Row 2:** At bound-off sts, cast on 4 sts, insert right needle from back to front under both loops of first bound-off st leaving loops on needle, work to end. **Row 3:** Knit bound-off loops with last cast-on st.

ONE-ROW HORIZONTAL BUTTONHOLE

The horizontal one-row buttonhole is the **neatest buttonhole** and requires no further reinforcing. It is shown worked from the right side (lower buttonhole) and from the wrong side (upper buttonhole).

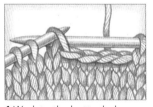

1 Work to the buttonhole, bring yarn to front and slip 1 stitch purlwise. Place yarn at back and leave it there. *Slip next stitch from left needle. Pass the first slipped stitch over it; repeat from the * 3 times more (not moving yarn). Slip the last bound-off stitch to left needle and turn work.

2 Using the cable cast-on with the yarn at the back, cast on 5 stitches as follows: *Insert the right needle between the 1st and 2nd stitches on the left needle, draw up a loop, place the loop on the left needle; repeat from the * 4 times more, turn the work.

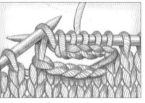

3 Slip the first stitch with the yarn in back from the left needle and pass the extra cast-on stitch over it to close the buttonhole. Work to the end of the row.

VERTICAL BUTTONHOLE

Vertical buttonhole slits are made by working **two sections** with separate balls of yarn at the same time or individually. If the latter, work the first side to desired depth (end at buttonhole edge). Work 2nd side with 1 row less, ending on wrong side. Turn work, cut 2nd ball of yarn. Then with yarn from first side, rejoin by working across all stitches.

Finish and strengthen by making a **horizontal stitch** at upper and lower joining points.

Seed stitch Vertical buttonholes can be worked on narrow bands. Not suited for large buttons or stress, it is best used for decorative purposes, such as on pocket flaps. Seed stitch is ideal because the edges lie flat.

Double buttonholes Because stockinette stitch rolls inward, vertical buttonholes should only be used on stockinette stitch for double bands, as shown. To make a neater edge, add a selvage st on either side of the slit.

Closed double buttonholes When the band is complete, fold it, match buttonholes and reinforce embroidering with buttonhole stitch. Note that the band is worked with a slip stitch at center to make a neater folding edge.

CONTRASTING-YARN BUTTONHOLE

Another method is to work the buttonhole stitches with contrasting yarn, slip the sts back to left needle, and reknit them with main-color yarn. Leave the contrasting yarn in the buttonhole.

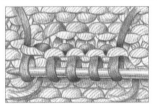

1 From back of work, using main color and a crochet hook, pull through a loop in each st on lower edge of buttonhole, and pick up 1 st from side edge. Slip these 5 loops from hook to a cable needle.

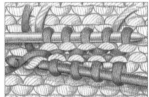

2 Working along the top edge, pick up 4 loops and 1 from the side. Transfer the 5 loops to a cable or double-pointed needle. Cut the yarn, leaving a strand about 8 inches (20 cm) long.

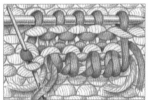

3 Fasten down each loop to fabric with yarn needle. Remove contrasting yarn. Use this method to add a ribbon band for reinforcement. Cut the space for the buttonhole on the ribbon before you pick up the loops and anchor them over the ribbon.

EYELET BUTTONHOLE

One-stitch eyelet: version A Eyelet buttonholes are small and are ideal for small buttons and children's garments. Work as follows: **Row 1:** Work to the buttonhole, knit 2 together, yarn over. **Row 2:** Work the yarn over as a stitch on next row.

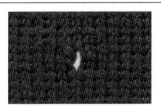

One-stitch eyelet: version B Row 1: Work to buttonhole, yo. **Row 2:** Slip yo, then yo again. **Row 3:** Slip 1 st knitwise before yarn overs, knit them together, leaving them on left needle. Pass sl st over st just made. Knit yarn overs together with next st on needle.

Two-stitch eyelet: version A Row 1: Work to buttonhole, k2tog, yarn over twice, ssk. **Row 2:** Work the yarn overs as follows: purl into the first yarn over and then purl into the back of the second yarn over.

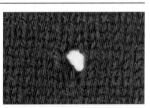

Two-stitch eyelet: version B Row 1: Work to buttonhole, yarn over twice, k2tog tbl. **Row 2:** Work to the yarn overs, purl the first yarn over, and drop the second yarn over from the needle.

OVERCAST BUTTON LOOP

Button loops are worked after the piece is complete and are generally used where only one or two buttons are needed. Loops are ideal for plackets in fine yarns, baby garments, or closures on jackets or coats.

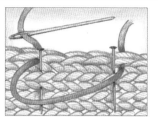

1 Mark beginning and ending point of loop on side edge. Using a yarn needle and yarn, bring needle up at lower edge. Insert needle at upper marker. Pull yarn through, leaving a loop.

2 Make a double strand by bringing the needle up at the lower marker once more. Depending on the size of the loop, this can be done once more to make a 3-strand core.

3 Work the buttonhole stitch over all the loops by bringing the yarn to the left of the needle. Then insert the needle under the loops and over the yarn, pull the yarn through and tighten.

CROCHETED BUTTON LOOP

The button loop should be just large enough to allow the button to pass through. If the loop is too large, the button will not stay securely fastened.

1 Mark the placement as for the overcast button loop. With a crochet hook, pull up a loop at the upper marker and work a crochet chain to the desired length.

2 Remove hook from the loop and insert it through the fabric at lower marker, then through last loop of chain. Draw loop through the fabric. Catch the yarn and pull it through the loop on the hook.

3 To work a row of single crochet over the chain, insert hook under the chain and pull up a loop. Catch the yarn and pull through both loops on hook. Fasten off last loop and weave in ends.

FINISHING BUTTONHOLES

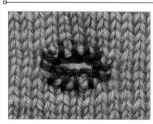

Sometimes even the best buttonholes need a bit of **reinforcing.** The buttonhole stitch shown is good for both single and double buttonholes.

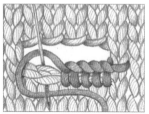

Buttonhole stitch Work around clockwise with needle pointing toward the center. Don't work the stitches too closely or you may distort the buttonhole.

The overcasting method is good for simple eyelets used to make small buttonholes.

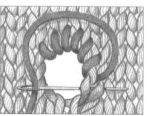

Overcasting This reinforcing technique is worked by overcasting evenly around the buttonhole.

Finishing Touches

The most important part of finishing is all the little details that don't show when the sweater is worn. Careful attention to these details improves the look and fit of your garments.

Knit fabric stretches and must be treated somewhat differently than woven fabric. To help stabilize your knits, you can add **seam binding** to shoulder seams and **ribbon facings** to the fronts of cardigans.

For ease of wear, you can add **zippers** to skirts and jackets. Try making matching buttons or attach purchased buttons in ways that prevent the fabric from stretching.

Your finishing materials and the yarn for your garment should be compatible in their cleaning. If not, dry clean, or attach any notions so that you can remove them easily before cleaning.

RIBBON FACINGS

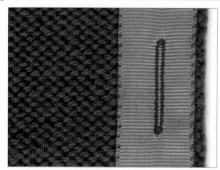

A ribbon facing is sewn in place and finished with machine-sewn buttonholes.

Ribbon facings, usually **grosgrain** ribbon, are generally sewn to the inside of the band, but decorative ribbon can also be used on the outside at the edges. On the buttonband, the ribbon helps support the button. On the buttonhole band, the ribbon adds stability to the buttonhole openings.

You can knit in buttonholes and then cut matching openings in the ribbon and join the two edges with the buttonhole stitch. Or once the ribbon is in place, you can machine sew the buttonholes through the knitting and the ribbon and cut through both layers.

Wash and dry the ribbon before attaching to preshrink it. The ribbon should be applied to blocked pieces. Cut two pieces to fit along the front edges with a ¼ inch seam allowance on each end. Fold the seam allowance under and pin or baste the ribbon to the band.

Pin the center and work out to either side for an even edge. With matching sewing thread, sew band in place, easing in the knitting. Work the butonhole band first. After machine- or hand-sewing the buttonholes, check the length with the buttonband. Making buttonholes can shorten the buttonhole side slightly.

TECHNIQUE

TAPING A SEAM

A narrow **twill tape or seam binding** can be used along seams to prevent them from stretching. This can be done after seaming and is especially good for areas such as shoulders that may need to be stabilized. The tape can also be used to ease in a shoulder that is too wide.

Cut a piece of tape the length of the desired shoulder width and whip stitch the tape on either side along the shoulder seam, easing in the fullness as desired.

Buttons

Buttons can add a striking contrast or they can blend in subtly with the knit fabric. You can also make perfectly matching crochet buttons, which are shown below.

The button should be appropriate to the yarn. For example, leather or stone buttons work best on tweedy, rugged yarns for outdoor garments, and fancy glass buttons are best suited to tailored or dressy styles.

Take along your swatch or a yarn sample when you buy buttons to find a good match. If possible, purchase an extra button or two to replace any you may lose.

Match the size of your button carefully to the size of your buttonhole so that the button will fit properly.

Buttons that cannot be washed should always be removed before cleaning. When you purchase buttons, look for any special care instructions on the package.

You also can leave a tail 2–3 inches long on the wrong side of the work as you first insert the needle to sew on the button. After you have attached the button, pull the needle to the wrong side of the buttonband, leaving the same amount of extra thread, and tie a secure knot.

CROCHET BUTTON WITH RING

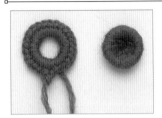

This button is made with a small plastic ring about ½ inch wide. Leaving a 6 inch tail, make a slipknot and work single crochets tightly around the ring. Join the last single crochet to the first stitch. Cut the yarn, leaving an 8 inch strand and pull through the last loop. Thread the 8 inch strand through a yarn needle and pick up the outside loop from every other single crochet. Gather them together and pull the strand to the back. Tie this strand tightly to the other one and use it to sew on the button.

SEWING ON A SHANK BUTTON

Sewing on a button with a thread shank adds **space** between the button and the buttonband. The button is able to slip in and out of the buttonhole more easily, and the button lies flat when it is closed.

Leave extra space in the thread loops that attach the button to the buttonband and then wrap the thread at least two or three times around those threads before tying the knot. It may help to insert a toothpick between the button and the buttonband when making the loops to elongate them as you attach the button.

TECHNIQUE

SEWING ON BUTTONS

To sew on buttons, you can use yarn (if it goes through the button), matching **thread**, or **perle cotton**. When sewing on metal buttons, which tend to cut the thread, you may wish to use **waxed dental floss**. Double the thread and tie a knot on the end. Then slip your button onto the needle and thread. You can further secure the button, which is especially desirable on garments that receive heavy wear, such as jackets. After going into the button and the fabric several times, wrap the thread around the button a few times and go back to the wrong side.

Add a **small button** or square of knitting or felt on the wrong side to keep the button in place.

Knotted thread has a tendency to pull through knit fabric. Lock it in place by inserting thread into the fabric on the right side and through the doubled thread. Clip the knotted end.

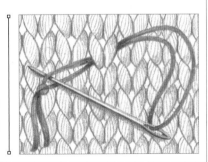

Zippers

Several different types of zippers can be added to knitted garments. Heavier zippers that **separate** are used for jackets and cardigans. These have metal or molded plastic teeth and are strong and durable. Regular **dressmaker zippers** are used for skirt waists or on the back of close-fitting necks. These have a nylon coil.

You can purchase zippers in stores that sell sewing notions or online. Many online sources will make zippers to your specifications (length, color of the tape, and coil) and offer various options for zipper heads and pulls.

Sew zippers into knit garments **by hand** rather than by machine. The opening should be the same length as the zipper so that the seam doesn't pucker or stretch. If your zipper is longer than the opening, fold the tape and sew it into place.

A challenge in adding a zipper to knitted fabric is that the fabric can stretch. To **stabilize** the edges of the garment, work a selvage such as the two-stitch garter selvage. If the edge is not smooth enough or if it is too stretchy, work a crocheted slip-stitch edge. Another method to stabilize the edge is to insert blocking wires along the edges before you sew in the zipper. You will need four **blocking wires** that are slightly longer than the length of the opening in your garment. Weave one blocking wire into the wrong side of your work along the edge and another four or five stitches away from it, so that the two blocking wires are parallel. Do this on both sides of the opening.

Place the knitting on a flat surface or insert a piece of cardboard, a blocking surface, or other firm and thin mat under the zipper opening. This will help you pin the zipper in place without catching another layer of knitting. Pin the zipper tape into place and baste one side of the zipper. Then backstitch along the zipper teeth without removing the blocking wires, although you may find it helpful to remove the pins.

Finish the tape by **whip stitching** it down as shown in the instructions below. Then pin and baste along the second side, add a row of backstitch along the zipper teeth, and whip stitch the tape. You may have to open the zipper to work on the second side. When you are done, remove the pins, if you haven't done so, and the blocking wires. **Steam block** the opening lightly with the zipper closed. Use a pressing cloth to avoid damaging plastic or nylon zipper teeth.

When planning to insert a zipper, you must decide whether you want the teeth to show. Some zippers have brightly colored zipper teeth, particularly plastic coil zippers often used in children's garments, and they add color and interest to a finished sweater. For a more subtle closure, you may wish the zipper teeth to be covered by the edges of your knitting or use an invisible zipper (on skirts or necks). If the zipper teeth are to show, then pin the knit fabric at the edges of the teeth. If the zipper teeth are to be covered by the fabric, pin your work a stitch or two in from the edge.

ADDING A ZIPPER

Whip stitch the zipper in place on the wrong side, then backstitch it on the right side close to the edge of the knit fabric.

1 To apply the zipper, work from the right side of the piece or pieces with the zipper closed. Pin the zipper in place so that the edges of the knit fabric will cover the teeth of the zipper and meet in the center.

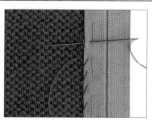

2 After pinning, baste the zipper and remove the pins. Turn the zipper to the wrong side and whip stitch in place. Turn the zipper to the right side, and backstitch in place.

Square and Rectangular Shawls

The simplest square and rectangular shawls are constructed by casting on the desired number of stitches and knitting in one direction.

For stitch motifs with a particular direction, it is possible to construct the shawl in two parts, either by knitting from the edges to the center or from the center to the edges. The center can be joined or grafted invisibly.

Some square shawls use a center-out cast on and are con-structed like the medallions on page 63. A similar method can be used to construct a rectangular shawl circularly, although in this case the shawl is begun by casting on a row of stitches and then joining to work in the round.

Most often, square shawls are folded in half and worn over the shoulders, but squares can also be constructed with openings so that they can be draped over the front as well as the wearer's back.

SQUARE SHAWLS

LEFT A stitch pattern based on garter stitch works best when designing a square shawl **worked diagonally**. Cast on 1–5 stitches. Increase 1 stitch at each edge on right-side rows and work even on wrong-side rows. When the diameter of the square is the width desired, decrease 1 stitch at each edge on right-side rows and work even on wrong-side rows. The increases and decreases can be positioned a few stitches from the edge of the square to create a border.

RIGHT To make a shawl knit froom the **outer edge to the center**, with a circular needle, cast on 4 times the number of stitches needed to create one side of the square. Place a marker for the beginning of the round and place 3 additional markers to divide the stitches into 4 equal sections. Join, being careful not to twist the stitches. Decrease before and after each marker in every other round, until 8 stitches remain. Change to double-pointed needles when there are too few stitches to fit comfortably on the circular needle. Cut the yarn, leaving a long tail, and thread the tail through the open stitches. Paired directional decreases, such as a k2tog and a SKP, give the diagonal lines a pleasing appearance.

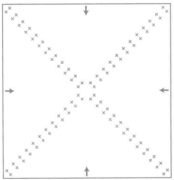

RECTANGULAR SHAWLS

For a shawl worked in **one direction**, determine the desired width and length. Choose a stitch pattern. Make a gauge swatch in the desired stitch pattern. Cast on the number of stitches equal to the desired width, considering the multiple in the pattern stitch and any border stitches. Work in rows to the desired length. Bind off.

For a rectangular shawl with matching edges, work it in two parts from the **edges to the center**. Cast on the correct number of stitches and work until the piece is half the desired length. Place the stitches on scrap yarn or a stitch holder. Work the second part to match the first, and graft the two halves.

To work from center to the edges, start with a provisional cast on. Knit to half the desired length and bind off. Place the cast-on stitches on the needle and work the second half of the shawl.

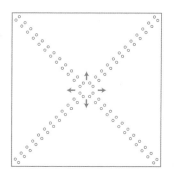

CENTER-OUT SQUARE SHAWL

With double-pointed needles and a **center-out cast-on method**, cast on 8 stitches, having 2 stitches on each needle. Knit 1 round, then increase 1 stitch at the beginning and end of each double-pointed needle in every other round—8 increases in every other round. Change to circular needle when necessary to accommodate the large number of stitches, placing a marker between each set of increases. Continue in this manner until the piece is the desired size. Bind off.

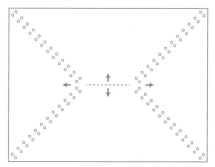

CENTER-OUT RECTANGULAR SHAWL

To work a rectangular shawl from the center out, with a circular needle, cast on the number of stitches required for the center section of **one long side of the rectangle** and place a marker, cast on 1–3 stitches for one short side and place marker, cast on for the **other long side**, place marker, cast on the same number of stitches for the **other short side**. Place a marker and join, being careful not to twist the stitches. Knit 1 round. Increase 1 stitch on each side of each marker in every other round until the shawl is the desired depth. Bind off. Sew the center opening closed. A provisional cast on can also be used and grafted to close.

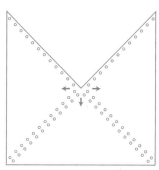

THREE-QUARTER SQUARE SHAWL

For a three-quarter square shawl worked from the neck down, **cast on 9 stitches or start with a garter tab cast on**, ending with a total of 9 stitches: 3 for each border and 3 for the body of the shawl. On the first shawl round, knit 3, place a marker, increase 3 times over the next 3 stitches, place a marker, knit 3—3 stitches increased. Work one row even. On the next row, knit 3, slip marker, increase 1, knit 2, increase 1, place a marker, increase 1, knit 2, increase 1, place marker, increase 1, knit 2, increase 1, slip marker, knit 3. Work an increase row every other row as follows: Knit 3, slip marker, [increase 1, work to next marker, increase 1, slip marker] 3 times, knit 3—6 increases. Continue in this manner until the shawl is the desired size. Bind off.

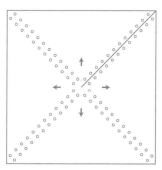

DIAMOND-SHAPED SHAWL

For a diamond-shaped shawl with a center opening, cast on **10 stitches or start with a garter tab cast on** ending with 10 stitches: 3 for each border and 4 for the body of the shawl. On the first shawl row, knit 3, place marker, increase 4 times over the next 4 stitches, placing a marker after every 2 stitches, knit 3. Work one row. Work an increase row every other row as follows: K3, slip marker, [increase 1, work to the next marker, increase 1, slip marker] 4 times, knit to end—8 increases. Continue in this manner until shawl is the desired size. Bind off.

Triangular Shawls

Many traditional shawls, which are typically **symmetrical**, have a triangular shape, but triangular shawls are common and popular shapes for modern shawl knitters as well. Some recent triangular shawls are designed to be **asymmetrical**, a shape that is suitable for a narrow shawl or scarf. The longer legs of the triangle can be wrapped around the neck one or more times. Symmetrical triangles also can be knit from the center out, just as other medallions are.

Most triangular shawls are worked flat, back and forth in rows, and they are shaped by increases or decreases. It is the positioning of the increases and decreases at the edges of the triangle that determines whether the triangle is symmetrical or asymmetrical. A triangle with the same number of increases or decreases on the right side as on the left will be **symmetrical**. If there are more increases or decreases on one side than on the other, the triangle will be **asymmetrical.** Right triangles can be worked by casting on for one edge and decreasing on one side only. The row spacing of the increases or decreases affects the slope of the sides. Increases or decreases placed close together (say, every other row) make a **wider angle**, whereas those with more rows between them create a more **gradual shaping**.

A simple symmetrical triangle can be knit by casting on a few stitches and increasing at each end on every other row. Another way to knit a triangular shawl is to cast on at one corner and increase on one side to the center, then decrease at the same edge back down to the original number of cast-on stitches. If the rate of increasing is different to the rate of decreasing, then the shawl will be asymmetrical. Often asymmetrical triangular shawls constructed in this way can be blocked to have a crescent shape.

Other simple triangles can be knit from the **apex to the base** by simply increasing at the edges or along the center vertical distance of the triangle. More commonly, triangular shawls knit from the neck down are shaped using **both center increases and edge increases**. Shawls of this type begin with a **garter tab**, as demonstrated below.

GARTER TAB CAST ON

With scrap yarn and crochet hook, chain 5. With shawl yarn and knitting needle, pick up and knit 3 stitches. Knit 2 (6) rows.

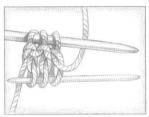

Carefully remove scrap yarn and place stitches on a double-pointed needle.

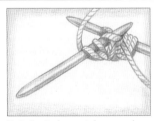

Knit 3 stitches, pick up and knit 1 (3) stitch(es) along the side edge, knit 3 stitches from the double-pointed needle—7 (9) stitches. Work row 1 of shawl pattern.

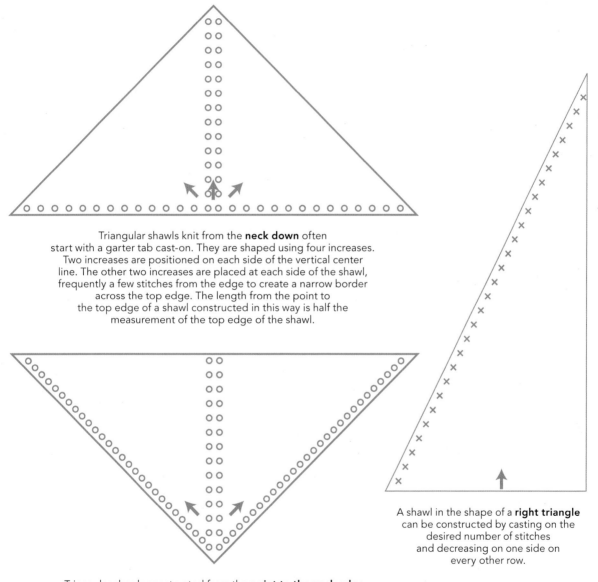

Triangular shawls knit from the **neck down** often start with a garter tab cast-on. They are shaped using four increases. Two increases are positioned on each side of the vertical center line. The other two increases are placed at each side of the shawl, frequently a few stitches from the edge to create a narrow border across the top edge. The length from the point to the top edge of a shawl constructed in this way is half the measurement of the top edge of the shawl.

Triangular shawls constructed from the **point to the neck edge** begin with a small number of stitches. They are shaped with four increases worked in every other row. Increases are worked at each edge and on each side of the center. The increases can be positioned a few stitches from the edge to form a border at the sides of the triangle.

A shawl in the shape of a **right triangle** can be constructed by casting on the desired number of stitches and decreasing on one side on every other row.

Circular and Half-Circular Shawls

Shawls can be knit to form circles using many of the same methods and cast ons as for center-out circles. Start with a **center-out cast on** and knit from the center to the shawl edges as you would for a circular medallion.

In a **pi shawl**, each section is twice as deep as the previous section with double the stitch count. Work with double-pointed needles for the cast on and first few rounds. Then switch to circular needles, increasing the needle's cable length as the shawl becomes larger.

A **half-circular shawl** is knit back and forth, not in rounds.

Because a shawl is a large piece, most knitters find it more comfortable to knit half-circular shawls on circular needles.

A **half-pi shawl** starts with about half the number of stitches in a full circle shawl—usually about seven to nine stitches. These are increased in the next row, and then the increases and number of rows are the same as the number of increases and rounds in a full-circle pi shawl. To make a half-pi shawl with a finished top edge, start with a garter tab cast on and work the border with the shawl as you knit. Do not include the garter edge stitches in your stitch count.

CENTER-OUT CIRCULAR SHAWL

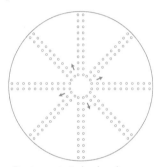

Center-out circle shawls worked in the round can be **shaped with rays that emanate from the center**. For a smooth-edged circle at least 8 sets of increases should be worked, forming 8 wedges.

Cast on 8 stitches using a center-out cast on method. Knit one round. **Next round** Increase one stitch in each stitch—16 stitches. Work 3 rounds even, placing a marker after every second stitch and slipping the markers every round. Work an increase round every 4th round as follows: *Work to 1 stitch before marker, increase 1 stitch, work to marker, slip marker, increase 1 stitch; repeat from * around—16 stitches increased. When the shawl is the desired size, bind off. A circular shawl should be pinned carefully into shape and blocked.

HALF-CIRCULAR SHAWL

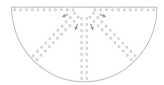

A half-circle shawl is worked in rows and often begins with a **garter tab cast on** to set up the border stitches. The half-circle is shaped with rays emanating from the top center edge formed with sets of increases and increases worked at the side edges that form a border across the straight top edge. Decide how many stitches wide the top border should be and cast on twice that number of

stitches plus 1 stitch for each wedge desired. The example shows 4 wedges. Knit one row. In next row, work border stitches even and double wedge stitches, placing a marker after right-hand border stitches, between each wedge, and before left-hand border stitches. Work 3 rows even. **Next row** Work to first marker, slip marker, [increase 1 stitch, work to 1 stitch before next marker, increase 1 stitch, work to the marker, slip marker] 4 times, work the remaining border stitches—8 stitches increased. Repeat the increase row every 4th row until the shawl is the desired size. Bind off.

PI SHAWL

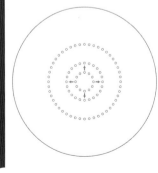

To make a pi shawl, cast on a small number of stitches, usually between 8 and 10. On the next round, **double the number of stitches**. Work three rounds and double the stitch count again. Continue to shape the shawl by doubling the number of rounds worked before each increase round and doubling the stitch count in each increase round. When the shawl is the desired size, bind off.

HALF-PI SHAWL

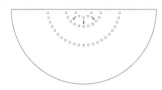

A half-pi shawl can be **worked in rows** using the same method as the pi shawl. Double the stitch count in each increase row and double the number of rows worked between each increase row.

Circular and Half-Circular Spiral Shawls

Like many circular shawls, those with spiral patterns are based on **center-out circles**. Circular shawls of this type are similar to those knit with rays that radiate out from the center, but the increases or yarn overs are staggered so that they form a spiral pattern. **Closed increases**, such as make one or knit front and back, are used to knit solid fabrics, and **yarn overs** are used for lace shawls. Most often circular shawls with spiral shaping have eight wedges, but any number of wedges from five to ten or more is possible. Although it is often convenient to start circular shawls on double-pointed needles, it is more comfortable to knit large shawls on circular needles. If the shawl is lacy, needles

with sharp points make it easier to knit lace motifs.

Half-circular shawls with spirals begin like half-circular shawls that radiate from the center. They are knit flat, back and forth, often on circular needles, to hold the many stitches in a large shawl.

For a circular shawl, you can begin by casting on the number of stitches that equals the number of wedges in the shawl. In a half-circular shawl, cast on double the number of stitches for the number of wedges. For a full circle, you will join to knit in the round; for a half circle, you will knit flat. The shawls can be knit in any textured stitch pattern.

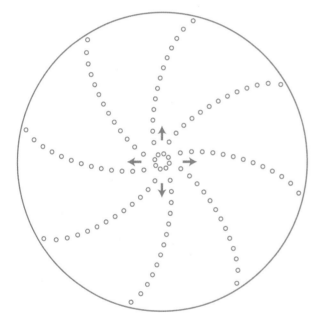

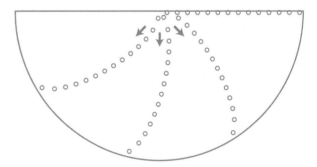

For a circular shawl worked in rounds where the increases form a decorative spiral, **cast on the number of stitches equal to the number of wedges** and knit one round. In the next round increase 1 stitch in each stitch. Place a marker for the beginning of the round and before each wedge section. Increase every other round by working 1 increase at the beginning of each wedge. When shawl is the desired size, bind off. Note that a yarn over increase is the most visible increase for a decorative spiral.

For a half-circle worked with a spiral increase pattern, **work in rows**. The increases can be set up to work a border along the top as you go by casting on the number of stitches required on each side and keeping them even as you work. **Cast on the number of stitches equal to the number of wedges, plus border stitches**, and work one row. Work the border stitches, place a marker, and then double the wedge stitches, placing a marker between each wedge and before the remaining border stitches. Work the next row even. Increase at the beginning of each wedge section every other row until the shawl is the desired size. Bind off.

Crescent Shawls and Short-Row Shaped Shawls

A symmetrical crescent shawl can be constructed from the neck down, starting with a few stitches and increasing at six points on every other row. This kind of shawl often begins with a **garter tab cast on** and has three segments.

Another simple crescent can be knit from **side to side**. In this case, cast on a few stitches at one of the corners and increase only on one side. Knit evenly until the shawl is as long as desired, then decrease along the same edge until you reach a point that matches the cast-on end.

Bottom-up symmetrical crescent shawls are constructed by knitting past the center stitch for an inch or two, and then turning your work to knit past the center stitch on the wrong side for an equal distance. Repeat for longer rows until you reach the top. Often the short rows are knit above a border.

Top-down short-row crescent shawls are knit by casting on the number of stitches for the top. Short rows are knitted from the neck down by knitting to a few edge stitches and then turning your work and knitting back, leaving the same number of stitches unworked on the opposite side. Each subsequent short row is reduced by that number of stitches.

Heart-shaped shawls are knit from the top down, often starting with a garter tab. On these shawls, there are six increases every other row: two at each edge and one on each side of a center stitch.

CRESCENT SHAWLS

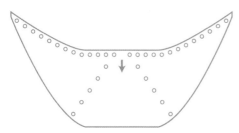

A crescent-shaped shawl can be worked from the **neck edge**. Cast on a small number of stitches or begin with a garter tab cast on. For example, begin with 12 stitches, 3 for left edge, 6 for shawl body, and 3 for right edge. Place markers after 3 right edge stitches, and every 2 stitches before 3 left-edge stitches. Increase 1 stitch after each marker every other row until the shawl is the desired size.

A crescent-style shawl can be constructed very simply by working from **corner to corner**. Cast on 3–5 stitches for the top left-hand corner. Increase on one side and work the other side without shaping. When the shawl is the desired depth, work even until the shawl is the desired length minus the length of the corner to where the shaping begins. Begin to decrease at the same rate and on the same side as the increases until the number of stitches cast on remains. Bind off.

SHORT-ROW CRESCENT SHAWLS

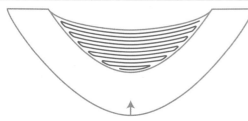

To construct a short-row crescent from **lower edge to top**, use **increasing** short rows. Cast on the number of stitches to equal the measurement of the lower edge of the shawl. Work several stitches past the center of the shawl and turn. Work to the same number of stitches past center and turn. Continue in this manner, working the same number of stitches after the previous turn in every short row, until the shawl is desired size. Hide the holes created by the short rows by using any of the methods on pages 139–141.

To construct a **crescent shawl from the top down**, cast on enough stitches for the length of the top edge. For a very deep crescent, cast on more stitches than for a shallow crescent. Use **decreasing short rows** by working to a few stitches before the end of the row and turning. Work to the same number of stitches on the other side. On each subsequent row, knit to the same number of stitches before the previous turn and knit to the same number of stitches at the other end. Work to the desired depth of the shawl and work a row over all the stitches. Bind off.

ASYMMETRICAL TRIANGULAR SHAWL

To create a shawl in the shape of an asymmetrical triangle, cast on a few stitches for the lower corner. **Increase at different rates on each side.** For example, on the right-hand side increase every other row and on the left-hand side work the increases every 4th row. Work the increases a few stitches in on each side to assure a smooth edge. When the triangle is the size desired, bind off.

ZIG-ZAG EDGE SHAWL

This zig-zag-edged shawl is formed by **offsetting short-row wedges** to form a crescent. Cast on the number of stitches required for the desired depth of the shawl. Work a wedge using short rows: on each right-side row, knit to a few stitches before the end, then turn and work to the end of the wrong side of the piece. When the first triangle is completed, work to an inch or two before the thin side of the wedge, turn and work back, cast on the same number of stitches left on the thin edge, and complete the second wedge as the first. Continue to add wedges until the shawl is the desired length. Work a few rows over all stitches at the neck edge and bind off.

HEART-SHAPED SHAWL

A heart-shaped shawl can be worked from the neck-down and is **shaped with 6 increases.** Cast on as for a neck-down triangular shawl, with a few stitches or using a garter tab cast on. Increases are positioned with 2 on each side of the center stitch and 2 each at the beginning and end of the row. A decorative way to increase along the sides is to work yo, k1, yo after the first stitch and before the last stitch. Work an increase row every right side row until the shawl is the desired size. Bind off.

SHORT-ROW CIRCULAR SHAWL

Circular shawls can be knit flat using short rows. The circle is formed by **working several short-row wedges,** as for the shape on page 64. Cast on the number of stitches that will equal the radius of your shawl or half the number of the desired length of the top edge when the shawl is worn folded in half. Work 2 rows. Then work to a few stitches before the end of the row, turn, and work to the end. Work to the same number of stitches before the last turn, then turn and work to end. Continue in this manner until the wedge is the desired size. Work 1 row over all the stitches, work back, and continue to work wedges in this way until a complete circle is formed. To graft the ends together, begin with a provisional cast on, otherwise bind off and sew the ends together.

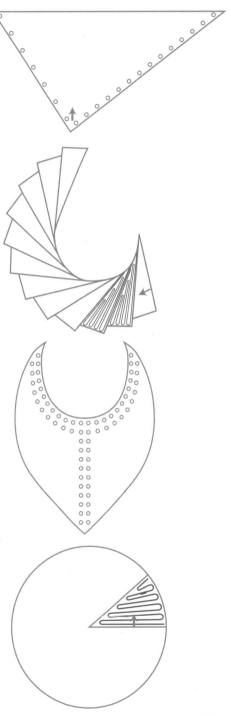

Shetland Shawls

A special type of square shawl is the Shetland shawl. It has a **center square** that is surrounded by a **border** and completed with **edging.** On hap shawls, the center square is knit in garter stitch. In a lace shawl, the center square can be knit in garter stitch or in a lace motif.

In the traditional method of knitting a Shetland shawl, a few stitches are cast on at one **outside corner** of the square. These stitches are knit to form an **edging** that extends along one length of the outer square of the shawl. Using mitered corners, the edging is knit around the other three sides to form an open square. The stitches on the inside of the edging are picked up to make the **trapezoidal border.** Mitered corners are formed by decreases at the ends of each side, worked at regular intervals. When the border is complete, a row of live stitches remains. These are picked up to knit the center square. Stitches along the side borders are worked with the rows of the center square. When the center square is complete, it is grafted to the live stitches at the top border. Shawls were constructed this way because they were knit on long straight needles—the only needles available at the time.

More **modern methods,** shown below of knitting Shetland shawls begin with the center square, which can be knit horizontally or diagonally When the square is completed, the live stitches are placed on a circular needle, and stitches are then picked up on the other three sides of the square and the shawl is worked in the round. The picked-up stitches are used to construct the trapezoidal border. The shawl is finished by attaching edging to each side.

The center square is worked either horizontally or diagonally. If worked horizontally, cast on using a provisional cast on and leave the top edge open.

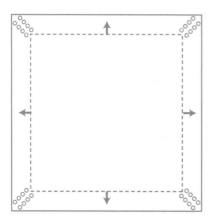

When the square is completed, pick up stitches along all 4 sides of the square. If the square was worked horizontally, end the square with a right-side row and place the stitches on a circular needle, pick up and knit stitches along the left-hand side, knit the cast-on stitches, and pick up and knit along the right-hand side of the square. Work in the round, increasing twice at each corner in every other round—8 stitches increased every other round. When the inner border is the desired depth, bind off.

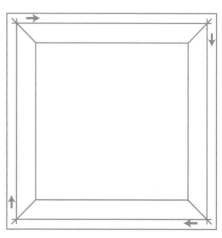

The outer border can be worked the same as the inner border, or it can be worked as an edging, and joined perpendicularly (see page 43). Be sure to join the edging 3 times to each corner. When the edging has been worked around the entire shawl, bind off and sew the bound-off edge to the cast-on edge.

Faroese Shawls

Faroese shawls are constructed from **two triangular side panels, a trapezoidal back panel, edging, and shaping at the shoulders** to keep the shawl from slipping off. The overall shawl looks somewhat like a pair of butterfly wings. Traditional Faroese shawls are knit from the bottom up in garter stitch and are shaped by closed increases in solid fabric or yarn overs in lace motifs and by decreases along the sides and center panel. Typically one stitch would be decreased on each side of the shawl every other row. The decreases are made inside the vertical border. Stitches also are decreased gradually to shape the center panel. When the triangular sections of the shawl are decreased and worked to the top 3 or 4 inches (8 to 10 cm), the shawls are shaped at the shoulders using a separate series of decreases.

The bottom of the shawl can be embellished with fringes, or a lace motif can be knit as a wide border along the bottom. An allover lace pattern can be used in this style shawl.

When you are knitting a Faroese shawl, be sure to cast on loosely so that the bottom edge is elastic.

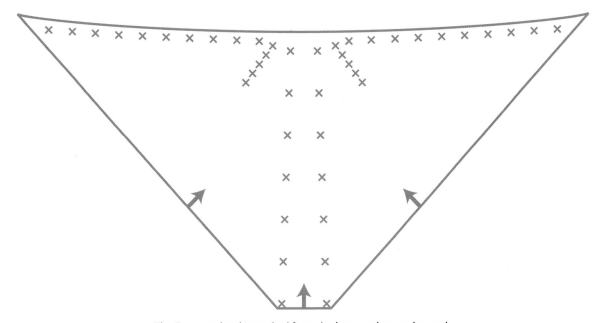

The Faroese shawl is worked from the **lower edge to the neck edge and shaped with decreases.** Cast on the total number of stitches for the bottom of the shawl. Decrease 1 stitch each side every other row. These decreases can be positioned a few stitches away from the edge to form a border for the top edge of the shawl. The gusset is decreased more gradually. Place markers to mark the center stitches for the lower edge of the gusset and work the decreases inside the markers. Use the row gauge to calculate how frequently to work the gusset decreases for a 2- or 3-inch (5-or 7.5-cm) gusset at the neck edge. When the shawl measures approximately 6 inches (15cm) less than the desired depth of the shawl to the back neck, begin to shape the shoulders, decreasing every other row in the center of the triangular sections so that the triangular sections end with stitches measuring 1 inch (2.5cm) or less at the top.

Ruanas

A **ruana** is a woolen covering, similar to a poncho, with a long back and open sides. Often the back, knitted as a single piece, is longer than the sides. It is divided at the shoulders so that there are two panels for the front. The area around the neck may be shaped to form a V-neck.

Knitted ruanas can also be con-structed from **side to side** In this case, stitches would be bound off at the center front and then cast on for the second front. Increases and decreases or short rows can be used to shape the neck.

Ruanas can also be constructed from **two separate rectangles**.

Ruanas typically are knit from heavier yarns, especially yarns such as mohair or bouclé. Ruanas can be embellished with fringes. The basic shape can be changed by substituting a half-circular shape for the back panel rather than a rectangle.

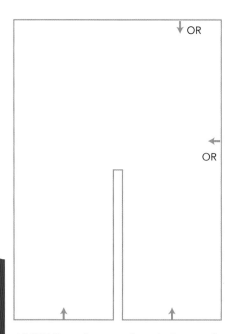

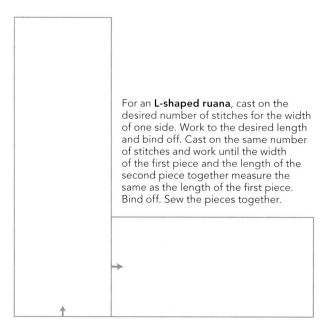

For an **L-shaped ruana**, cast on the desired number of stitches for the width of one side. Work to the desired length and bind off. Cast on the same number of stitches and work until the width of the first piece and the length of the second piece together measure the same as the length of the first piece. Bind off. Sew the pieces together.

ABOVE To work a ruana from the **lower edge of the back**, cast on the appropriate number of stitches to equal the desired width. Work even to the desired length. Place half the stitches on scrap yarn or a stitch holder and complete one side of the front. Place the held stitches on the needle and work the second side to match the first. To work the ruana from **side to side**, cast on double the number of stitches for the desired length. Work even to half the desired width and bind off half the stitches for the front opening. In the next row, cast on the same number of stitches over the bound-off stitches. Work until both sides are the same. Bind off.

A ruana also can be worked by knitting two **front pieces separately** and joining them by working across one piece, casting on additional stitches and knitting across the second piece. Work the back to desired length.

Hats

At its most basic, a hat consists of a **brim or band** and a **crown**. There are endless ways to vary the shape and size of these components. Hats also may have a **cuff**, **visor**, or **earflaps**.

TOP

CROWN ——————□

□———————— **RISE**

CUFF

CROWN

The portion of a hat that covers the head is called the **crown**. The portion of the crown that forms the sides of the hat is called the **rise**, and the crown is usually shaped at the top.

BRIM

BUCKET HAT

The **brim** is the lower projecting portion of the hat. A brim can be shallow or wide, depending on the style.

BAND

BERET OR TAM

Some hats simply have a 1 to 2 inches (2.5 to 5 cm) deep **band** around their base, rather than a projecting brim. Bands are often worked in a rib pattern to be slightly smaller than the head circumference, allowing it to stretch to fit the wearer snugly.

CUFF

If you knit a band to be double the desired width when worn, you can fold it back to form a **cuff**. Because the wrong side of the cuff will show when folded back, knit the cuff in a reversible stitch pattern or plan ahead to knit the desired pattern on the wrong side. Like bands, cuffs often are knit in rib patterns for stretchability.

VISOR

NEWSBOY CAP

A **visor**, or **bill**, is an extension of the brim in the front of a hat that provides extra shade for the face. A visor is created by knitting in a dense stitch pattern that is naturally rigid or by sewing the brim to create a pocket into which a plastic or cardboard crescent is inserted.

EARFLAPS

CHULLO

Earflaps can be knit as part of the body of the hat or stitched separately and attached. Earflaps are often finished with cords that tie under the chin.

CORRUGATED RIBBING

Corrugated ribbing is a classic choice for **Fair Isle** hats and sweaters.

1 With main color knit 2. When changing colors, be sure to bring the main color under the old color

2 With contrasting color, bring yarn to front between the needles and purl 2. Bring the yarn over the main color.

3 On the wrong side, purl 2 with main color, bringing contrasting color to the back between the needles, knit 2.

CLOSING TOP OF HAT

After the stitches have been decreased, cut the yarn, leaving a long tail. With a yarn needle, thread the tail through the open stitches. Keep the stitches on the needles to thread the yarn through the stitches twice. Remove the needles and pull the yarn tightly to close the hat top. Pull the tail through to the inside and weave in the end.

HAT FINISHED WITH I-CORD

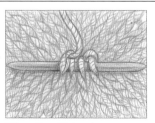

When the stitches have been decreased, knit all the stitches onto one double-pointed needle. Work I-cord to desired length. For a decorative knot, work the I-cord for an extra inch before fastening off, and tie knot.

Mittens and Gloves

Mittens and gloves have many of the same components. They begin with a **cuff**, they have a **hand** region that covers the back and palm of the hand, and they have a separate **thumb** that extends from the lower part of the hand. Mittens are **shaped at the top**, whereas gloves have separate **coverings for each finger**.

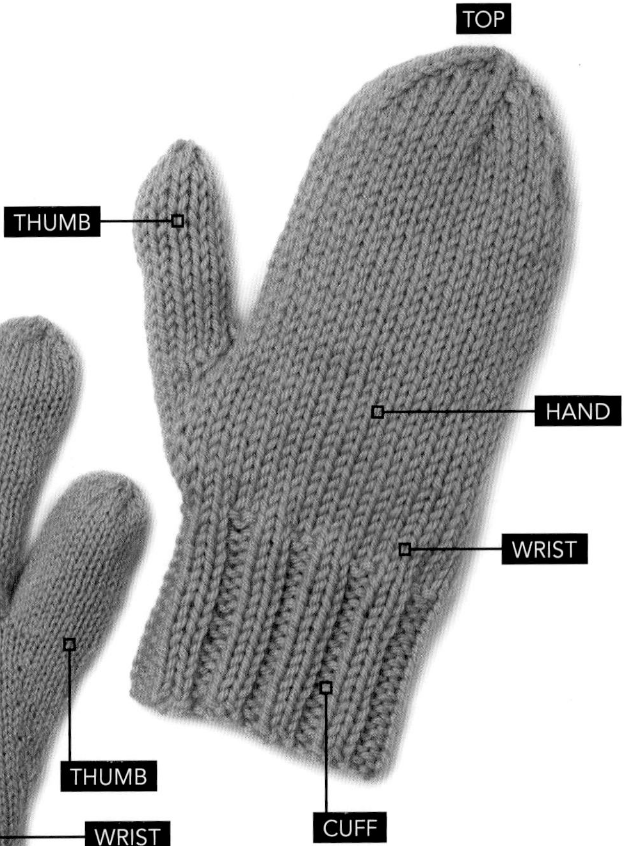

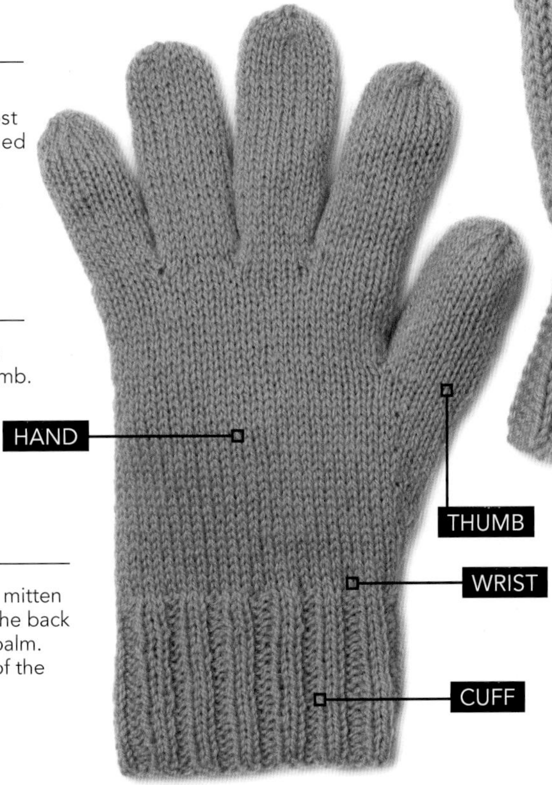

THUMB

TOP

HAND

WRIST

CUFF

The cuff of a mitten or glove covers the wrist. Most mittens and gloves designed for cold weather will have tightly knit cuffs, typically worked using **ribbing**.

WRIST

The wrist is the area above the cuff and below the thumb. Like the rest of the mitten or glove hand area, it is worked more loosely than the cuff.

HAND

THUMB

WRIST

CUFF

HAND

This is the part of the mitten or glove that covers the back of the hand and the palm. It is the **widest** part of the glove or mitten.

CUFF

THUMB

The thumb extends from the hand region of both gloves and mittens. Some gloves and mittens will have a gusset for the thumb. The **gusset** is a small triangular area intended to provide additional ease.

Other styles of gloves and mittens will not require gussets. In this case, an opening is left for the thumb, these stitches are picked up after the hand is complete, and the thumb is worked.

GLOVE FINGERS

When the hand is as long as desired, the circumference has to be **divided** to form the fingers in order to knit the **tubes** that will cover each finger. Stitches forming the area between the fingers, known as the **fourchette**, must be added between those from the hand and palm sides of the glove.

MITTEN TOP

When the hand is as long as desired, the circumference of the mitten is **decreased**. The decreases can be positioned at the **sides** of the hand, where the palm and back of the hand meet, or **within the hand**.

NO-GUSSET THUMB

 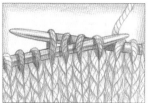 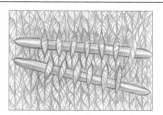 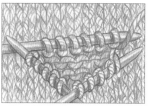

1 Knit to desired thumb placement. With scrap yarn, knit half the desired number of thumb sts minus 2, slide these sts back to right needle and with main yarn, knit them again, continuing pattern as established. Continue in pat until hand is complete.

2 When the hand is complete, thread one double-pointed needle through the row below the scrap yarn. Thread a second double-pointed needle through the row above the scrap yarn. Carefully remove the scrap yarn.

3 Rejoin main color, pick up and k 2 sts along RH side of opening, work sts on bottom of thumb opening, pick up and k 2 sts along side of opening, knit sts from top double-pointed needle. Divide sts on 3 dpn and complete thumb.

SIDE-SEAM THUMB GUSSET

1 When cuff is complete and one or two rounds have been worked, work to 2 sts before end of rnd, place marker, k1, M1, k1, place marker.

2 Next round Work to marker, sl marker, inc 1 st, work to 1 st before marker, inc 1 st, sl marker, work to end of rnd. Rep inc rnd evenly over length of gusset until desired number of sts is between markers. This is total number of thumb sts minus 5. Work to end of rnd.

3 Place sts between markers on scrap yarn, cast on 2 sts over opening in next rnd, work in pattern until hand is complete.

ASYMMETRIC THUMB GUSSET

 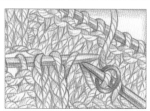 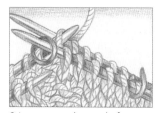 

1 For left hand: k to 2 sts before center of rnd, place a marker, M1R, k4, place marker.

2 Inc every other rnd after first marker until total number of thumb sts minus 4 is between markers, place these sts on scrap yarn. Cast on 4 sts and cont to end of hand.

3 For right hand: k to 2 sts before center of rnd, place a marker, k4, M1L, then place marker. Increase every other rnd before 2nd marker. Complete as for left hand.

SHAPED THUMB GUSSET PLACED BELOW INDEX FINGER

For left hand, work to where center of index finger will be positioned on palm side of hand, generally 2–4 sts before center of round, place markers and work increases as for side-seam gusset on page 162.

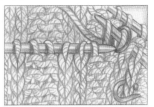

For right hand, work to where center of index finger will be positioned on palm side of hand, generally 2–4 sts after beginning of round, place markers and work increases as for side-seam gusset on page 162.

MAKING THUMB

1 Place the stitches from the scrap yarn on 2 double-pointed needles.

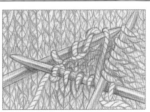

2 Pick up and knit stitches along the thumb opening.

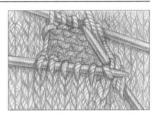

3 Work in the round until the thumb is the desired length.

TRADITIONAL MITTEN TOP

Four decreases are worked in *every* round to create a pointed effect. The decreases are paired and positioned with a k2tog at beginning of round, SKP and k2tog at center of round, and SKP at end of round. The decreases may have one or two stitches between each pair.

SOCK TOP SHAPE

This flat top maintains the sides of the mitten. Two sets of paired decreases are worked *every other* round with 2 sts between each pair. Decreases are worked as foll: K1, k2tog, k to 3 sts before center of round, SKP, k1, k1, k2tog, k to 3 sts before end of rnd, SKP. When just under half of sts rem, place evenly on 2 needles and graft.

ROUND TOP

This top is round and shaped by decreasing 6 stitches evenly around in every other round. When 6–8 sts remain, cut yarn, leaving a long tail, and draw tail through open sts twice to close.

Socks

Each sock has seven parts. The parts of the sock described here and shown in the photo on the right are those found in a typical sock knitted from the cuff to the toe. Basic instructions and photos for knitting both cuff-down and toe-up socks appear on pages 166–167.

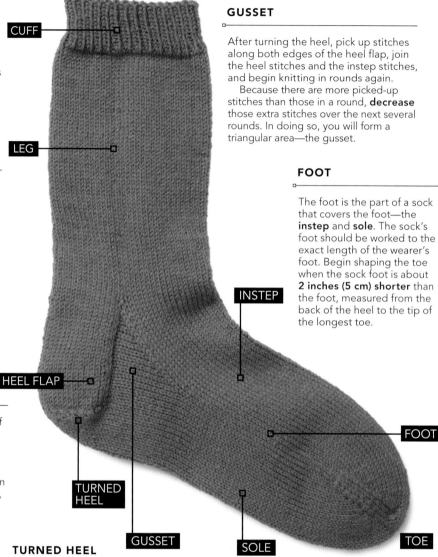

CUFF OR TOP

This is the part of a sock that covers the top of the leg and should be constructed so that the top does not slide down. It is often knit in **stretchy ribbing**, plain or fancy, and the length can be varied.

LEG

This is the part that covers the leg down to the start of the heel, and it is the area **most visible** when the sock is worn.

HEEL FLAP

The leg is divided so that half the stitches are used to construct the heel flap. The heel flap covers the back of the heel and is constructed by **working back and forth** in rows. Often additional fibers, such as nylon, are added to make the flap more durable.

TURNED HEEL

To turn a heel, use **short rows** to form a cup into which the heel will fit. This process is called **turning** because you turn frequently when knitting the short rows.

GUSSET

After turning the heel, pick up stitches along both edges of the heel flap, join the heel stitches and the instep stitches, and begin knitting in rounds again.

Because there are more picked-up stitches than those in a round, **decrease** those extra stitches over the next several rounds. In doing so, you will form a triangular area—the gusset.

FOOT

The foot is the part of a sock that covers the foot—the **instep** and **sole**. The sock's foot should be worked to the exact length of the wearer's foot. Begin shaping the toe when the sock foot is about **2 inches (5 cm) shorter** than the foot, measured from the back of the heel to the tip of the longest toe.

TOE

There are many ways to shape a toe, but the most common is to work a series of **paired decreases**, with each decrease round separated by an even round.

CUFF

LEG

HEEL FLAP

TURNED HEEL

GUSSET

INSTEP

FOOT

SOLE

TOE

6 DESIGNING

JUDY BECKER'S CAST ON

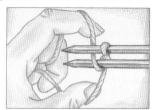

1 To cast on to work a sock from the toe up using Judy Becker's cast on, use two double-pointed needles held parallel. Make a slip knot and place it on back needle. Holding yarn as for long-tail cast on, *bring index finger yarn from back to front over the front needle and under back needle close to slip knot.

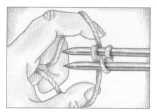

2 Bring the thumb yarn from back to front over the back needle and under the front needle.

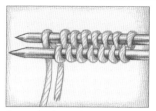

3 Repeat from the * in step 1 until the desired number of stitches has been cast on.

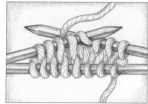

4 Turn needles so that working yarn is coming from back needle ready to work. With a 3rd double-pointed needle, knit half the sts from back needle and with 4th needle, knit 2nd half, cont around, knitting remaining sts onto 2 needles. Place a marker for the beginning of the round and begin to increase to shape the toe.

KITCHENER STITCH

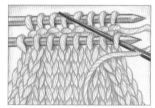

1 To graft a sock toe using Kitchener stitch, divide the stitches evenly on two double-pointed needles, being sure that the center of the heel lines up with the center of the needles. With the working yarn coming from the back needle, thread a yarn needle. Insert the yarn needle purlwise in the first stitch of the front needle and draw the yarn through, leaving the stitch on the knitting needle.

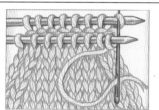

2 Insert the yarn needle knitwise in the first stitch on the back knitting needle. Draw the yarn through, and leave the stitch on the knitting needle.

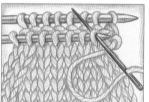

3 Insert the yarn needle knitwise in the first stitch on the front needle, draw the yarn through, and slip the stitch off the knitting needle. Insert the yarn needle purlwise through the next stitch on the front needle. Draw the yarn through, leaving the stitch on the knitting needle.

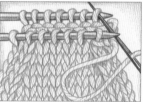

4 Insert the yarn needle purlwise in the first stitch on the back needle, draw the yarn through, and slip the stitch off the knitting needle. Insert the needle knitwise in the next stitch on the back needle. Draw the yarn through, and leave the stitch on the needle.

TIP

SOCK KNITTING

• To tighten the join between a heel flap and gusset, pick up stitches **through the back loop** of the chain edge along the heel flap. By doing so, you twist the stitches and make them tighter.

• To avoid the small hole that sometimes appears over the gusset, **pick up an extra stitch or two**. Then decrease the extra stitches on the next round.

• To **avoid ladders**, adjust the tension at the point where you switch to a new needle, whether you are using double-pointed needles or two circular needles, or using the magic loop method.

• For a rounder toe on cuff-down socks, **decrease on every round** on the last four decrease rounds.

CUFF-DOWN SOCKS

Knitting socks circularly from the cuff down is the traditional way of constructing socks in Western cultures. Early socks were knitted in this manner using sets of double-pointed needles, and there still are more sock patterns written for cuff-down socks than for toe-up socks. Modern knitters have a choice of using double-pointed needles, two circular needles, or one long circular needle (magic loop method).

Socks constructed from the cuff down begin with a **stretchy cast on**, such as the long-tail or German-twisted cast on. Most socks of this type begin with a **ribbed cuff**, but it is possible to use a hemmed cuff, picot cast on, or other decorative edging to begin your socks.

There are many ways to shape the heel, but a standard method, shown below, uses a **heel flap,** which is knit flat in rows. The heel flap often features a slip-stitch pattern to give it additional strength. When the flap is completed, the **heel is turned**, also by knitting flat, and shaped using short rows.

To form the **gusset**, stitches are picked up along the edge of the heel flap and the sock is rejoined into a tube. The stitches are decreased gradually along the side of the instep so that the circumference of the tube is reduced to the number of stitches in the leg. Then the tube is knit in rounds until it is about 2 inches (5 cm) shorter than the foot length. The **toe** is then shaped by decreases.

CONSTRUCTION OF A CUFF-DOWN SOCK

1 With a set of five double-pointed needles, cast on the appropriate number of stitches for your sock, keeping in mind the stitch multiple for the cuff pattern. For the k1, p1 rib an even number of stitches is cast on. Work in the round until the cuff is the desired length.

2 The leg, worked here in stockinette stitch, is knit to the desired length before dividing the stitches in half to begin the heel.

3 Half the stitches are worked in rows on two needles only for the heel flap. The instep stitches wait on the original needles.

4 The heel is turned using short rows and paired decreases to close the holes and decrease the stitches on the bottom of the foot.

5 Gusset stitches are picked up and knit along the sides of the heel flap. These stitches are worked in the round with the heel and instep stitches and decreased gradually until the needles hold the original number of stitches. If desired, the stitch count can be adjusted here to accommodate a foot that is much wider or narrower than the leg.

6 The foot is worked in the round until the measurement from the back of the heel is approximately 2 inches (5 cm) shorter than the desired length to the tip of the toe.

7 The toe is shaped using paired decreases and closed with Kitchener stitch.

TOE-UP SOCKS

Many knitters like to knit toe-up socks because you can check while knitting that you have enough yarn for your project. Knitting socks in this way allows you to determine how much yarn you have left for the leg once you have finished the foot and heel. This method of sock construction also eliminates the need to graft the toe closed.

There are many ways to start toe-up socks, some of which are easier to accomplish on two circular needles or one long circular needle using the magic loop method than on double-pointed needles. If you like to knit with double-pointed needles, you can start with a **short-row toe**, as illustrated below. You can also start by casting on with circular needles and then switching to double-pointed needles.

After completing the toe, toe-up socks are knit in rounds until the heel. Many toe-up socks feature **short-row heels**, although you can knit toe-up socks with heel flaps as well. The construction of the short-row heel shown below is the same as the short-row toe.

When the heel is complete and the stitches in the tube are equal to the circumference of the foot, knit the leg of the sock. When binding off a toe-up sock, use a **stretchy bind-off** method, such as the tubular bind off or the sewn bind off. Toe-up socks can also be finished with decorative bind offs, such as a picot edge or lace.

CONSTRUCTION OF A TOE-UP SOCK

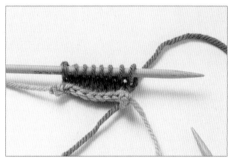

1 Begin the toe-up sock with an appropriate cast on. Here a provisional cast on is used.

2 When the appropriate number of rows is worked and all the cast-on stitches are on the needles, the toe is worked in rounds and shaped with increases until the desired number of stitches is on the needles for the foot.

3 When the foot is 2 inches (5 cm) shorter than the desired length of the foot from the tip of the toe to the back of the heel, a short-row heel is worked. An afterthought heel is also an appropriate choice.

4 When the heel is complete, the leg is worked to the desired length. The cuff is then worked. An elastic or loose bind off is used to finish the sock.

BLOCKING AND CARING FOR SOCKS

Although it is not strictly necessary to block socks, doing so evens out the stitches and improves their overall appearance. Even if you don't block socks you've knit for yourself, you may want to block them if your socks are a gift.

To **wet block socks**, place them in a basin of lukewarm water with a little soap or woolwash. Let them soak until the water permeates the yarn—usually about 20 minutes. Some types of woolwash do not need to be rinsed out. If you are using one of them, agitate the socks gently and carefully squeeze the water out. If you are using ordinary soap or shampoo, rinse the socks before squeezing out the excess water. Roll your socks in a colorfast towel to remove as much additional moisture as possible. Place the socks on **sock blockers**, if you have them, or dry them flat on a clean towel or drying rack.

Note that socks knit from all-wool yarns should be blocked and washed with care so that they do not shrink or felt. This is especially true of all-wool yarns used in stranded stitch patterns.

Socks receive more wear and tear than most other knitted garments, especially around the heels and toes. You can repair a favorite pair of socks by **replacing** those areas or by **darning holes** as soon as you spot them.

Lacy sock blocking on antique sock blocker

REPLACING HEELS

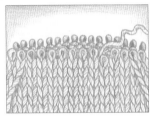

Carefully unravel the heel stitches to the beginning of the heel.

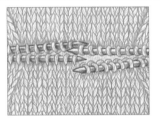

Place open stitches on double-pointed needles.

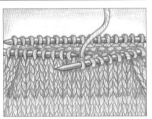

Rejoin matching yarn and knit the heel using the afterthought heel method.

REPLACING TOES

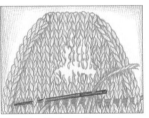

Thread a lifeline of smooth contrasting thread below the weakest place.

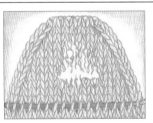

Snip a thread below the hole and unravel it all the way around the sock toe.

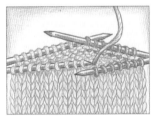

Place double-pointed needles in the round with the lifeline, divide evenly, being sure the beginning of the round lines up with the center of the heel, remove the lifeline, and reknit the toe.

Embellishments

Embroidery

Embroidery is used to add another dimension to your work once the knitting and blocking is complete. Embroidery is most effective on simple stitch patterns—stockinette stitch is the best.

Many types of yarn can be used for embroidery. Select one that is smooth enough to go through the knitted fabric. Be sure that the weight and content of the yarn is appropriate for the knit piece. Yarns that are too thin will sink into the fabric, and a thick yarn will stretch out the piece. The embroidery yarn should have the same care properties as the yarn used for your sweater and should be colorfast.

Complex patterns can be drawn on lightweight nonfusible interfacing and basted in place. Embroider over the interfacing and through the knit fabric. Cut away the interfacing once the stitching is complete. If the knitted fabric is lightweight, back the embroidery with a nonfusible interfacing on the wrong side of the work.

Work evenly and not too tightly, using a blunt needle with an eye large enough to accommodate the yarn but not so large that it will split the stitches. Thread the yarn by folding it around the needle and inserting the folded end into the eye. It is best not to make a knot at the end of your yarn, but to weave it through to the place where you will begin your embroidery.

Back stitch is used for outlining and lines. Draw the needle up. In one motion, insert the needle a little behind where the yarn emerged and draw it up the same distance in front. Work from right to left, by inserting the needle where the yarn first emerged.

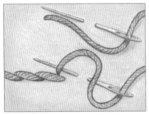

Stem stitch is used for stems or outlining. Bring the needle up, then insert it a short distance to the right at an angle and pull it through. For stems, keep the thread below the needle. For outlines, keep the thread above the needle.

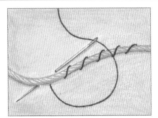

Couching is used to catch yarn laid on top of a knit piece. Place the yarn as desired, leaving a short strand at either end. Make stitches over the yarn as shown. To finish, thread the short strands and pull them through to the underside of the piece.

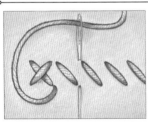

Cross stitch is a filling stitch. Pull the yarn through and make a diagonal stitch to the upper left corner. Working from right to left, make a parallel row of half cross stitches. Work ba ck across the first set of diagonal stitches in the opposite direction, as shown.

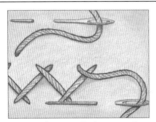

Herringbone stitch is used to hem, to fasten down facings, or as a filling stitch. Working from left to right, bring the needle up, then across diagonally and take a short stitch. Go down diagonally and take a short stitch.

Blanket or buttonhole stitch can be used to apply pieces such as pockets, to reinforce button-holes, or for hemming. Bring the needle up. Keeping the needle above the yarn, insert it and bring it up again a short distance to the right, as shown. Pull the needle through to finish the stitch.

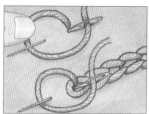

Chain stitch forms a line of chains for outlining or filling. Draw the needle up and *insert it back where it just came out, taking a short stitch. With the needle above the yarn, hold the yarn with your thumb and draw it through. Repeat from the *.

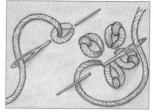

Lazy daisy stitch is used to make flowers. Work a chain stitch, but instead of going back into the stitch, insert the needle below and then above the stitch in one motion, as shown. Pull the needle through. Form new petals in the same way.

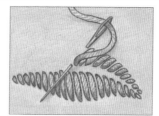

Satin stitch is ideal as a filling stitch. Be careful not to pull the stitches too tightly to avoid puckering. Bring the needle up at one side and insert it at an angle, covering the desired space in one motion. Repeat this step.

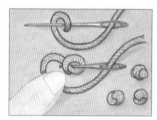

French knots can be used for flower centers or worked in bulky yarn to form rosettes. Bring needle up and wrap thread once or twice around it, while holding thread taut. Reinsert needle close to where thread emerged.

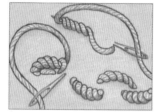

Bullion stitch is similar to French knots. Bring needle up. Reinsert it as shown and wrap yarn four to six times around it. Holding yarn taut, pull needle through. Reinsert needle a short distance from where it emerged and pull it through.

Duplicate stitch covers a knit stitch. Bring needle up below stitch to be worked. Insert needle under both loops one row above and pull it through. Insert it back into stitch below and through center of next stitch in one motion.

SMOCKING

Smocking or the honeycomb stitch uses a ratio of three or four reverse stockinette stitches to one knit stitch, depending on the weight of yarn used. The fabric reduces approximately one-third when the smocking is complete. Run a contrasting yarn under the knit stitches to be smocked.

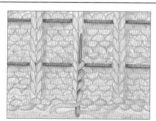

1 Beginning with the second knit rib at the lower right edge, bring the needle up the right side of that rib to the fourth stitch.

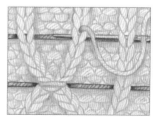

2 *Insert the needle from right to left into the fourth stitch (shown here after a few stitches have been smocked) of the first and second ribs. Bring the needle through and pull to join the ribs; repeat from the * once to complete a smocking stitch.

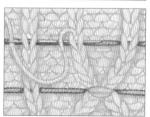

3 Bring the needle up the next four stitches on the left side of the second knit rib and work the smocking stitch, joining the second and third ribs by inserting the needle from left to right. Repeat steps 2 and 3 to the top of the piece.

Knitting with Beads

Knitting with beads is an age-old art. The easiest method, **beaded knitting**, has beads spaced at planned or random intervals. The beads are added by threading them directly onto the working yarn. These beads usually fall over the stitches rather than between them. Beaded knitting is worked most often with one type or color of bead, but with advance planning as you thread, you can work out a sequence with several types or colors of beads. The techniques on the opposite page are for beaded knitting.

Another method, a traditional one first developed in the eighteenth and nineteenth centuries, was used for purses and other elaborately decorated items. It is called **bead knitting** (sometimes known as purse knitting). This method, also worked by threading the beads onto the working yarn, is done by placing one bead between each stitch, so that the knitting stitches are completely hidden by beads. You can work intricate patterns in bead knitting by threading beads in reverse of the design (which must be completely accurate) and then working the beads into the knitting.

Most beads are made from glass, wood, plastic, clay, and papier-mâché, but they can also be made from pearls, gems, buttons, and some stones. Match your beads to the yarn by using luxurious beads on silks and other shiny yarns for evening wear and rougher beads and stones on tweeds and wools for day wear. When considering whether your beads and yarn are an appropriate match, just remember that beads will add weight to your project. Heavy yarns with vast numbers of beads will not be comfortable to wear and are likely to stretch out. Fragile yarns should be beaded with care, because some are not strong enough to withstand the beading process without fraying or becoming worn. If your yarn is too thick to thread and bead, you can sew beads onto the finished pieces. When choosing suitable yarns and beads, make sure you can wash the beads if you are using a washable yarn. If you plan to dry clean the garment, make sure the beads can be dry cleaned too.

Work stitches **firmly** on either side of the beads to keep them in place and from falling to the back of the work. To avoid edges that curl or that are difficult to seam, don't work beads close to the edge of your pieces.

Be creative when you add beads. Add beads in pattern indentations, increases and decreases, at the sides or centers of cables, or in the openings created by eyelet stitches.

THREADING BEADS

For both beading methods, thread beads onto balls of yarn before you knit. The threading needle must be large enough to accommodate the yarn, but small enough to go through the beads. Because this combination is not always possible, you can use an **auxiliary thread** to thread the beads. Using a sturdy thread, loop it through a folded piece of yarn and then pull both ends of the thread through the eye of the needle. Pass the bead over the needle and thread it onto the yarn. (It may help to pass a bead back and forth over the

folded yarn a few times to crease it.)

Beads are available prestrung or loose. To thread prestrung beads, carefully open the strand and insert the needle into the beads through the strand. Store threaded beads in a plastic bag or jar to keep them from tangling as you knit.

YARN WEIGHT VS. BEAD SIZE

yarn weight	prestrung beads	placing a bead
LACE	size 8	sizes 6 or 8
LIGHT FINGERING	size 8	size 6
FINGERING/SOCK	sizes 6 or 8	size 6
SPORT	size 6	size 6
DK	size 6	size 5
WORSTED	size 5	size 5 or larger

Courtesy Laura Nelkin of Nelkin Designs, www.nelkindesigns.com.

STOCKINETTE STITCH

You can add beads in stockinette stitch on wrong-side rows by making a knit stitch (a purl on the right side of the work) on either side of the bead to help anchor it.

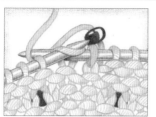

From the wrong side On a purl (wrong-side) row, work to one stitch before the point you wish to place a bead. Knit this stitch. With the yarn still at back of the work, slip the bead up to the work and knit the next stitch.

On right-side rows, beads are placed without the purl stitches on either side. The bead will lie directly in front of the stitch. Work the stitch firmly so that the bead won't fall to the back of the work.

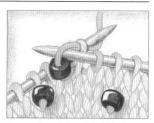

From the right side Work to the stitch you wish to bead, then slip the bead up in back of the work. Insert the needle as if to knit and wrap the yarn around it. Push the bead to the front through the stitch on the left needle and complete the stitch.

GARTER AND REVERSE STOCKINETTE STITCH

Add beads to garter stitch by working the wrong-side rows so that the beads fall to the right side of the work. Work right-side rows with no beads.

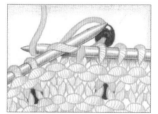

Garter stitch With the yarn at the back, slip a bead close to the work, and then knit the next stitch from the left needle. The bead will sit between the two stitches.

Beads can be added in reverse stockinette stitch on right-side (purl) rows.

Reverse stockinette stitch Work to the stitch where the bead will be placed, and insert the needle into the next stitch as if to purl. Push the bead up to the front of the work and purl the stitch.

SLIP STITCH

Adding beads with a slip stitch is done on stockinette stitch from the right side of the work. The bead falls directly in front of the slipped stitch.

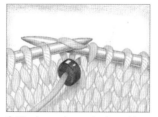

1 Work to where the bead is to be placed. Bring the yarn and the bead to the front of the work and slip the next stitch knitwise.

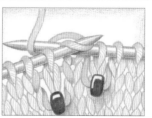

2 Bring the yarn to the back, keeping the bead to the front, and knit the next stitch firmly.

Knitting with Sequins

Adding sequins is a glamorous way to embellish simple sweaters and other items. Sequins come in various shapes, colors, and sizes and can be added all over to make a sequined fabric, placed at planned intervals, or set into specific motifs in certain areas. Sequins are a bit more difficult to work with than beads because they are usually larger, more awkwardly shaped, and sometimes difficult to separate. As with beads, always work sequins a stitch or two in from the edges for easier seaming. Accuracy is important when you work with sequins, because they are difficult to rip out once knit.

Sequins come with holes at the top or in the center. The **hole placement** determines how the sequin will lie, which will affect the finished look of your sweater.

Special care may be needed for sequined garments. Some sequins can be hand washed but not dry cleaned. Don't press or steam them. Check them for colorfastness.

Thread sequins onto a ball of yarn before you begin, using an auxiliary thread. String shaped sequins onto the yarn with the cup side facing the ball, so that the cup, which has more facets, will face out once it is knit. Add enough sequins to knit a full ball of yarn.

STOCKINETTE STITCH

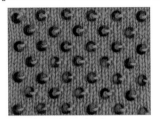

A purl stitch worked on one side of a sequin on stockinette stitch helps the sequin to lie flat. This is done on the right side (knit rows).

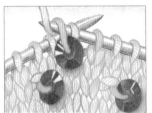

From the right side with a purl stitch Knit to the stitch where the sequin will be placed. Bring the yarn to the front and slide the sequin to the work. Purl the stitch.

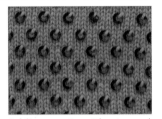

Adding sequins without a purl stitch on stockinette is more time consuming but may be desirable for certain garments where the sequins must be anchored.

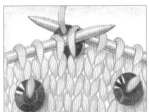

Without a purl stitch Work to where the sequin will be placed and inset the right needle into the back loop of the next stitch. Push the sequin close to the back of the work and then through the stitch with your finger while you finish the stitch.

GARTER AND REVERSE STOCKINETTE STITCH

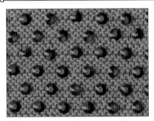

When you work sequins into garter stitch on wrong-side rows, the sequin will fall between the two stitches on the right side of the work.

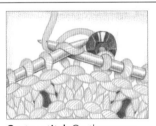

Garter stitch On the wrong-side row, work to where the sequin is to be placed and, with the yarn at the back, slip the sequin close to the work. Knit the next stitch, leaving the sequin between the two stitches.

Sequins can be worked on purl rows (the right side of reverse stockinette stitch).

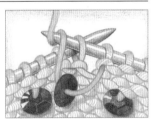

Reverse stockinette stitch Work to the placement of the sequin. Twist the next stitch on the needle by slipping it through the back loop and placing it back on the left needle. Push the sequin close to the work. Purl the twisted stitch, pushing the sequin through the stitch.

Additions

Your finished knitting can be a base for adding a wide variety of creative extras. You can apply pieces of knit fabric, leather, or felt. You can also add ribbon, petals, purchased appliqués, cords, pompoms, tassels, beads, stones, or knit bobbles. Look in craft or millinery supply stores to find creative additions or make your own from the instructions that follow.

Additions such as ribbon, leather strips, and cords can be woven or laced into eyelets, lace stitches, loosely knit areas, or dropped-stitch spaces. You can create a plaid effect by weaving in strands of contrasting yarn.

Apply additions **securely**. They should not bind, pull, or pucker the knit fabric. If you plan to appliqué large areas, make sure that they will still have the same flexibility as the rest of the piece. **Baste** trims or additions to the sweater to check placement before attaching. Additions that need to be cleaned differently than your garment should be detachable.

CORDS

 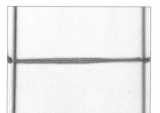 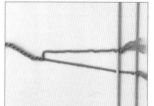 

Twisted cord is made by twisting strands of yarn together. The thickness of the cord will depend on the number and weight of the strands. Cut strands three times the desired finished length and knot them about 1 inch (2.5 cm) from each end.

1 If you have someone to help you, insert a pencil or knitting needle through each end of the strands. If not, place one end over a doorknob and put a pencil through the other end. Turn the needles clockwise until they are tightly twisted.

2 Keeping the strands taut, fold the piece in half. Remove the needles and allow the cords to twist onto themselves.

I-cord is made on double-pointed needles. Cast on about 3–5 stitches. *Knit 1 row. Without turning the work, slip the stitches back to the beginning of the row. Pull the yarn tightly from the end of the row. Repeat from the * as desired. Bind off.

TECHNIQUE

SPOOL KNITTING

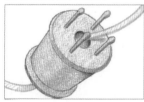 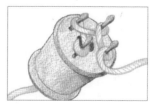 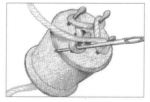 

1 Spool knitting creates a tube. Use a purchased knitting spool or attach four small nails to a wooden thread spool. Thread yarn down through spool, using a yarn needle if necessary.

2 Wrap the yarn around each nail counterclockwise and pull tightly.

3 Lay yarn over first wrap on the nail. Pull first wrap over yarn with yarn needle or crochet hook. Work each stitch, pulling yarn at lower edge of spool to tighten it.

4 To bind off, move last knitted stitch to the nail at its left. With yarn needle, pull bottom stitch over top stitch. Repeat this step until 1 stitch remains. Fasten off.

FRINGE

Simple fringe Cut yarn twice the desired length plus extra for knotting. On the wrong side, insert a hook from front to back through the piece and over the folded yarn. Pull yarn through. Draw ends through and tighten. Trim yarn.

Knotted fringe After working a simple fringe (with longer strands to account for extra knotting), take half of the strands from each fringe and knot them with half the strands from the neighboring fringe.

Knitted fringe This applied fringe is worked side to side. Cast on stitches to approximately one-fifth the desired length of the fringe. Work garter stitch to desired width of fringe band. Bind off 4–5 stitches.

Unravel remaining stitches to create fringe, which may be left looped or cut. Apply fringe at garter stitch border to garment.

TASSEL

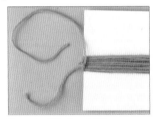  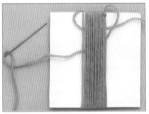 

Tassel with shank Wrap yarn around a piece of cardboard that is the desired length of the tassel. Thread a strand of yarn, insert it through the cardboard and tie it at one side, leaving a long end to wrap around the tassel.

Cut the other edge to free the wrapped strands. Wrap the long end of the yarn around the upper edge and insert the yarn into the top, as shown. Trim to even the strands.

Tassel without shank Wrap yarn around cardboard the length of the tassel, leaving a 12-inch (30-cm) strand loose at either end. With a yarn needle, knot both sides to the first loop and run the loose strand under the wrapped strands. Pull tightly and tie at top.

Cut the lower edge of the tassel and, holding the tassel about ¾ inch (2 cm) from the top, wind the top strands (one clockwise and one counterclockwise) around the tassel. Thread the two strands and insert them through to the top of the tassel.

POMPOM

You can use pompoms as a decorative trim, at the ends of cords, on hats or hoods, and for children's garments. They are easy to make.

1 With two circular pieces of cardboard the width of the desired pompom, cut a center hole. Then cut a pie-shaped wedge out of the circle.

2 Hold the two circles together and wrap the yarn tightly around the cardboard. Carefully cut around the cardboard.

3 Tie a piece of yarn tightly between the two circles. Remove the cardboard and trim the pompom.

8 Tables and Tools

KNITTING NEEDLE SIZES

Millimeters	U.S. Size
2.00 mm	0
2.25 mm	1
2.75 mm	2
3.25 mm	3
3.5 mm	4
3.75 mm	5
4 mm	6
4.5 mm	7
5 mm	8
5.5 mm	9
6 mm	10
6.5 mm	10½
8 mm	11
9 mm	13
10 mm	15
12.75 mm	17
15 mm	19
19 mm	35
25 mm	50

CROCHET HOOK SIZES

Millimeters	U.S. Size*
2.25 mm	B-1
2.75 mm	C-2
3.25 mm	D-3
3.5 mm	E-4
3.75 mm	F-5
4 mm	G-6
4.5 mm	7
5 mm	H-8
5.5 mm	I-9
6 mm	J-10
6.5 mm	K-10½
8 mm	L-11
9 mm	M/N-13
10 mm	N/P-15
15 mm	P/Q
16 mm	Q
19 mm	S

US TO METRIC CONVERSIONS

MULTIPLY	BY	TO GET
inches	2.54	centimeters
ounces	28.35	grams
yards	0.91	meters

METRIC TO US CONVERSIONS

DIVIDE	BY	TO GET
centimeters	2.54	inches
grams	28.35	ounces
meters	0.91	yards

EQUIVALENTS WEIGHTS
(ounces to grams)

¾ oz = 20 g

.88 oz = 25 g

1 oz = 28 g

1½ oz = 40 g

1¾ oz = 50 g

2 oz = 60 g

3½ oz = 100 g

5 oz = 141 g

Standard Yarn Weight System

CATAGORIES OF YARN, GAUGE RANGES, AND RECOMMENDED NEEDLE AND HOOK SIZES

Yarn Weight Symbol & Category	**0** Lace	**1** Super Fine	**2** Fine	**3** Light	**4** Medium	**5** Bulky	**6** Super Bulky	**7** Jumbo
Type of Yarns in Category	Fingering 10-count crochet thread	Sock, Fingering, Baby	Sport, Baby	DK, Light Worsted	Worsted, Afghan, Aran	Chunky, Craft, Rug	Super Bulky, Roving	Jumbo, Roving
Knit Gauge Range* in Stockinette Stitch to 4 inches	33–40** sts	27–32 sts	23–26 sts	21–24 sts	16–20 sts	12–15 sts	7–11 sts	6 sts and fewer
Recommended Needle in Metric Size Range	1.5–2.25 mm	2.25—3.25 mm	3.25—3.75 mm	3.75—4.5 mm	4.5—5.5 mm	5.5—8 mm	8—12.75 mm	12.75 mm and larger
Recommended Needle U.S. Size Range	000–1	1 to 3	3 to 5	5 to 7	7 to 9	9 to 11	11 to 17	17 and larger
Crochet Gauge* Ranges in Single Crochet to 4 inch	32–42 double crochets**	21–32 sts	16–20 sts	12–17 sts	11–14 sts	8–11 sts	6–9 sts	5 sts and fewer
Recommended Hook in Metric Size Range	Steel*** 1.6–1.4 mm	2.25—3.5 mm	3.5—4.5 mm	4.5—5.5 mm	5.5—6.5 mm	6.5—9 mm	9—16 mm	16 mm and larger
Recommended Hook U.S. Size Range	Steel*** 6, 7, 8 Regular hook B–1	B–1 to E–4	E–4 to 7	7 to I–9	I–9 to K–10 1/2	K–10 1/2 to M–13	M–13 to Q	Q and larger

* GUIDELINES ONLY: The above reflect the most commonly used gauges and needle or hook sizes for specific yarn categories.

** Lace weight yarns are usually knitted or crocheted on larger needles and hooks to create lacy, openwork patterns. Accordingly, a gauge range is difficult to determine. Always follow the gauge stated in your pattern.

*** Steel crochet hooks are sized differently from regular hooks—the higher the number, the smaller the hook, which is the reverse of regular hook sizing.

This Standards & Guidelines booklet and downloadable symbol artwork are available at: YarnStandards.com

Needle Inventory

Use this chart to catalog which needles you already own. There are multiple slots per needle type (straight, dpn, circular) so you can write in specific lengths, if desired.

US	0	1	2	3	4	5	6	7	8	9	10	10½	11	13	15	17	19	35	50
MM	2	2.25	2.75	3.25	3.5	3.75	4	4.5	5	5.5	6	6.5	8	9	10	12.75	15	19	25
STRAIGHT NEEDLES																			
DOUBLE-POINTED NEEDLES																			
CIRCULAR NEEDLES																			

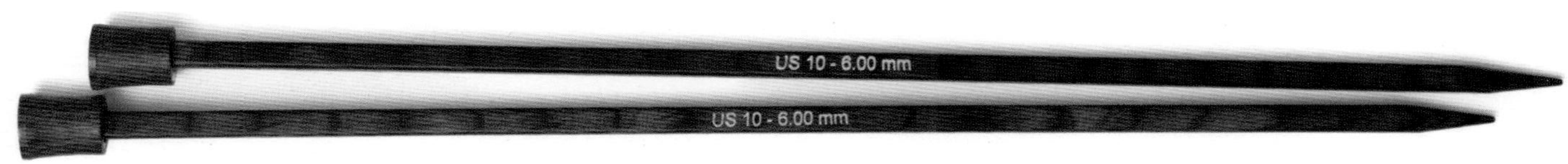

US 10 - 6.00 mm

US 10 - 6.00 mm

Bibliography

Barbara Abbey, *Knitting Lace*, Viking Press, New York, 1974, penguin.com.

Judy Becker, "Magic Cast-On for Toe-Up Socks," *Knitty*, Spring 2006, http://www.knitty.com/ISSUEspring06/FEATmagiccaston.html.
-------, "Persistent Illusion: Knitting and the Search for Reality," *Judy's Magic Cast On Blog*, http://www.persistentillusion.com/blogblog/techniques/magic-cast-on/magic-cast-on-2

Beth Brown-Reinsel, *Knitting Ganseys*, Interweave Press, Loveland, Colorado, 1993, interweave.com.

Nancy Bush, *Knitted Lace of Estonia*, Interweave Press, Loveland, Colorado, 2008, interweave.com.
-------, *Folk Socks: The History and Techniques of Hand Knitted Footwear*, Interweave Press, Loveland, Colorado, 1994, interweave.com.

Rosemary Drysdale, *Entrelac: The Essential Guide to Interlace Knitting*, Sixth & Spring Books, New York, 2010, sixthandspring.com.
-------, *Entrelac 2: New Techniques for Interlace Knitting*, Sixth & Spring Books, New York, 2014, sixthandspring.com.

Nicky Epstein, *Knitting Never Felt Better: The Definitive Guide to Fabulous Felting*, Sixth & Spring Books, New York, 2007, sixthandspring.com.

Margaret Radcliffe, *Circular Knitting Workshop: Essential Techniques to Master Knitting in the Round*, Storey Publishing, North Adams, Massachusetts, 2012, storey.com.

Priscilla A. Gibson-Roberts and Deborah Robson, *Knitting in the Old Way, Expanded Edition*, Nomad Press, Ft. Collins, Colorado, 2004, nomad-press.com.

Priscilla A. Gibson-Roberts, *Ethnic Socks and Stockings: A Compendium of Eastern Design and Technique*, Knitter's Magazine Books, Sioux Falls, SD, 1995, knittinguniverse.com/xrx_books.

June Hemmons Hiatt, *The Principles of Knitting: Methods and Techniques of Hand Knitting, Revised and Updated*, Touchstone Book, Simon and Schuster, New York, 2012, simonandschuster.com.

Nancy Marchant, *Knitting Brioche*, North Light Books, Cincinnati, Ohio, 2009, northlightshop.com.
-------, *Knitting Fresh Brioche*, Sixth & Spring Books, New York, 2014, sixthandspring.com.

Sharon Miller, *Heirloom Lace*, The Shetland Times Ltd., Lerwick, Shetland, 2002.

Susanne Pagoldh, *Nordic Knitting*, Interweave Press, Loveland, Colorado, 1991, interweave.com.

Deborah Pulliam, "Traveling Stitches: Origins of Fair Isle Knitting," 2004. *Textile Society of America Proceedings*, Paper\467.

Alasdair Post-Quinn, *Extreme Double-Knitting*, Cooperative Press, Cleveland, Ohio, 2011, cooperativepress.com.

Richard Rutt, *A History of Hand Knitting*, Interweave Press, Loveland, Colorado, 1987, interweave.com.

Alice Starmore, *Aran Knitting, New and Expanded Edition*, Dover Publications, Mineola, New York, 2010, doverpublications.com.
-------, *Alice Starmore's Book of Fair Isle Knitting*, Dover Publications, 2009, doverpublications.com.

Mary Thomas, *Mary Thomas's Book of Knitting Patterns*, Dover Publications, New York, 1972, doverpublications.com.

Barbara G. Walker, *A Treasury of Knitting Patterns, Reprint Edition*, Schoolhouse Press, Pittsville, Wisconsin, 1998, schoolhousepress.com.
-------, *Second Treasury of Knitting Patterns, Reprint Edition*, Schoolhouse Press, Pittsville, Wisconsin, 1998, schoolhousepress.com.
-------, *Charted Knitting Designs: A Third Treasury of Knitting Patterns, Reprint, Edition*, Schoolhouse Press, Pittsville, Wisconsin, 1998, schoolhousepress.com.

-------, *A Fourth Treasury of Knitting Patterns, Reprint Edition*, Schoolhouse Press, Pittsville, Wisconsin, 2000, schoolhousepress.com.
-------, *Mosaic Knitting, Reprint Edition*, Schoolhouse Press, Pittsville, Wisconsin, 1997, schoolhousepress.com.
-------, *Knitting from the Top, Reprint Edition*, Schoolhouse Press, Pittsville, Wisconsin, 1996, schoolhousepress.com.

Martha Waterman, *Traditional Knitted Lace Shawls*, Interweave Press, Loveland, Colorado, 1998, interweave.com.

Elizabeth Zimmermann, *Knitter's Almanac: The Commemorative Edition*, Dover Publications, New York, 1981, doverpublications.com.
-------, *Knitting Around*, Schoolhouse Press, Pittsville, Wisconsin, 1989, schoolhousepress.com.

Vogue Knitting, The Ultimate Hat Book: History, Technique, Design, Sixth & Spring Books, New York, 2012, sixthandspring.com.

Vogue Knitting, The Ultimate Sock Book: History, Technique, Design, Sixth & Spring Books, New York, 2007, sixthandspring.com.

The Best of Vogue Knitting: 25 Years of Articles, Techniques and Expert Advice, Sixth & Spring Books, New York, 2007, sixthandspring.com.

Credits

Standard Yarn Weight System, page 178, courtesy of the Craft Yarn Council, www.yarnstandards.com.

Toe-Up Socks Cast-on Method, page 165, based on "Judy's Magic Cast-On," developed by Judy Becker, author of *Beyond Toes: Knitting Adventures with Judy's Magic Cast-On.*

Yarn Weight vs Bead Size, page 172, courtesy Laura Nelkin of Nelkin Designs, www.nelkindesigns.com.

Index

"And the best part is, as far as new discoveries and variations are
concerned, there is no end in sight. Are we knitters not fortunate?"
— ELIZABETH ZIMMERMANN
Vogue Knitting: The Ultimate Knitting Book
by the Editors of *Vogue Knitting* Magazine 1989